BRITISH BOOKPLATES

MEDIOCRIA ★ FIRMA ·

N.Bacon eques auratus & magni
sigilli Angliae Custos librum hunc bibliothecae Cantabrig.dicauit.
1574.

BRITISH BOOKPLATES
A PICTORIAL HISTORY

EX·LIBRIS· E·GVY·DAWBER

BRIAN NORTH LEE

DAVID & CHARLES
NEWTON ABBOT   LONDON   NORTH POMFRET (VT)

British Library Cataloguing in Publication Data

Lee, Brian North
    British bookplates.
    1. Book-plates, British
    1. Title
    796' .5.   2994 E5
    ISBN 0-7153-7785-X.

Typeset by ABM Typographics Limited
and printed in Great Britain
by Alden Press, Oxford
for David & Charles (Publishers) Limited
Brunel House Newton Abbot Devon

Published in the United States of America
by David & Charles Inc
North Pomfret Vermont 05053 USA

CONTENTS

INTRODUCTION

There have always been areas of research largely left to the amateur, and bookplate history is among them. The reasons for this hinge chiefly on the complexity of so vast and yet specialised a subject—but the fact that it is so has been a stimulus to those with an eye for uncharted fields, for there is something beguiling in the prospect of an exploration which could fill lifetimes of leisure. This work has quietly progressed over a century, and as scholarship is indebted to past students and collectors for their devotion and their findings it should also be grateful that many of their collections are now in museums and libraries for benefit of their successors. The serious recording of bookplates, or *ex-libris,* has always been inextricably linked with the history of collecting.

It was early in the nineteenth century that attention turned to bookplates as items worth collection and study, but only two collectors before 1850 are known to us by name. They were a Miss Jenkins of Bath who was collecting in 1820, and Daniel Parsons who wrote on the subject in 1837 and contemplated a history of them in 1851. This, however, came to nothing, and it was not until 1880 that the Hon. J. Leicester Warren (later Lord de Tabley) privately published *A Guide to the Study of Book-plates.* His was the first scholarly investigation of *ex-libris* in Britain, but its publication was commercially premature. In a letter to his sister in 1894, quoted in a privately printed *In Memoriam* to de Tabley, he comments on how fashionable bookplates had become, and continues: 'When I began collecting them, C— came into my room and said she hoped I would keep it dark, for people would suppose me mad! The curious thing was that for ten years after my book came out, it remained perfectly dead. Then, all of a sudden every copy went and I could have sold three or four editions with the greatest ease'. 1890 seems to have been the year when collecting took wing, for by February 1891 a meeting was convened and the Ex Libris Society was formed; this flourished for eighteen years, produced an excellent *Journal,* and gave rise to publication of practically all the other standard works on the subject.

Until the demise of the Society at the end of 1908 enthusiasm for bookplates remained unabated, and it survived to encourage the publication of James Guthrie's *The Bookplate Magazine* and *The Bookplate* in the early 1920s. By that time, however, attention was more keenly concentrated on interesting contemporary design, and the fashion for collecting was much on the wane. There remained nevertheless a small group of serious students and collectors, in touch with each other as members of the Bookplate Exchange Club which derived from the old Society, whose interest was academic and whose researches and notes have furthered knowledge of the use and vicissitudes of these marks of ownership. In 1971 The Bookplate Society was formed, and within that Society and outside there has been a serious turning of attention again to *ex-libris*; books on the subject leave bookshop shelves with surprising rapidity, original plates offered by booksellers are in demand, and there are other clear evidences of keenness for collecting and study.

There is every reason for it. Many of the ephemeral printed legacies of an age are historically important, for they may define areas of social and graphic history otherwise lost. In Britain bookplates have been used since the sixteenth century; they are thus a unique record of past book collectors, they assist the genealogist, and—since they were many people's only graphic commissions—are evidence of individual response to the artistic styles and preoccupations of centuries. They may also betray in a fascinating way the individuality of owners or artists, or an amalgam of the two where friendship forged their creation; and they furnish modest but not unimportant examples of the work of some of our best graphic artists and book illustrators.

On these grounds alone bookplates are an absorbing subject, and this book is written as much for those who are not collectors as for those who are. A cursory examination reveals that *ex-libris* are also relevant to other aspects of artistic activity and have stylistic parallels in areas as diverse as monumental and trade card design, ornamentation of old cartography, the engraving of silver and painting of armorial porcelain, for which they sometimes provided models. With these points in mind the aim has been to illustrate the range of bookplate design and the predominance of particular styles at various times, both of bookplates and of book labels, their humbler but no less historically important counterparts. Any selection brings disappointments to enthusiasts, but balance was the rationale, and the task was difficult with probably more than 100,000 possible illustrations to choose from.

The needs of the collector have, of course, been considered in choice of illustrations. Ideally a good collection of bookplates provides a fairly representative selection of most periods and is a source for their study, which can be furthered by consulting the permanent collections. In the case of elusive plates, and for everyday reference, we have to turn to illustrations in published works, and these have had two disadvantages: famous examples have often been featured at the expense of others, and some of the books showing them are both costly and scarce. The several 'picture' books published in the past, including both series of Griggs' *Examples of Armorial Book Plates* and J. J. Howard's *Armorial Book-plates. Baronets,* were deliberately limited in scope and are hard to find. In attempting in some degree to rectify this omission here, it seemed most helpful to illustrate less familiar as well as classic examples in order to provide a pictorial working reference. For the would-be collector some practical hints follow the essay, and one can only add that at a basic level bookplates are an engrossing sphere of collecting that still denies the need for a deep purse. Yet their greater importance and interest lies in the rewards of quiet and patient investigation, and in the genealogical, artistic and social evidences which they afford the scholar.

BRITISH BOOKPLATES

Most buyers of old books and browsers in second-hand and antiquarian bookshops must have stopped to examine and perhaps admire the armorial or pictorial designs or labels sometimes found pasted inside. Called bookplates, or *ex-libris,* these links with past owners are sufficiently varied to arouse our curiosity. Ranging in size from twenty inches to a fraction of a postage stamp—though normally of intermediate size—their history covers five hundred years and they have been used by all kinds of people. If the plate encountered is a crest with the name Charles Dickens beneath, the book is unlikely to remain long on the shelves, whatever its subject; but even where the name is unknown the mark of ownership may still merit attention, for it brings personality to a volume and is a way of declaring allegiance to it. Sometimes it is a little work of art, perhaps by an artist we particularly admire.

No one more aptly suggested its purpose than Edward Gordon Craig, who wrote, 'A bookplate is to the book what a collar is to the dog', and the analogy could be extended by the fact that in some old libraries books had a kind of lead as well! As a dog's collar maintains hold of the wearer and, when he strays, tells the world to whom he belongs, so bookplates serve our books. This, to Craig—and essentially he is right—is all bookplates NEED to do, but many tell a different tale, for some books are prized possessions. If a beloved dog has a finer collar than utility demands, why should we deplore it? The artefact is token of our estimation, and while the pride is in a dog, or our books, there is small cause for complaint. We may, in contrast, take issue with those bookplates, and there are some, whose tone echoes Pope's couplet on the collar of the Prince of Wales' dog, 'I am His Highness' dog at Kew, Pray tell me, Sir, whose dog are you?', but while such arrogance from an acquaintance (he could hardly be a friend) irritates, from a stranger and at a distance in time it is distinctly engaging.

Essentially, the design of bookplates reflects the diversity of those who had them made, and is the more fascinating for it. Here is an individual mark in a literal sense, and from it we may trace a man's attitude towards his books, and perhaps learn something of him by his choice of subject and inscription. That is not to deny the existence of thousands of undistinguished plates, especially Victorian ones, which artistically tell a dull tale of casual conformity; these may be bibliographically and genealogically important or useful, but they are of peripheral significance to a study of bookplate design as a branch of graphic art. Equally it would be wrong to exaggerate the degree to which better designs always reflect their owners, for few examples are totally out of step with current fashion, and here the key is the degree of conformity. Yet any marked independence of design is probably a result of personal preference or whim, even where we see the typical work of a graphic artist favoured by the bookplate user.

Occasional variations of inscription are nearly always deliberately chosen, and can be fascinating. Admittedly, few British bookplate inscriptions have been as individual as German ones, where the proffered bounty implied on a famous plate of c.1500, reading 'LIBER BILIBALDI PIRCKHEIMER, SIBI ET AMICIS', strongly contrasts with the admonition of a librarian of the Benedictine monastery at Wessenbrun, c. 1730, whose inscription reads in translation, 'I am the rightful possession of the Cloister of Wessenbrun. Ho there! Restore me to my master, so right demands'—a change of heart which perhaps human behaviour wrought. Nevertheless, the familiar 'Ex Libris' or, on labels, 'His Book' were sometimes eschewed for more telling legends. 'MR. POLLITT'S BOOKPLATE' inscribed on his Beardsley design (see No. 127) is perhaps a unique phraseology with a real sense of dignity and direct address to the borrower, while the label reading 'THIS BIBLE APPERTAY-NETH UNTO MEE GEORGE ANDERSON, Burges, Merchand, and Master of the Church-works, in the Honourable Citie of ABERDENE, (see No. 214), adopts that delightful word 'appertayneth' and shows a civic as well as personal pride in his work. Another curious label (see No. 243) inscribed 'Hic Liber est JUSTINI Penton-villæ Archidiaconus; Quem siquis abstulerit—in Sarta-gine coquatur—In Purgatorio rotatur—et Anathema sit! Amen!!', suggests a sense of fun in that the culprit being cooked in a baking pan is enough to allay that ultimate fear of roasting in Hell and being forever damned (unlike similar inscriptions written in ancient Russian books, which were definite promises). Lady Oxford and Morti-mer's 'Given me by my Lord' on her beautiful Vertue bookplate (see No. 54) seems suitably respectful, not least because her husband easily and somewhat wantonly spent most of the £500,000 fortune she brought him. It lacks the warmth of Selina Countess of Huntingdon's 'Given me by my dear Lord', though this was in manuscript and doesn't appear on her poorly engraved later bookplate. David Garrick, and others (see No. 226), used a quotation from Menagiana: 'La première chose qu'on doit faire quand on a emprunté un Livre, c'est de le lire afin de pouvoir le rendre plutôt', and one hopes his friends heeded it. Does, perhaps, the individual legend on an Eric Gill label reading 'From a bedroom in Arundel Castle' indicate a willingness to let guests borrow and finish reading bedtime books which ensnared their attention? It is a pleasant idea. Certainly the more severe and rare 'Stolen from' on labels is blatant enough to encourage the *ex-libris's* removal should the books be ever sold, and shows small trust in one's visitors. Many Victorians had a liking for gently rebuking verses and apt and often expansive quotations on their book labels, but in view of their length several of these must speak for themselves among the illustrations. The best-known of such verses begins, 'If thou art borrowed by a friend' (see No. 250); and a very tedious cliché it became.

Inscriptions are sometimes very curious. The most precisely dated English plate must be that of Samuel Bracebridge, Treasurer at the Inner Temple, dated 'Feb 2d. 1733 4 o'Clock' (see No. 53); yet even this cannot compare with the posthumous bookplate of John Vennitzer, a German cutler, which records his birth at Nuremberg at 22 minutes past 5 in the afternoon on the 14th day of May, 1565, though these details were probably believed of astrological significance. The Richard Towneley 1702 Early Armorial records he was then 'Aetatis: 73'; one questions his delay in commissioning a bookplate, and has in answer perhaps a glimpse of the suddenness with which bookplates became fashionable at this time. So far as individuality of occupation is concerned it would be hard to better the label reading 'ISAAC LUNSON, PSALMODIST, SATLEY, County of DURHAM', but the psalm which Thomas Wentworth sings on his final bookplate is not of David! It reads, 'His EXCELLENCY, The Right Honourable THOMAS Earl of STRAFFORD, Viscount Wentworth, of Wentworth Woodhouse, and of Stainborough, Baron of Raby, Newmarch, and Oversley; Her Majesty's Ambassador Extraordinary, and Plenipotentiary to the States General of ye United Provinces, and also at the Congress at Utrecht; Colonel of Her Majesty's own Royal Regiment of Dragoons; Lieutenant General of all Her Forces; First Lord of the Admiraltry (sic) of Great Britain and Ireland; one of ye Lords of Her Majestys most Honourable Privy Council; and Knight of the most Noble Order of ye Garter. 1712'. Rarely is there originality in engravers' inscriptions, but that on the cluttered pictorial for Joseph Rix (see No. 124) is signed 'FRAT: CARISS: 1857', which enables identification of the monogram signature; and a Chippendale for John Anderson M.D. records the gratitude of the engraver, whose daughter's life was saved by the doctor, 'P Simms sculpsit et dono dedit ob filiam unicam a morbo vindicatam', and could be a lead to this unknown engraver's place of residence. It is possible to illustrate few of these plates here—since curiosity is not our criterion—but these examples show something of the bookplate's diverse interest.

One hopes few treasured books ever stray far today, for though all bookplates can remind friends of obligations, surprisingly few give enough information for strangers to direct books homeward. The quality of *ex-libris* design today is perhaps seen to be at risk where an inscription follows a name, for the lettering is often the weakest part of composition and least relished by many graphic artists—unless they have the skill of Reynolds Stone or Leo Wyatt to make every engraved letter memorable. An unfortunate corollary is the modern reaction to any sort of individuality construable as ostentation; the mentality which is making, for instance, that formerly fascinating posthumous mark, the gravestone, largely a thing of no account. At the heart of the matter, however, is probably an attitude towards the use of bookplates in an age where they are fewer and of generally higher artistic quality than in the past: the *ex-libris* is reserved for more cherished volumes, those we don't lend, while paperbacks and other cheap editions are both lent and left to fend for themselves. It is no new idea. Edmund Gosse, having ensured that all his books contained bookplates (see No. 145), retorted when confronted by the borrower, 'Oh! certainly I will lend you this volume, if it has not my bookplate in it; of course, one makes it a rule never to lend a book that has'. To return, however, to the helpfulness of precisely denoting ownership, 'It is a custom more honoured in the breach than the observance'. Even Craig—for all his talk of dog collars—disregards his dictum, for many of his designs remain incognito unless you have his *Nothing, or the Bookplate* at hand for identification, though his idea of putting a map on the plate of his mother, Ellen Terry (see No. 161), was a brilliant stroke, and an idea later adopted by the Lord Chancellor, Lord Jowitt.

Problems of precise identification can also, for these and other reasons, be acute for those investigating old bookplates, and they sometimes leave the bibliographer with questions unanswered and preclude a thorough knowledge of bookplate history. An early pictorial plate with name but no arms may ever remain unidentified unless a print occurs with an annotation by its owner; this is an added reason why we should deplore removal of bookplates from the books they properly belong to, for it may separate them from clues to ownership. Not even armorial plates are always identifiable, for where arms are single and a Christian name occurs over generations in a family, the design may be an uncertain guide, for styles overlap in use; provincial engravers often worked in outworn styles they were familiar with long after these were superseded in fashionable centres. Apart from this, heraldic inaccuracy is common, for few engravers thoroughly understood blazoning, and there was a very casual attitude to finer points of heraldry like marks of cadency. Impaled arms are generally more helpful, for marriages may be traceable, and dated bookplates are a great bonus, but only where they record the year the engraving was done. This qualification is necessary because a number of plates show misleading dates. That on Sir Francis Fust's elaborate bookplate (see No. 47) is a case in point, for it records the creation of the baronetcy in 1662, though the copper cannot have been engraved before 1728, when Sir Francis succeeded to the title.

The establishing of bookplates in Britain was frankly undistinguished. The 1574 Nicholas Bacon gift plate, shown as frontispiece, is our first recorded printed bookplate, and only two others—the Holand (see No. 1) and the Tresham (see No. 2)—certainly belong to that century. There were in contrast seventeen times as many printed book labels to 1600, and labels remained notably more popular until 1700. Comment on them will follow, but so far as bookplates are concerned the tardiness of their adoption is more clearly understood by comparison with their origin in Germany. About twenty German examples belong to the fifteenth century, and of the three earliest, probably all c.1470, two record gifts to the Carthusian monastery at Buxheim: the Brandenburg and von Zell plates. The third is the Igler, also a woodcut, a quaint pictorial depicting a hedgehog. From this modest beginning the gathering momentum of bookplate use in Germany is easily traced, and doubtless it had much to do with the willingness of Dürer and his followers to design and engrave bookplates for friends and notable families, and to continuation of this work in copper-engraving by the Little Masters. Coincidence with the greatest period of engraving the world has seen so assisted the bookplate's establishment in Germany that in its first seventy years it attained an artistic excellence never since equalled. In other words, it emerged at the right moment for its utility to be matched with a beauty which scholars and book-lovers would find hard to resist.

No such flowering of the engraver's art accompanied the bookplate's adoption in Britain, and as a result neither did significant styles develop nor did they become popular until the threshold of the eighteenth century. Establishment seems, indeed, almost too strong a word, for little over a hundred bookplates in a century and a quarter is a very modest showing—and armorial stamps on the bindings of books of the period were a familiar alternative. It took a long time for bookplates to catch the popular imagination, and their use until about 1698 was apparently limited to three categories of people: individualists who took a particular fancy to bookplates, those who hit upon the idea of reprinting coppers or using armorial engravings in their possession as ex-libris, and those who wished worthily to record gifts or bequests of books to college and institutional libraries.

An idea of their scattered incidence may be gleaned from known early gift plates. The Bacon armorial (see frontispiece) marks a gift to Cambridge University Library in 1574, but it was almost forty years before the next, an armorial for William Willmer's gift to Sidney Sussex College, Cambridge in 1613, and over half a century more elapsed before Faithorne's portrait plate of Bishop Hacket marked the latter's bequest to Cambridge University Library in 1670. The Dowager Countess of Bath's armorial gift plate was engraved the next year, probably for various gifts to different places (some examples survive in Trinity College Library, Dublin), and between then and 1700 come Archbishop Sancroft's rather dull armorial gift plate to Emmanuel College, Cambridge and the quaint woodcut armorial for books given to St. Alban's Grammar School by Sir Samuel Grimston. A bequest armorial of Dr. Richard Baylie, Dean of Salisbury, dated 1668, survives in books in the Cathedral Library; and though not a gift plate, the pictorial Winchester Cathedral ex-libris (see No. 19) merits attention as the only 'institutional' plate probably ascribable to the seventeenth century. What is here particularly significant about these eight plates is that none resembles any other, which indicates that choice of a bookplate (as distinct from gift labels, of which there were already many) was at that period independently decided upon and without models.

A number of armorials served other as well as bookplate purposes. The Bacon woodcut was used as illustration to Legh's Accedence of Armorie, and the Holand plate's frame was almost certainly from an Album Amicorum; both John Marsham's armorials (see No. 9) occurred on title-pages, and the Littleton plate by Marshall (see No. 7) may well have appeared in a book long before it served as frontispiece to Littleton's Reports in 1683. The larger Pepys portrait was frontispiece to his The State of the Navy, and Thomas Gore's Faithorne armorial (see No. 13) was similarly used in his Catalogus de re heraldica. There is reason to suppose that several other plates served similar purposes as well, and were adopted as ex-libris subsequently. Even Baylie's bequest plate is a second state, and its inscription is a later printing, but where this and others first appeared is still not ascertained.

Marshall's and Faithorne's plates, with Hollar's armorial for John Aubrey (see No. 4) and Pepys' portraits by White after Kneller (see No. 11), are the leaven of the seventeenth century bookplate. William Marshall's Littleton armorial (see No. 7) is notably earlier than the others—and it is pleasing that he enters our story at all—but it pales by comparison with Faithorne's few bookplates (see Nos. 13, 14). Here perhaps alone among earlier ex-libris is excellent composition perfectly matched with superlative engraving, and it is arguable that no other British example matches the magnificence of the large Gore plate. It would be absurd to pretend that the vast majority of British marks of ownership are more than tolerably good or even merely passable engravings; they do not pretend to be, for Fincham's catalogue of artists shows that most bookplate engravers were little-known city or provincial practitioners who could, no doubt, provide what was required at no great cost. There are, of course, very notable exceptions, but the fact that perhaps a greater proportion of these are illustrated doesn't alter the general truth. Nor does it decrease the interest or importance of the subject, for reasons given in the introduction.

Another interesting seventeenth-century artist who engraved bookplates was David Loggan, and though the rare Astry armorial (see No. 8) is illustrated his two Isham plates are more familiar. They are also in a sense the more interesting, since the correspondence regarding them survives—which is very unusual. Loggan's sincere attachment to Sir Thomas Isham is evident from their correspondence (see No. 8). Two letters relating to the bookplates are worth quoting for reasons which will be explained, quite apart from their quaint spelling, the phonetics of which almost bring back Loggan's voice for us. The first, of 8th January, 1675/6, reads: 'Sr, I send you heir a Print of your Cote of Armes, I have Printet 200 wich I will send with the plate by the next return, and bege the favor of your kind Exceptans of it, as a small Nieue yaers gieft, or a acknowledgment in part for all your favors, if any thing in it be amies I shall be glade to mend it I have taken the Heralds painters direction in it, it is wery much used a mongst persons of Quality to past ther Cotes of Armes before ther bookes, in stade of wreithing their names'. Five days later, on the 13th, he writes again: 'I ame sory that the Cote is wronge I have taken the heralds direction in it, but the Foole did give it wrong the plate and prints wher send before your Letter

Came. the altering of the plate will be very troublesom. And therefor you shall be presented with a Newe on, wich shall be don with out falt, and that wery sudenly. And if you plase Sr to give this plate and the prints to your Brothers it will serve for them'. Two points are of particular interest. Anyone familiar with heraldry on bookplates will know only too well that 'the Foole did give it wrong' rather often, for heraldic oddities and inaccuracies often bedevil the researcher. What is more important, and mystifying, is Loggan's suggestion that bookplates were very much used, for the surviving evidence strongly suggests that in England at least this was far from the case at this time.

It was not, however, to be so for much longer, for having spasmodically appeared for a score of years before, the Early Armorial style assumed its typical and mature character in the 1690s and retained popularity until about 1720. The Andrew Barker plate (see No. 15) shows its earlier form, with inscription on a broad cut-and-curled label. The sudden burgeoning of the Early Armorial style from 1698 is a manifestation most easily understood by reference to what is known as the 'Brighton' Collection. Its discovery is explained in Gambier Howe's introduction to the *Catalogue of the Franks Collection*. Bought by de Tabley from a Brighton bookseller, who believed it to contain arms cut from a peerage, 637 of its 640 prints are unquestionably bookplates. Franks thought them the work of Sturt, but Gambier Howe, recognising the work of several hands, suggested they may have been from John Senex's workshop at the 'Globe' in Salisbury Court, Fleet Street. However, Anthony Pincott's research into Oxford and Cambridge college bookplates—a number of which occur in the Collection—suggests the workshop of William Jackson (see Nos. 22, 23, 36, 41), and his convincing case is stated in *The Bookplate Society Newsletter* for June 1974. There seems little doubt that de Tabley's purchase was a pattern book, and its importance is as evidence that the sudden fashion for bookplates after 1698 was largely attributable to Jackson's work.

The robust and confident line of Early Armorials is fairly stereotyped, but examples illustrated show that several hands were at work under Jackson, and that very occasionally acanthus mantling was replaced by a cloth stiffly folded, tied and tasselled; the plates of bishops also allowed a refreshing variation. The 'Brighton' series clearly reveals that the Jacobean style co-existed with the Early Armorial for some years and that it was fully mature even in turn-of-the-century examples. An optional style obviously advantaged engravers seeking clients for bookplates, and the Jacobean's maturity is easily explained. The term seems incongruous at this period, but de Tabley suggested it because of such bookplates' compositional similarity to ecclesiastical woodwork, mouldings and ornament in the latter part of the seventeenth century, and it also reflects trade card decoration and engraved cartouches on maps and silver plate, etc., of that time. The style was therefore fully fledged before it was taken up in the ambience of the bookplate's sudden popularity. In contrast, thirty years

later we can trace through *ex-libris* design the growing acceptance of the Chippendale, or Rococo, style.

Broader areas of society were very soon using bookplates, as is evident from the numerous examples extant and the growing incidence of bookplate engravers in centres other than London. Though there are exceptions in the last hundred years, bookplate engravers have mostly fitted into one of two categories: notable artists—willing to turn their hand very occasionally to bookplate work for favoured clients or friends—and less distinguished practitioners, doubtless glad of any engraving work which came along, though few of them until the early 1800s made a speciality of bookplate work. To turn, however, for the moment to the years to 1760, surviving evidence gives some sort of picture of the way bookplate usage developed, though the usual lack of signatures, dating and indication of where the lesser engravers lived impedes a comprehensive view. Hogarth, Vertue, Pine, Baron and Wale did little bookplate work, and it was largely pictorial (see Nos. 55, 54, 56, 80, 51); Gribelin engraved about sixteen armorials; and the two B. Coles and the Bickhams were responsible for about sixty signed plates between them. Another twenty-five known London engravers did some bookplate work in this period, but the majority of them emerged towards 1760 with the arrival of the Chippendale style. Elsewhere in the country, Michael Burghers, M. Cole and James Cole worked in Oxford, William Stephens and William Henshaw in Cambridge, J. Skinner in Bath, Richard Mountaine and William Haskoll in Winchester, Francis Garden (or Gardner) in perhaps London or Exeter, William Milton in Bristol, Mordecai and Levi in Portsmouth and Portsea and Matthew Skinner in Exeter. Of those in the provinces only Burghers was noted as an engraver, but they made a significant contribution to *ex-libris* design, and in social spheres Jackson never reached. Use of bookplates inevitably increased where people saw them in books in friends' libraries or those of colleges; this must also have influenced choice of style, and accounts, for instance, for the popularity of book labels, as distinct from plates, in early eighteenth-century East Anglia.

Reference has already been made to Isham's plates by David Loggan, and an interesting fact the correspondence provides is that Loggan sent 200 prints of the first plate; it was, of course, a gift, so we learn nothing from it of the cost of bookplates at the time, but there is elsewhere slight evidence of this. Jackson appears, from his dealing with colleges, to have been an astute businessman, for he was willing not only to engrave but undertook the pasting in of plates, and anyone having tackled this laborious job will know what an added incentive his offer must have been (when the future King Edward VIII early in the present century had a bookplate made by Philip Tilden, he commented, 'Now I want a nice comfortable illness, so that I can sit up in bed and stick them in'). Exeter College, Oxford, for instance, in 1704 paid Jackson 5/od (25p) for the plate, but £2.15.od (£2.75) for prints and pasting. Pasting in, however, was not always required: Lincoln College paid £3.4.6d

(£3.22½) for 3,000 prints and the copper plate, and the Society for Propagating the Gospel paid £1.1.6d (£1.7½) for their bookplate. In 1752/3 Gray's Inn Library paid John Pine £3.13.0d (£3.65) for 2,000 prints. So far as individual commissions were concerned, William Milton was in 1746 paid 10/6d (52½p) by Thomas Goldney of Clifton for a bookplate (presumably the price of the engraving), while William Stephens of Cambridge charged Samuel Kerrich 10/6d (52½p) for 800 prints, adding, 'I have done but 800 because you seem'd in doubt whether you shou'd want quite 1000 at present'.

Jacobean armorials were symmetrical and formal, and though Hardy thought them stylistically less satisfactory than Early Armorials, not all of us would agree. In their distinctive form, with mantling exchanged for a distinctive frame, and often with brackets, escallop-shells, and fish-scale, diaper or lattice patterning as a lining round the arms, they allowed a greater scope for invention, and their ornament was certainly an ideal complement to the lozenges of ladies' bookplates. At any rate, their composition didn't deter the efforts of less skilled engravers—but nor, for that matter, did the more severe demands of the Chippendale style which followed, with a result that many frankly ludicrous attempts at engraving survive in books and bookplate collections. The essence of Chippendale, or Rococo, composition was a light fancifulness, a defying of the laws of gravity, and choice of these terms for the style needs no explanation. The scallop ceases to be a mere ornament and becomes the framework itself, convoluted, frilly and intricate, with festoons of flowers. As time went by—and a heavy ornateness set in—pictorial excrescences abounded, including kilted shepherdesses, sheep, cherubs, dragons, trees, fountains and baskets of flowers. Earliest examples date from just after 1740, and Chippendales became so popular that they outnumber the bookplates of any other style until the so-called 'die-sinker' armorial became the norm in the early nineteenth century.

Pictorial bookplates—to many collectors more immediately appealing for their variety of design and the individuality they reveal—found quiet favour in the 1700s. Portraits were an exception, which is regrettable after the distinction of the Hacket and Pepys plates, but among a handful of examples James Gibbs' by Bernard Baron (see No. 80) is in the first rank. Depictions of actual scenes, as in the earlier Winchester Cathedral plate (see No. 19) also remained rare, but the best include another Baron ex-libris, for use of the incumbent of Ecton in Northamptonshire, and Mynde's rather handsome Tower of London plate for the Public Record Office, then housed there (see No. 81). The bookpile, which first appeared about 1699, was more often used, and White Kennett's is a fine ecclesiastical example (see No. 61); but the style was decidedly stolid, with its regimented three tiers of books around the arms or inscription. Including variations of state, there are probably less than 200 of them, but this style was chosen by a number of Irishmen, and continued in modest use in the nineteenth century. It is hardly surprising that library interior scenes and, later, less stereotyped arrangements of books became more popular, but these will be discussed later.

The two classes of pictorial bookplate which significantly caught the imagination of book-users were allegorical and landscape subjects, in that order chronologically, and though these naturally overlap they are very easily defined: the latter depict the real, and the former a combination of things real and imaginary. The first allegorical was an ugly composition with cherubs and eagles for Thomas Gore, by Michael Burghers, c.1680, and the next seems to have been Louis du Guernier's plate for Lady Elizabeth Cairnes, c.1715; significantly, both artists came here from the continent, where the style was very popular. It is rather surprising that it took so long to establish itself here, especially as seventeenth-century engravers had such a predilection for elaborate allegory on title-pages, etc., and in this connection it is worthy of note that William Marshall's title-page for the second part of Quarles' *Emblems*, 1635, was adapted as a bookplate in the next century by George Fage. It is not, however, correct to suggest, as Castle did, that fully allegorical plates resulted from the inclusion of cherubs, satyr heads and other fanciful details in Jacobean armorials; this inclusion certainly encouraged the style's development, but its origin was at the hands of good engravers who set out to produce fully pictorial designs. Though the style was later despised, notably by Hamilton (who should be read on the subject), it is full of interest, and in no area was it more difficult to select for this book illustrations representative of such a diversity of work.

A number of intriguing and occasionally fine allegorical bookplates, of varying subject, belong to the first half of the eighteenth century, the majority of them by unknown engravers. Amongst the most handsome examples of this style and period are George Vertue's plate for Lady Oxford's books (see No. 54) and Hogarth's *ex-libris* for John Holland (see No. 55), but they were by leading artists for friends. The more flamboyant series—varying in size—which Pine engraved for Cambridge University Library (see No. 56) must have been influential in encouraging a taste for this kind of plate, for all who used the Library would be familiar with those grandiose pictorials, and the germ of an idea for a personal bookplate doubtless sprang from those and other allegorical compositions seen in engravers' stock and pattern books. Cherubs were the most popular subjects, with Minerva and/or Apollo next in favour (though these were more familiar on premium plates of academic institutions, which must unfortunately lie outside the scope of this work, though they would make a fascinating study in themselves). The Muses, Bellona, and Pegasus also appear occasionally, and some medical men chose Aesculapius, or his rod and the caduceus. It was, after all, the century of the Grand Tour; the classical world was being widely discovered, depictions of antique figures or landscapes offered pictorial bookplate designs a dignified personality attuned to contemporary taste, and their significances would be readily understood. Just how involved and detailed a composition was sometimes envisaged in the compass of the bookplate's small size is seen on John Boswell's plate (see No. 59); it is not a particular success

—so few allegoricals really were—but it was ambitious. Excepting a handful of examples, it was not until Bartolozzi (see No. 101) and his pupils and followers engaged in *ex-libris* design towards the end of the century that grace matched artistic imagination, but by then the style was more securely established, and they furthered its success. A small evidence of this is the appearance from about 1780 of several allegorical stock patterns, which had been common in armorial design throughout the century.

Landscape plates were not much in evidence until after 1750, and few are of specifically identifiable subjects; an attractive generalisation of some corner of the natural world is more familiarly seen, and was obviously less difficult to find an engraver for. Among landscape bookplate engravers the name which springs immediately to mind is Thomas Bewick (see No. 105), who indeed with his wood-engravings popularised a particular kind of plate: the vignette, with the owner's name often graven on a rock, sometimes with the tower of St. Nicholas' Church, Newcastle discerned in the distance. Attractive as these are—as a transference to bookplates of the world of his incomparable tail-pieces—ascription of them to Bewick himself has been too ready, and probably all but a handful were the work of his pupils and workshop; Mark Lambert chronologically but not artistically furthered the tradition with steel-engraved designs of rather mechanical flatness. The vignette was, however, only one aspect of landscape bookplate work, for compositions of varying subject and mood were becoming popular at the time, in parts of the country far from Newcastle. A distinct type—familiar in the work of the Bewick school, but of slightly earlier origin—is the 'monumental' plate, which often achieves such a weighty sense of mortality that it seems an odd choice for bookplate design; and a like inevitability hangs over some of the then-popular urn plates, which provide an interesting comparison with commemorative sculpture of the period in churches. A number of urn designs, including James Tobin's (see No. 98), have the adjunct of a snake seizing its tail as symbol of eternity, which is a more acceptable reminder of our destiny than the grave-digging scene, with skull and bones laid bare, on a bookplate for John Warner, D.D. Excluding, however, such extremes, it must be admitted that many *ex-libris* reflecting a gentle but melancholic sensibility are very attractive.

Another favoured pictorial arrangement, with close parallels in earlier and contemporary decorative work of all kinds, was the trophy, but this most often served simply as a frame for a shield of arms. Trophies of military subjects—the most familiar—have an older history than landscape plates, for among several early examples the Royal Hospital at Dublin's bookplate (see No. 87) dates from soon after 1710, and is unusually large and impressive; but the style really only emerged after 1750. There have been few trophies of musical instruments, but they include an attractive book label for Joseph Tylee (see No. 227), who was organist at Bath Abbey, and other subjects have included drama and agriculture. Actual military scenes have been rarely depicted, but the William Skinner bookplate (see No. 83) is a good example, and another for John Bullock probably shows a representation of the Siege of Quebec. Likewise, few plates relate specifically to the sea and shipping. Captain Locker's simply shows the sails and rigging of a ship (see No. 84), and another for John Le Mesurier (see No. 85), Governor of Alderney, is a useful topographical document portraying the harbour at Alderney before the breakwater was built. William Milton of Bristol engraved a fascinating little series of *ex-libris* for men who traded by sea, probably with the West Indies, among which the Laroche scene (see No. 86), with its busy harbour, most cleverly contrives to incorporate a Chippendale armorial, and is full of curious detail.

Finally, in what can be but a brief summary of the range of pictorial bookplate design at this time, there are library interiors and arbitrary arrangements of books, which naturally, in view of the bookplate's purpose, found a rather wider appeal. A high proportion of them are wretchedly poor pieces of engraving, and many designs comprising a miscellany of books show volumes so haphazardly placed and juxtaposed that those responsible would risk exclusion from others' libraries. Quite a number of library scenes show the ministrations of cherubs, even as early as c.1730, when they inhabited the Countess of Oxford and Mortimer's library under the close supervisory eye of Minerva (see No. 54). They also served a dual purpose, for, apart from their classical connotations, a design showing a bookcase or shelves of ordered books was benefited by the addition of a figure or two if tedium in composition was to be avoided. In later years, however, less ambitious arrangements of books became more familiar, and here—as in choice of bookplate design in general—details often merit a closer scrutiny than they are generally given. The titling of particular volumes is a case in point, for it is, after all, by items such as this that a bookplate owner tells us something of his concerns and interests. Joseph Rix's decidedly ugly plate (see No. 124), for example, shows his religious leanings, for its books include 'Biblia Hebraiaca' and 'Biblia Sacra'; and the two volumes of George Cornelius Gorham's *The History and Antiquities of Eynesbury and St. Neot's in Huntingdonshire and St. Neot's in Cornwall,* etc. (the title reduced to *St. Neot's*) both relate to the place where he lived and suggest a concern for local history.

In armorial design, the Chippendale having enjoyed its ever more circuitous and wayward line for thirty years gave way to spade shield and festoon plates—those chaste little designs, so symmetrical and elegant, which at their best seem the almost perfect complement to leather-bound books of the 1780–1810 period. Apt and uncluttered, they generally contrive a delicate balance of arms and ornament, yet as the illustrations will show are in no sense stereotyped. It is no wonder they became so acceptable, but their curious history may seem inexplicable today, with our advantage of a historical perspective. The fact is that after about thirty years their charming ornament was deliberately eschewed for plain and dull shields—such as that for Edward Gibbon (see No. 120)—and worse was to follow. From earliest times in Germany, and through much of the bookplate's history in this country, its service as a mark of ownership had gone hand in hand with a recognition of its potential as an attractive adornment; but this was to be drastically changed. An article by the author on the bookplates of the Hoare family (see Nos. 58, 100, 103) shows the change being effected. Charles Hoare, after using lovely allegorical and library interior bookplates, turned in later years to a very simple spade shield, and his brothers Henry Hugh and Henry Merrik used armorial plates of frankly debased design. It seemed, suddenly, as if only understatement and dull uniformity in *ex-libris* design could be the mark of the man of breeding and importance; there was a turning away from that individuality which lent interest and sometimes distinction to earlier examples. Yet if the resultant denial of taste may seem somewhat inexplicable to us, it had not a little to do with a notable change on the commercial side of bookplate commissioning: there were now stationers throughout the country willing to undertake bookplate production for those who wished to use them—and more people wanted them than ever before.

So it was that the steel-engraved armorials generally called 'die-sinkers' came into popularity, and the truly vast quantities of these plates, though uninteresting in themselves, yet have a quite revealing story to tell. Anyone who believed himself someone clearly felt a bookplate essential; it betokened possession of a library, became *de rigueur,* and—a distinct advantage—could be obtained inexpensively. No longer was it necessary, as in earlier times, to go to cities and centres of national life and seek out copper-engravers. Unentitled arms or crests were sometimes purloined, as the Dickens crest shows (see No. 144), and both high and low in general used very similar *ex-libris.* Their die-sinkers—useful though they may be genealogically—have become the bane of the bookplate collector's life, and except where there is the added attraction of famous ownership the prices some ambitious booksellers place on them nowadays are ludicrous.

It is, however, too easy to dismiss armorial bookplate design between 1810 and 1860 in a summary fashion, for there was occasionally interesting and artistic work in the period, though it has been cursorily treated in bookplate literature. Among others, the Jewitt brothers (see Nos. 137, 138) were responsible for very fine wood-engraved plates in the middle of the century, and their meticulous designs nicely exemplify the peculiar skill of some of the engravers of their age: a marvellously achieved detail which requires the aid of a magnifying-glass for full enjoyment. The Jewitts, of course, did much work for book illustration, and some years later it was to be popular book-illustrators who helped to bring about a renaissance of the pictorial bookplate from the 1860s.

Such a statement nevertheless needs qualification, for it should not be supposed that illustrators like the Dalziels, Randolph Caldecott, Kate Greenaway, Walter Crane and Aubrey Beardsley (see Nos. 133, 131, 128, 155, 127) did much *ex-libris* design. Some of them did very little of it, and then only for friends, but their small essays into this field—along with the isolated plates of men like Sir Edward Burne-Jones (see No. 130) and Sir John Millais

(see No. 126)—made for much interest when attention turned to bookplates in the final decades of the last century. There is little doubt that the documentation of some of their work in the pages of *The Ex Libris Journal* from 1891, and in the standard works of that time on the subject, led to more numerous commissions from graphic artists of the first rank and encouraged their participation in bookplate design. This involvement has continued to the present day, but the disbanding of the Ex Libris Society in 1908 has left an unsatisfactory situation in respect of it by removing the best vehicle for the showing and proper listing of important work (and though Guthrie tried to continue this with his magazines in the 1920s, his efforts were short-lived). This was an unfortunate situation, but it is not hard to explain why it should be. Book illustrations have a public to see and evaluate them; bookplates are made for individuals, and are essentially private. Yet at the same time, and paradoxically, the vigour and well-being of *ex-libris* design depends—like its continuance—on a degree of helpful and encouraging publicity.

Returning to stylistic innovations, there was soon after 1860 a reaction to stereotyped armorials which was to have far-reaching consequences. This was firstly and chiefly due to the outstanding copper-engraved work of Charles William Sherborn (see No. 139), who was rightly called the Victorian 'Little Master' and engaged chiefly on the making of bookplates. His earliest works continued, with modifications, the old die-sinker tradition in their design, but he soon began to show both the influence of the early German engravers and a mastery of their techniques, and his 400 plates—which occupied him up to his death in 1912—are superbly engraved. Another artist of notable skill, but in the etching of *ex-libris,* was G. W. Eve (see No. 140), whose work covers the latter part of the same period; and the bookplates by members of the Wyon family (see No. 141) show great assurance, and even greater prolificness. Chatting one day with Sir Augustus Franks at the British Museum, Allan Wyon was asked whether he had any plates to spare, and three weeks later he sent Franks a parcel of a thousand of them from their workshop. These men established the tradition which has dominated copper-engraved armorial composition ever since, and its furtherance was much encouraged by the willingness of the Royal Academy to include a few examples of bookplate work in its annual exhibition in the period covering the turn of the century. The tradition which Sherborn began may be traced through Robert Osmond, J.A.C. Harrison and George Taylor Friend (see Nos. 167, 166, 189) to Leo Wyatt (see No. 190), who is still busily at work today—and Stephen Gooden (see No. 188) owed something to it in his armorial plates.

In pictorial work, after the very strongly individual compositions of the book illustrators who went immediately before, there arose in the mid-nineties a fashion for predominantly large and ornate designs, many of them showing distinctly languid and serious-minded pseudo-classical female figures, and one regrets that space precludes three or four full-page bookplates to adequately represent this manifestation. Several flamboyant examples can, however, be studied in *The Studio* Special Winter Number, 1898–9, and very fine they are. Anning Bell (see No. 149) and his pupils, and Ospovat—a young Russian artist—were leading exponents of the style, but in course of time it degenerated into a mere pretty-prettiness; but by then more potent and exciting influences were shaping the predominant character of twentieth-century work. The fact that this is not easy to summarise is, however, more indicative of its fertility than of a falling apart and lack of cohesion; for though modern design has been remarkably varied, it is—for those familiar with bookplates and book illustration—as easy to approximately date as the work of other periods, even where an artist sets out to create a composition in an earlier idiom. It is also apparent that though fewer *ex-libris* have been commissioned in this century than ever before, they have been sought chiefly by people who have felt the pulse of significant graphic creativity and wished to further it.

The most important move after 1900 was towards the eradication of fussiness and undue complexity of design, and here the influence of Edward Gordon Craig (see No. 161) was considerable, for his bookplates and views on what was apt were published and well-known. His criteria, as has already been observed, were simplicity and directness, and Lovat Fraser (see No. 165) shared his ideal in his spirited exploitation of the reed pen (they were, like Brangwyn (see No. 153), also able to use colour to a degree which modern economics would unfortunately make impracticable). Entirely independently, D. Y. Cameron (see No. 157) was working in the same direction in his bold and arresting etched designs; and in wood-engraving Eric Gill (see Nos. 193, 194) recognised that a simple pictorial device accompanied by good lettering could make *ex-libris* both personal and memorable. Indeed, he knew exactly how to create the sort of plates which would enhance the inside boards of all kinds of books: a skill which could hardly fail to be acknowleged, for most people use only one bookplate but have a diverse range of publications on their shelves.

Since 1908, when Gill first tackled bookplate designing, most of the finest wood-engravers in Britain have engaged in it with distinction, and they can still convince us that wood-engraving belongs to the ornamenting of books in a very particular way. The mantle of Gill himself fell upon Reynolds Stone (see No. 197), who from the 1930s has worked on lettered, armorial and pictorial plates with a skill and industry surpassing that of his mentor, if the term is appropriate to a practical tutorship of only two weeks. More recently, Diana Bloomfield (see No. 201) and Leo Wyatt have followed directly in Stone's footsteps, but a great many others have found their approach to lettering also refined by his example. In wood-engraved pictorial work, the catalogue of artists who have created bookplate designs reads like a *Who's Who* of the luminaries of the art's revival, and includes Sturge Moore, Eric Ravilious, John Farleigh, Lucien Pissarro, John Buckland Wright, Robert Gibbings, Joan Hassall and George Mackley (see Nos. 163, 175, 178, 196,

179, 195, 198, 199). Nor is it in any sense an art in eclipse, for John Lawrence, Richard Shirley Smith, Michael Renton and Simon Brett (see Nos. 207, 202, 203, 205) are among a number of the younger generation who are busily and attractively at work.

While the acknowledged inheritors of a tradition enjoy from time to time the benefit of bookplate commissions, the most common and logical reason for a particular artist being approached is quite simply an admiration for his or her work. The criterion of the commissioner is here quite distinct, for he requires of his *ex-libris* either a typical statement of that artist's craft and sensibility or an amalgam of this with symbols of his own personal interests and preoccupations—and the latter can, incidentally, as many bookplate designers will tell you, be a daunting prospect. The work shown here of etchers such as Strang, Legros and Muirhead Bone (see Nos. 160, 159, 158) belong in the first category, as does that of artists including Arthur Rackham and Austin Spare (see Nos. 180, 183). It is significant, too, that their forays into bookplate design were few. Elsewhere, as in the work of Rex Whistler (see No. 187), we may trace not only a response to claims of personal interest on the part of clients but the maturing and development of the artist's own style; and an acquaintance with the *ex-libris* made by a graphic artist more familiar for his other works can sometimes reveal an integral and perhaps very personal part of his work and give a new perspective or understanding.

The attempt to encapsulate here the stylistic development and variety of four hundred years of bookplates was an exacting task. Some readers will regret the exclusion of artists whom they recognise as important; others may take issue with bookplates selected as representative, feeling that other designs have a greater right or appeal; and it may be suggested that undue attention has been focussed on a particular period. This is inevitable, for interest tends to be specialised and collectors, for instance, are likely to turn first to plates relating to their particular area of investigation. One hopes it will be recognised, however, by both specialists and other readers, that the book endeavours to be a history. Had it been entitled 'The Finest Bookplates of Four Hundred Years' the selection would necessarily have been different. That such a work would have included many of the *ex-libris* shown here is as it should be; the fact that plates shown here would not pass that test is also right. No apology is made for the failure to refer in this essay to all the artists whose work is shown, for the illustrations and the notes on them are the heart of the book; nor did it seem wrong to mention here several artists whose work is not represented. These references may encourage personal research; and the measure of the book having served its purpose will be whether it draws attention to the graphic and historical importance and interest of bookplates.

The history of British *ex-libris* would, however, be incomplete without the inclusion of book labels, which, though generally humbler marks of ownership, made their appearance in this country before bookplates, and for a century and a half were more commonly used. The earliest were very unassuming typographic inscriptions, some impressed from type by hand on a title-page, others—like the earliest recorded label, for Robert Reid (see No. 208)—pasted in. About fifty labels were printed in Britain in the sixteenth century, and two factors probably accounted for their increasing incidence after the turn of the century. The first was that librarians at Oxford, Cambridge and elsewhere were grateful for gifts of books and found labels a suitable record of the presentation and perhaps a modest means of flattering the donors, as is evidenced by the many examples still extant in college and institutional libraries; the second was that printers became familiar with their use, and probably sometimes made gifts of them to favoured clients. The usual custom was for labels to be cut to an appropriate size for pasting in; but on occasion they were printed, like a number of early book-plates, on large sheets of paper and included among the sheets at binding.

In view of the usage referred to above, and the lack of impact of small and totally lettered labels, it is not surprising that ornamental borders were used, even on isolated examples as early as the 1560s. These were pleasantly varied and decorative, and of the *ex-libris* included here, the Tredway, Bendish and Anderson labels (see Nos. 209, 213, 214) show the use of printers' ornaments, which was the most common form of embellishment. The Ashmole, Large and Sandcroft labels (see Nos. 210, 211, 212), among others, used an attractive alternative: a compartment frame or engraved cartouche. Choice of decoration seems generally to have been a matter of using what came to hand, and either ornaments or odd pieces of engraved work lying about among the stock in the printing-house might be pressed into service for the enhancement of typographic inscriptions, as they have continued to be ever since—though to a lesser degree today. It will be noticed, also, that four of the labels cited were for personal use, which increased in the early part of the seventeenth century.

Evidence suggests that, unlike bookplates, which would probably be printed at one time in sufficient quantity for the books in a library, book labels were often printed either singly or in very small numbers. The Large and Sandcroft labels, for instance, are apparently unique, and only two prints of the Ashmole are known, one of them undated but printed some time after the other. This usage seems to have remained common for some time, in view of the scarcity of early examples; and as late as 1701 George Newland, a Dublin clothier, and his wife Susannah, used three quite diverse printed labels with different and precise dates during the year. Whatever the quantity printed, however, book labels were only jobbing printing and were in consequence given generally little attention. The otherwise handsome George Anderson label of 1626 is a case in point, for the ornament has gone awry at the top left-hand corner; but it seems that Anderson was satisfied with it. Indeed, few users of early labels appear to have fretted about the finer points of typography, for there are countless examples with odd fleurons interposed or border lines failing to meet. The mark of ownership was the thing; and the rest didn't seem much to matter. A series of labels printed at Cambridge between 1694 and 1702 for William Ray and others, for example, used an ornament border which remained in the forme and out of alignment for eight years!

Occasionally the same engraved decoration occurs on several book labels and can help to identify the place of printing. The border of the Martha Simcox label of 1670 (see No. 216) had been used in the previous year for Martha Richards, for whom the inscription after the name reads: 'At the THEATRE in OXFORD, Octob. 9. Anno Dom. M.DC.LXIX'. This is useful information, for they are the only two prints of the border seen; but it also unfortunately raises a question which vexes the documentation of book labels, for the wording of the Richards label suggests that it was probably printed as a keepsake. Visits to printing presses were welcomed, and it was customary to pay a small fee as token of one's gratitude. In return a small printed keepsake, with the visitor's name printed on it, would often be given, and a verse which was sometimes included on it explains the custom:

Since you have seen what we with pleasure show,
'Tis hop'd your generous Bounty you'll bestow;
To give a Trifle for a free Access
Is made a Law at every Printing-Press.

It may be that the idea of employing these otherwise useless pieces of paper as book labels was suggested by printers, for many labels inscribed 'His/Her Book' have otherwise the appearance of keepsakes; but it nevertheless prompts the question of what constitutes a book label. The only answer can be that any printed name pasted into a book to denote ownership becomes an *ex-libris* by use. Fortunately the Richards print shows clear evidence of removal from a book, and elsewhere manuscript additions can make the position clear; but many leave unanswered questions since they were removed from books in the heyday of bookplate collecting around the turn of the present century. Some idea of the occasional size of the keepsake market can be gleaned from John Evelyn's diary for 24th January 1684, where he wrote: 'The frost continuing more and more severe, the Thames before London was still planted with boothes in formal streetes, all sorts of trades and shops furnish'd and full of commodities, even to a printing presse, where the people and ladyes took a fancy to have their names printed, and the day and yeare set down when printed on the Thames; this humour tooke so universally, that 'twas estimated one printer gain'd £5 a day, for printing a line onely, at sixpence a time, besides what he got by ballads, etc.'.

Throughout the seventeenth and early eighteenth centuries book labels of usual size retained a generally unremarkable form, and few show much striving for notable individuality in their design; new ornaments appeared in course of time, but since some of them continued in use over many years they are of little help as indications of approximate date. There were, however, a number of exceptions among labels of larger size, and several of them are illustrated here. Few book labels on so large a scale speak in such plain terms as that of Nathaniel Johnston (see No. 217), for it has no ornament at all; and few of any size are so specific as to residence. It would nevertheless be dwarfed by comparison with a 1701 book label for Mrs. Margaret Combridge of Penshurst, which had a massive woodcut type and was, according to Hamilton's description of it, 18¼″ (456mm) high. Elizabeth Grey's *ex-libris* (see No. 218)—which has an inscription so apposite to its decoration—is both handsome by book label standards and of particular interest as one of several which employ very old engravings; it was printed in 1697, but its border, which comprises four pieces of engraving placed together, depicts men in costumes of the 1615–20 period in attitudes of war. One suspects that it may not have pleased her, for there is evidence the border was pasted over, perhaps by an endpaper; and a similar label printed at the same time has the border entirely cut away. Other instances of early engravings being used are cited with the notes on the Grey label.

In the years after 1730 book labels became increasingly popular, particularly in East Anglia, but none is more impressive than the one for Fersfield Parish Church (see No. 219), printed on the press Blomefield set up at the rectory for the printing of his *History of Norfolk*; it must have been one of the earliest pieces of work from the press, and has a grandiose compartment frame. It is only very rarely that we are able to identify the press from which a label came, and for the printer to be named is even more uncommon; but an interesting example is a label for William Lloyd of Maes-Annod, 'Printed by J. Ross, Carmarthen, 1764', the second year of the existence of his press. The ornament which was used on the label of more typical size for Sheppard Frere (see No. 221) first appeared on one of 1714 for Thomas Thurlin, and it became the most familiar of the Cambridge-printed borders on labels of the 1730s. These borders are very often worth scrutiny, for sometimes in this period labels would be printed two at a time, with consequent small variations of setting. Compartment frames, generally small and engraved on wood or pewter, continued to be used—as the Kingston and Frome labels show (see Nos. 222, 224)—but to a lesser extent; and sometimes a mixture of engraved blocks and ornaments was contrived, as on John Tourner's label (see No. 223) of 1750.

This period also saw the rise of engraved labels, which had the advantage of being studied compositions and were in consequence generally more elegant than their printed counterparts. In the seventeenth century there had been only one engraved label, a very handsome and entirely lettered design for John Collet, whose grandmother Susannah was the sister of Nicholas Ferrar of Little Gidding; it is illustrated in *Miscellany,* No. 1, 1978. Soon after 1730, however, the potential of the engraved label was beginning to be exploited, and the John Bancks, of 1740 (see No. 225), is both a fine example and evidence of the appeal which these labels could have. The work of George Bickham the younger, who died in 1758, it is also an early instance of the use of Chippendale ornament, which was to shape bookplate design during the next thirty-five years. Compositions such as this and the Garrick, Tylee and Kaye labels (see Nos. 226, 227, 228) pose a problem of nomenclature, for if the page illustrating them is compared with the one which follows, it can be

seen that the term 'book label' becomes less apt where the decoration becomes substantial, and Richard Kaye has even contrived to show his arms in the little compartment at the top; yet the predominance of text on the William Mountaine design (see No. 229) denotes it assuredly an engraved label (this problem was not unknown to Gambier Howe when compiling the *Catalogue of the Franks Collection,* for he classifies the Kaye as a Chippendale armorial but the Tylee as an engraved label).

From 1760 until the century's end, and indeed beyond, the vast majority of traditionally-ornamented printed labels were merely serviceable; and Philip D'Auvergne's (see No. 239), which dates from before 1792 and is quite typical, indicates that though new ornaments were introduced, the basic character of labels underwent little change. There were, however, a number of curiosities, including a small group notable for the placing of ornaments in unusual patterns. For lack of space here, Catherine Houghton's and M. Wright's labels (see Nos. 231, 232) must represent these, but more ambitious arrangements were attempted—on occasion even affecting to portray a chandelier and imposing portico, as on a label for Richard Gunn in 1771. Most of these fanciful creations belong to approximately the same time. Perhaps the ultimate in crudity is the design with masonic symbols for J. Murden (see No. 234), one of two comedians who used book labels; but in such declarations of profession lies one of the useful evidences which labels of the time afford: proof of the increasingly widespread use of *ex-libris*. Random examples include a late Chippendale for John Whittingham, a Worcester glover; a quaint copper-engraving for John Troup, an Aberdeen blacksmith; printed labels with ornaments for Benjamin Belcher, a Bristol joiner and an upholsterer; and quite a number for doctors and surgeons, clergy and dissenting ministers.

The wider use of labels is also indicated by the considerable numbers with Georgian frames, often with festoons depending from wall pins. These, like their armorial counterparts, were the more pleasing successors of overwrought late Chippendales. It is also significant to note that they were common in two varieties: totally engraved, or with typographic inscriptions in readymade engraved frames—the latter doubtless advantageously priced. As a result we find Robert Ewing, a Glasgow baker, using an engraved label, while Lord Barrymore contented himself while he was a boy at Eton with a typographic facsimile (see Nos. 238, 240). Neither design, however, quite matches the compositional harmony of the very delicately engraved labels of James Hadley Cox and Lady Burnaby (see Nos. 236, 237). J. Jones of Sheffield (see No. 241), on the other hand, perhaps finding that such precise symmetry palled, chose a contrasting wreath of palm and oak. It is relevant here to reflect that this was an age in which circulating and subscription libraries abounded, most of which marked their wares with printed or engraved labels; and nothing so much encourages the increase of *ex-libris* as the sight of them in books one handles.

Since the early nineteenth century book labels have taken several guises. Traditional simply-ornamented inscriptions remained popular throughout the century, as the modest *ex-libris* of the authoress Charlotte Mary Yonge shows (see No. 246); but they have been eclipsed since, for was an outworn idiom. Over the same period an ornamental border enclosing inscription and a small vignette to lend individuality and a degree of distinction was sometimes chosen, as on the Haworth label (see No. 251); and some little blocks engraved in the Bewick manner were used in this way. Since the death of Charles Dickens, books from the libraries of a number of famous writers have been marked by a specially-printed label, but these show a preference for a ruled border such as we find on the one for Sir James Barrie's books (see No. 256). The most frequent feature of Victorian printed labels, however, was a wordiness which extended to suitable verses on the subject of ownership or borrowing, or admonitions already popular, such as 'The wicked borroweth and payeth not again.' The verses beginning 'If thou art borrowed by a friend', which F. Tylor chose (see No. 250), occurs on probably more than a hundred labels and became rather wearisome in its repetitious good-natured banter. Charles Cotton's choice of verse is more unusual (see No. 245), and Henry Charles Douglass has anthologised a few presumably favourite quotations from Crabbe, Bacon, Milton and Overbury (see No. 244). Some minutely and ingeniously engraved labels show a skill which has been too little attended to in appraisal of work of the period, perhaps because it belongs so essentially to a time we have too long denigrated; and we see something of its character in the Andrew Lang and John Huxtable labels (see Nos. 247, 248). That it was preferable to the copper-plate lettering of the Hayter (see No. 249) and other labels is not in question.

The renaissance—and it is not too grand a term—of the book label really began in the typographic and lettering revival effected by the vision and ability of Edward Johnston and his followers, for Eric Gill was his pupil at the Central School of Arts and Crafts. Gill can truly be said to have created the modern engraved label, and Reynolds Stone has been his more than worthy successor (see No. 254). Johnston wanted to see the art of lettering raised again to be a medium of artistic expression, and this is exactly what the wood-engraved label has become; it is also the proof of Stone's belief, expressed in his *A Book of Lettering,* that letters 'should look easy'. Leo Wyatt and others have inherited the tradition, and book labels now almost rival bookplates in popularity. The much rarer modern printed labels owe their inspiration to the private presses which were a part of the same movement from the 1890s, and the earliest worthy of comment here was the series printed at the Kelmscott Press in 1898 (see No. 252): dignified, simple and small, these labels were copied by admirers, and there has been a small stream of printed labels ever since, including examples from the Ashendene and Golden Cockerel Presses.

It remains to be seen what direction *ex-libris* design in general will take next, for each generation discovers its own idiom. None could deny that fewer bookplates and labels are made now than at any time during the past two hundred and fifty years, yet the standard of their design is very high. Commissions have much increased recently, and a wider interest in use of marks of ownership is apparent from the number of firms which now produce 'universal' bookplates: mass-produced designs to which one's name can be affixed. One has sometimes heard the comment that even very recent bookplates are old-fashioned. Perhaps it would be more to the point to say that they show a respect for traditional standards of art and craftsmanship, and mostly serve people who recognise the value of suitability. Whatever the answer, however, it seems *right* to mark one's books with an *ex-libris*: it indicates provenance, may help to guide them home, is a tangible expression of what our books mean to us, and is the continuation of a tradition in which many of our finest graphic artists have had a part.

BOOKPLATE COLLECTING

Since bookplate collecting has notably increased recently, a few words of advice—on questions most often asked—may help the would-be collector. Bookplates are easily housed, but many people find real difficulty in deciding how best to organise a collection. There is no single or easy answer to this, for it depends on particular interest. The following can only be a personal view, but it is written with two important facts in mind: the subject's real fascination lies in study and not acquisition, and a sizeable collection is a modest but important historical record and as such should be respected.

1 Though some suggest that specialisation is essential if you want a good collection today, a fairly comprehensive collection may still be built up by careful search; some great rarities have admittedly disappeared from circulation for ever, but one of the pleasures of examining even small collections is that they nearly always contain scarce and choice examples. Apart from this, early specialisation may be a mistake, for until you know the subject a little you will probably not know precisely where your particular interests lie. It is therefore better to collect in a general way; plates you eventually discard can always be used as exchanges later on.

2 One of the two most difficult practical decisions is how to organise a collection. Bookplates are small but many, and it is frustrating to know you have a particular plate and yet not be able to lay hands on it. Some collectors arrange plates in categories, and you may do this eventually to help study, but it is rarely wise for the beginner. No arrangement can be perfect, for the interest of bookplates is diverse, but an alphabetical sequence by owner is best for a start; with this method you immediately know whether you have a plate and will learn much about the subject from series of family plates. Having tried various arrangements, I now keep my British plates in two series: one alphabetical by owner, the other by artist since 1860. This plan aids study of the work of interesting artists of the past century.

3 The second most difficult decision is the method of mounting plates. If you begin with a plain-leaved book or scrap-book you may soon find yourself in difficulties with sequence. It is better either to mount them on cards which can be kept in boxes (unless you find examining a boxed collection tedious) or use loose-leaf books. I find loose-leaf stamp albums most convenient, and though some may think the squared paper supplied with them unattractive for bookplates, it helps to place them and provides useful lines for annotations; alternatively, one could have paper cut and holes punched to size. Except for large plates it would waste space to allot a page to each plate, but only those of the same surname or artist should share a sheet. You can then always change your scheme if a new arrangement seems preferable.

4 For the same reasons, and to prevent damage to plates, it is best to use peelable stamp hinges to mount your collection. If you later want light to stick them down, perhaps by the top corners, a simple wheat paste is ideal and easily made. Some gums and glues are harmful and lead to anxieties and disasters as they permeate the paper or if you ever try to soak plates from their pages.

5 Some collectors have cleaned old bookplates, even bleached them, but both actions are ill-advised in general. Bookplates with some marks of age are infinitely preferable to those made whiter than white. Bookplates are frail, and unless you know the techniques of cleaning and conservation it is better to leave them as they are.

6 Though bookplates in fine condition are, of course, to be preferred, you should hesitate before discarding imperfect or damaged prints of early plates, except where sure they are common examples. Quite a number of seventeenth and eighteenth-century plates are very rare, and several may be unique. If you study collections where you can (especially permanent ones, like the Franks Collection) you will come to recognise unfamiliar examples. The Franks and Marshall catalogues are invaluable references from this point of view, particularly for those who cannot go and examine the originals.

7 Studying many bookplates also quickly teaches you to recognise reprints (there are few forgeries, and most are documented). This valuable knowledge saves disappointment and expense, for though you may decide to keep a reprint as reference it is worth virtually nothing. Many fine plates have been reprinted or even reproduced so cleverly that they look like originals, generally quite legitimately for purposes of illustration. Beginners have been known, for instance, to mistake the Pepys portrait plate reproduced in Castle's *English Book-plates* for an original. Such mistakes rarely happen when one knows bookplates and learns to gauge the age of papers.

8 If you want to collect seriously you will need at least a modest library of reference books at hand. There are a surprising number of books and booklets on the subject, and they are of very variable usefulness. The bibliography on page 156 has therefore been arranged in two sections to give practical advice on essential and specialised texts.

9 Bookplates should never—well, hardly ever—be removed from books. There is no harm in damping a modern plate off the boards of a book on the bookseller's 10p shelf, but an old bookplate in situ is a different matter, and a plate of any period marking an association copy. In these cases you should either buy the book and keep it as part of the collection with its bookplate in place, or leave the book on the shelf. This good habit won't prevent you from having a fine collection of loose bookplates, for many were taken from their books in the past, but while glad of it remember that much bookplate history was lost by their removal. Not all removals, of course, were acts of vandalism, for when useless volumes went for pulping it was common for booksellers to retain boards with bookplates and sell them, sometimes at twopence a time. They must have been happy days for the collector.

1. BOOKPLATES

Frontispiece. Sir Nicholas Bacon

This hand-coloured bookplate marked about seventy volumes given by Bacon, at the suggestion of his friend Archbishop Parker, to assist the rebuilding of Cambridge University Library. Only nine of these now remain in books: eight in the University Library and another in a copy of Laurentius Valla, *Opera*, Basle, 1543, at Jesus College, Cambridge, whither it probably migrated some centuries ago. The only other recorded print is now in the British Museum Franks Collection. A little is known of its later provenance, but there is no evidence from what book it came. It belonged late in the last century to Dr. J. J. Howard, and at the disposal of his collection by Puttick and Simpson in 1902 was bought by Frederick Crisp for £25.10s (£25.50). He showed it at the Burlington Fine Arts Club Heraldic Exhibition in 1916, but when he died the print could not be found, though much of his collection was sold by Sotheby's. Then in 1935 Bernard Halliday published his Catalogue No. 196, offering the bookplate for five guineas (£5.25), and by sending a telegram G. H. Viner secured it. He later gave both this and his print of the Holand plate (No. 1) to the British Museum, thus completing its holding of the known English printed sixteenth century bookplates; the third, the Tresham (No. 2), was already in the Franks Collection.

This woodcut armorial had already been used as illustration in the second edition of Gerard Legh's *Accedence of Armorie*, 1568, where it replaced the arms of the first edition, Bacon having received a new armorial in the meantime; it also continued in use in four later editions. An account of the bookplate and of Legh's choice of arms as illustrations can be found in E. R. Sandeen's article, 'The origin of Sir Nicholas Bacon's book-plate' (*Transactions of the Cambridge Bibliographical Society, Vol. II, Part V, 1958*). It is here suggested that Richard Tottel of Fleet Street, the printer of *Accedence*, may have also printed the gift plate. Comparison of the armorial over five editions shows gradual wear to the block. By the third, in 1576, the block is more worn and there are gaps in the horizontal cross-lines of the lower left of the second quarter, a notable deterioration by comparison with the gift plate's slight wear, and later editions show even greater stress to the block. The significance of this lies in confirming that the gift plate genuinely dates from between 1568 and 1576, in accordance with the date it declares. The evidence of the lack of damage to the block also helps approximately to date the only known print of the arms uncoloured and without inscription, in the British Museum Bagford Collection (E.5963, No. 437). This was illustrated by Hardy in his *Book-plates,* where he asks, 'Can it be the bookplate of Bacon himself, to which, on the copies used for the books that he gave to Cambridge, was added the donatory inscription?' It seems very unlikely it was ever so used. As Sandeen points out, a copy of Bracton's *De Legibus Angliae,* now in the British Museum, has 'N. Bacon owner' scrawled across the first page in his hand, but there is no bookplate. Moreover, the lack of wear to the block suggests that the print dates from the time of the second edition in 1568. If Bacon had prints made for himself he had eleven years to use them, yet none has ever been found in a book, nor does the Bagford example show signs of pasting down. More probably it was a proof pulled before the block's use in the second edition. Sir Nicholas Bacon (1509–1579) entered Corpus Christi College, Cambridge in 1523, and was called to the bar at Gray's Inn in 1533. He became Lord Keeper in 1558 and received patent to exercise jurisdiction as Lord Chancellor the following year. He was married twice: firstly to Jane Fernley, by whom he had three sons and three daughters; and secondly to Ann, daughter of Sir Anthony Cooke, who bore him two sons, the younger of them the illustrious Francis.

1 Joseph Holand

The bookplate of Joseph Holand, 1585, almost certainly employs an engraving from an unidentified Album Amicorum, and G. H. Viner suggested that illustrations accompanying a paper on the subject by Max Rosenheim (*Archaeologia* LXII, 1911) indicate that the engraver may have been Theodore de Bry or one of his imitative contemporaries. The arms and crest are filled-in in pencil, and the name, date and motto are inked in. Two prints are recorded: one in the College of Arms (MS. Philipot p.e. 15), with the autograph title 'In this booke are conteyned the armes of the nobylytye of Ireland and of certeyne gentilmen of the same country. Joseph Holand 1585'; the other in the Viner Collection at the British Museum in an Elizabethan manuscript of 98 folios containing a series of Rolls of Arms in colour executed by Holand himself (215.1.13). The arms of the plate are Holand (or Holland), quartering Metsted, Merton, Walleys, Bathe and Appledor. Holand was a well-known antiquary and member of the old Society of Antiquaries, and T. Hearne's *A collection of curious discourses written by eminent antiquaries* (1720; reprinted with additions 1774) contains an essay 'Of the Antiquity and Use of Heralds', which is ascribed to Joseph Holand and dated 28th November, 1601. Hearne's introduction and preface deal largely with the foundation of that society which was the forerunner of the Society of Antiquaries, and met apparently at the 'Herald's Office', to which Holand was a frequent contributor. At the end of the work are a list and details of thirty-eight of the men involved, which gives the following information about Holand: 'He was born in the County of Devon, and was educated in the study of the common law in one of the Temples, London. He was an excellent herald, genealogist and antiquary, as appears from many of his writings now preserved in the library of the College of Arms in London. Among them are:- A collection of the names and arms of the nobility and gentry who lived in the County of Devon in and before the year 1585'. A note by Thomas William King, York Herald, in *Notes and Queries,* First Series, 4:354, 1851, adds the information that Holand 'was father of Philip Holand, who was Portcullis *tempore* James I; and Gibbon, Bluemantle, says he was a "collector of rarities"'. One of Holand's essays, 'Of the Antiquity, Variety and Reason of Motts [sic] with Arms of Noblemen and Gentlemen in England' has at its conclusion, in addition to the date 28th November, 1600, his signature and 'Fortitudo mea Deus', the motto upon the bookplate. (See *The Ex Libris Journal* for August-September, 1906, and G. H. Viner's *The origin and evolution of the book-plate,* The Bibliographical Society, 1946, reprinted from *The Library*.)

2. Sir Tho. Tresame, Knight

The bookplate of Sir Thomas Tresame, or Tresham (1543–1605), who at the age of fifteen succeeded his grandfather to the Rushton and Lyveden estates in Northamptonshire, is—like the two other recorded sixteenth century bookplates—most rare. The motto derives from the Magnificat, but the precise dating of the plate, June 29th, 1585, is a mystery. Hardy suggested that this 'no doubt refers to the date of the engraving, or probably, to the date at which the design for the engraving was finished by the artist'. This may be so, yet the known facts of Tresham's life leave one puzzled. After the death of his catholic grandfather it appears that the young Tresham was brought up a protestant. He was knighted in 1575, but by about 1580 it seems that he was converted back to catholicism, and on 18th August, 1581 he was summoned for harbouring Edmund Campion and consigned to the Fleet Prison. He was confined seven years in all, first in the Fleet, then at his house in Hoxton, then at Ely, and one wonders whether perhaps the plate's date coincides with his return home? Though released on bail in 1588, further imprisonment and heavy fines were to follow. His periods of freedom he occupied in architectural work; Fuller commented on his 'skill in buildings', and J. A. Gotch's *The buildings of Sir Thomas Tresham,* Northampton, 1883, gives a full account of three of his buildings in that county between 1575 and 1605; there is, however, some disagreement on the authorship of his designs. Tresham married Muriel, daughter of Sir Robert Throckmorton of Coughton, and his eldest son, Francis, was embroiled in the Gunpowder Plot.

3 William Courtenay, of Tremeer

A woodcut armorial, with the inscription in a rectangular border of printers' ornaments in the manner of contemporary typographic labels (see the author's *Early Printed Book Labels,* 1976, for similar examples). The blazon of the arms, 'He beareth, Or 3 Torteauxes', beneath the inscription is most unusual. William Courtenay of Tremeer in Lanivet succeeded his father at Tremeer in 1632. He married in 1613 Jane, daughter of James Basset of Tehidy. The present whereabouts of any prints of this plate is unknown, but it was shown in W. Griggs' *83 Examples of Armorial Book Plates,* 1884, from a print then owned by the Rev. J. I. Dredge, whose collection was dispersed in 1898.

4 (John Aubrey)

A Carolean armorial by Wenceslaus Hollar (1607–1677) for John Aubrey, FRS (1626–1697), the scholar and antiquary. Possibly the only *ex-libris* by the famous Bohemian engraver (but see No. 9), an account of whom appears in Aubrey's *Brief Lives,* it was executed after 1652, and probably not later than 1661. The plate occurs in various books in the Bodleian, while in one of Aubrey's notebooks (MS. Aubrey 6, fol.IIv) a manuscript addition shows a motto ribbon bearing 'J'aime mon Honneur que ma vie', accompanied by a list of the four quarterings: 1 & 4. Aubrey; 2. Danvers; 3. Lyte (see the illustration, showing additional manuscript notes, in Anthony Powell's *John Aubrey and his friends,* 1948). Prints are also found in the British Museum Hollar and Bagford Collections, the Pincott Collection, and in the libraries of Windsor Castle, Worcester College, Oxford and the Royal Society.

5 Coll. Talbott

This bookplate shows the arms of Talbot of Thorneton in Yorkshire quartering Ferrers, Bellars and Arderne, and has been ascribed by Sir Augustus Franks to John Talbot of Thorneton who died in 1659. He was described as 'Colonellus ex parte Regis'; his youngest son, described as 'capitaneus' and living unmarried in 1666, probably never became Colonel, and would in any case correctly have borne the coat with due difference. Though this bookplate could be as early as 1630, recent printings from the original copper are encountered. There is an early print in the de Tabley Collection, printed on a large sheet of paper which may have been pasted down; and a print with full borders, completely covering the inside of the front board, occurs in a copy of James Howell's *History of Naples,* 1654, in the library of the Society of Antiquaries. This book passed, probably at Talbot's death, to Sir William D'oyly, whose signature, and a note that he paid 6s 6d (37½p) for it, appears on the title-page (and matches his signature on a pay warrant in the possession of the late A. W. G. Lowther, FSA, who also owned the Howell volume). D'oyly died in 1677.

2

William Courtenay,
of *TREMEER* in the
County of *CORNWAL,*
Esquire.

He beareth, *Or 3 Torteauxes.*

3

4

TOUT JOUR FIDELE

Coll Talbott.

5

6 Sir Edward Dering

This quaint armorial dated 1630 was apparently used as a bookplate by Sir Edward Dering (1598–1644), the antiquary and politician. It is one of two similar engravings so used. This example shows no tinctures; the other engraving, likewise dated 1630, has twenty quarterings with the tinctures marked, a mantle of fleurs-de-lis, and the inscription in italics. The tower and group consisting of key, mace and oar occur on both. The plate illustrated was pasted inside the covers of perhaps only one or two books from the Surrenden Library, and a print was in the last century in the possession of the Rev Dr Haslewood, Vicar of Chislet in Kent. He also had a print of the other, of which a further example occurs among the Harleian MSS. at the British Museum (1432. fo. 279). This was described by Humphrey Wanly, 'library-keeper to Robert and Edward, Earls of Oxford' as 'A printed Cut of the Arms or Atchievement of Sir Edward Dering, Baronet, dated A.D. 1630, with a fanciful motto in misshapen Saxon characters; but by the hatching of the arms in order to show the colours, according to the way found out by Sir Edward Bysshe, I guess that it is not so old'. Both engravings are illustrated in J. J. Howard's *Miscellanea Genealogica et Heraldica* (2nd Series, i. 285 & iii. 56). Sir Edward Dering of Surrenden Dering was born in the Tower of London, where his father was deputy-lieutenant; he was educated at Magdalene College, Cambridge, knighted in 1619, and created a baronet eight years later. He had lost two wives by the time he was thirty, and in 1629 married his third wife, Unton, daughter of Sir Ralph Gibbs. It was about this time that he was appointed lieutenant of Dover Castle, to which post the bookplate alludes, but having bought the post it seems not to have met his expectations; he represented Kent in the House of Commons but later found himself in trouble both for his writings and his support of the king and was briefly imprisoned in his old home the Tower in 1641. His activities and enthusiasms as an antiquary explain the 'misshapen Saxon characters' of his bookplate's motto. He took these studies very seriously and was spoken of in the highest terms by Dugdale, who with Dering, Sir Christopher Hatton and Sir Thomas Shirley made an agreement in 1638—entitled 'Antiquitas rediviva'—each to concentrate on the history of his county yet to help the others with research. They took up and advanced the study of Anglo-Saxon, and worked much on Laws and Charters; of these there was much 'borrowing', which no doubt had something to do with Dering's holdings of these things and the consequent richness of the Surrenden Library (though later members of the family added to it). Much about the contents and dispersal of the collection and fuller details of Dering's life and activities, may be found in C. E. Wright's 'Sir Edward Dering: a seventeenth-century antiquary and his "Saxon Charters" ', which is Chapter 19 of *The Early Culture of North-West Europe* (H.M. Chadwick Memorial Studies), edited by Sir Cyril Fox and Bruce Dickins, 1950. A small portion of the Surrenden Library was sold in 1811, and the larger part was dispersed by Puttick and Simpson between 1858 and 1865, and there is a note as early as 1851 in *Notes and Queries* that several 'loose copies' of the armorial plates were in the Surrenden Collection. Dering's grand-daughter Elizabeth married Sir Robert Southwell, whose bookplate is illustrated (No. 18).

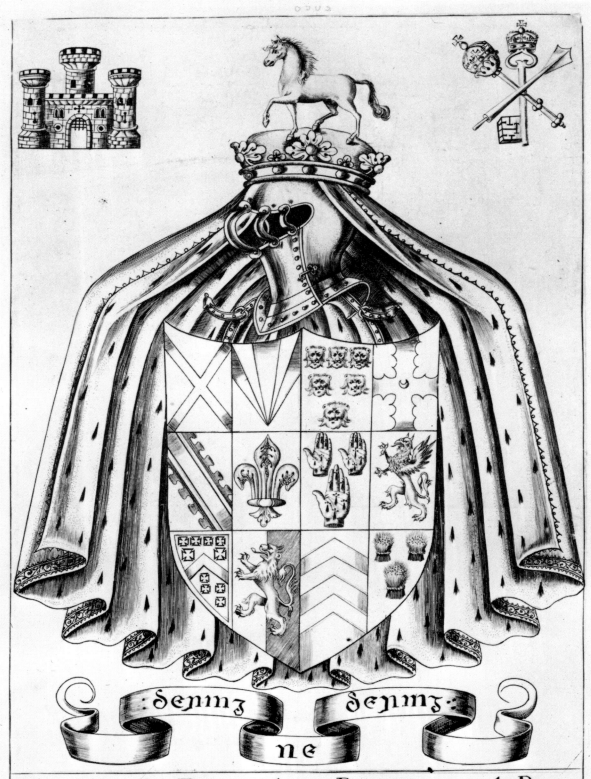

Dñs Edoardus Dering miles et Baronettus, in aula Regia
Priuatis Cameris adiuratus Locum=tenens in officio
Conestabulariæ Castri Douor, Vice=Custos Pro=Can=
cellarius, atq Hypo=Thalafsiarcha Quinq Portuum. Etc:
1630

7 (Sir Edward Littleton)

The first British bookplate to include its engraver's signature, this anonymous armorial bears the arms of Edward Littleton (1589–1645), who became Chief Justice of the Common Pleas and Lord Keeper. It is the only recorded *ex-libris* by William Marshall (fl. 1630–50), a prolific engraver of portraits and title-pages whose work in general has little distinction, but who made two historically-interesting youthful engravings of Donne and Milton. The bookplate, which was evidently made after Littleton's father's death and before his knighthood in 1635 (since the helm of a knight should be shown full-face), is of interest for its early use of tinctures to denote heraldic colour, a scheme of deliberately angled lines which had recently been devised by Father Silvester Petra Sancta. For a full account of the various quarterings of the arms, which concur with Littleton's arms in the stained glass of the Hall of the Inner Temple, with the arms formerly in the chapel at Frankley and with the arms on the patent issued on his being created Baron, see *The Ex Libris Journal* for April 1894. Most prints of this engraving being on large paper and showing no signs of having been pasted in books, its authenticity as a book-plate has been questioned, but two examples in the de Tabley Collection appear to have served in books. Littleton's career was not without anxieties in that stormy period, for in trying to please both king and parliament he pleased neither. He fled with the great seal to the king at York and, though ordered by parliament to return it within fourteen days or lose his appointment, he remained with the king's party and in 1644 raised and commanded a regiment, chiefly of legal gentlemen, for the king's service; his cares, however, undermined his health, and he died within the year. The bookplate was subsequently used as frontispiece in a copy of the so-called *Littleton's Reports,* now in Lincoln's Inn, and this copy has contemporary notes on the verso. Though, as has been said, no other bookplates by Marshall are recorded, the copper of his frontispiece to Quarles' *Emblems,* 1635 was later adapted as an *ex-libris* by George Fage; it occurs in two states, one reading 'G. Fage' and the other 'George Fage'. It was clearly printed from the copper when it was very worn, and the engraver's signature, a motto and the title 'QUARLEIS' have been removed, the last—which was central—having been replaced by Fage's name.

VNG: DIEV ET VNG: ROY

7

8 (Sir Samuel Astry)

This anonymous plate probably belonged to Sir Samuel Astry of Henbury (c.1631–1704), who was Clerk of the Crown in King's Bench, and the helmet indicates that it was engraved after he was knighted on 8th December, 1683. Its similarity to the better known bookplates of Sir Thomas Isham, engraved in 1676, strongly suggests it is likewise the work of David Loggan; it occurs in two states, the second re-worked, and both are in the Franks Collection. Loggan was born in Dantzic, c.1630, came to England before the Restoration, and is best remembered for his engravings of Oxford and Cambridge. An account of him and the text of his letters to Isham can be found in 'The correspondence of David Loggan with Sir Thomas Isham' by Sir Gyles Isham, Bart., in *The Connoisseur*, April and October, 1963. Passages from his two letters on the heraldic inaccuracy of the first Isham armorial have already been quoted (see pp. 9–10).

9 (John Marsham)

John Marsham of Whome's Place, Cuxton in Kent (1602–1685) was knighted in 1660 and created a baronet three years later. It is recorded in W. Griggs' *83 Examples of Armorial Book Plates*, 1884, that the Hon. Robert Marsham found it used as a bookplate in books belonging to his ancestor, though it was also used on the title-page of *Diatriba chronologica*, 1649. Its close resemblance to the design of the dedicatory shields in the first volume of Dugdale's *Monasticon*, 1655, to which Marsham contributed a preface, indicates it may have been engraved by Hollar or Daniel King. Marsham had a second *ex-libris*, which shows the badge of a baronet. This may also have been first engraved for a title-page; it appears in his *Chronicus canon Aegyptiacus*, 1672, but there differs from the bookplate prints in that the word 'Aristoteles' among the printing on the verso of the title-page is just above the plate mark at the top. Marsham was also a collector of manuscripts.

10 (Ralph Sheldon)

One of three bookplates for the antiquary Ralph Sheldon of Beoley in Worcestershire (1623–1684), who accompanied Charles II in his flight to Boscobel, and was party to his concealment in the oak. He married Maria, daughter of Viscount Rocksavage. A benefactor to the College of Arms, he was also a friend of Pepys and Evelyn. Sheldon's bookplates often have a shelf-mark added in manuscript; one of the other two is very similar to that illustrated and also displays a single coat, while the third is a large and squarish armorial which is quarterly of six and more often encountered than the smaller plates. See 'Bookplate of Ralph Sheldon' in *The Ex Libris Journal* for December 1895.

11 & 12 Sam. Pepys

Five bookplates are recorded for Samuel Pepys (1633–1703), three of them undoubted *ex-libris*. In the Pepysian Library at Magdalene College, Cambridge, there is, appropriate to a volume's size, a print of the large or small portrait plate pasted either facing or behind the title-page, some cut down in size to fit the book. At the end of the books is the cypher, or anchor, plate here shown, indicating Pepys' appointment as Secretary of the Admiralty. The portrait plate illustrated is the smaller one; both were engraved by Robert White after Kneller, and the larger served also as frontispiece to *The state of the Navy*, 1690. The other two bookplates, if such they are, must have been superseded, but one is of particular interest. By the engraver of Blome's *Guillim*, 1679, where a different cut of Pepys' arms appears, it is a full armorial inscribed, 'Samuel Pepys of Brampton in Huntingtonshire Esq, Secretary of the Admiralty to his Ma^ty. King Charles the Second: Descended of ye antient family of Pepys of Cottenham in Cambridgshire'; the arms are Pepys quartering Talbot of Cottenham. A photograph of this among loose bookplates at Cambridge University Library has a note on the back, 'The Armorial bookplate of Samuel Pepys in Codex Justinianus', but this is yet untraced. The other armorial has the same quarterings and fine mantling. See *The Ex Libris Journal* for November 1893. Two other plates by the engraver of Blome's *Guillim* are illustrated (Nos. 17, 18).

8

9

10

11

12

13 (Thomas Gore)

Thomas Gore of Alderton (1632–1684), writer on heraldry, was a member of Lincoln's Inn and married Mary, daughter of Michael Meredith of Southwoode in Gloucestershire. At one time a crony of John Aubrey, Gore later quarrelled with him, and it isn't hard to understand Aubrey's dissatisfaction with him for he must have been a most tedious and pernickety old bore. Even in his long-winded will, which he wrote out in duplicate in his own hand (and of which more anon), his every single reference to his parish reads 'Aldrington *alias* Alderton' in apparent deference to its ancient name; and his own written account of his visit to be made high sheriff of Wiltshire in 1680–1 shows excessive self-importance in its detail, beginning with his leaving his own front door, and of an order more appropriately reserved for the coronation of a monarch. In 1671 a letter from Aubrey to Anthony Wood contains the comment, 'If [Browne] writes or sees Mr Gore let him not tell him that he sawe me, for he is a fidling peevish fellow and something related to my adversarys', and the following year, again to Wood, he writes, 'I shall write to this purpose to my stiffe starcht friend T. G., Cuckold & Esq.'. The vicissitudes of their relationship may be traced in Anthony Powell's *John Aubrey and his friends*, 1948. Gore had a choice library, and used several bookplates. The most handsome is the large engraving by William Faithorne, illustrated here, which occurred both as a plate in Gore's *Catalogus de re heraldica*, 1668, and as a bookplate inserted by the edge in a copy of Segoing's *Armorial Universel*, 1654, together with a kind of index-plate which he had engraved for his family documents. The elder William Faithorne (1616–1691) was a pupil of John Payne and William and Robert Peake.

Joining the royalists he was eventually imprisoned, and though friends secured his release it was on condition that he left the country. He went to Paris, but was allowed to return in 1650, when he set up a print shop near Temple Bar. His portraits and frontispieces are of high quality, but the statement in the *Dictionary of National Biography* that 'he engraved numerous portraits, bookplates, maps, title-pages &c' is not proven in the case of the bookplates (unless it simply means illustrations for books), for only five are recorded. The other four are a large armorial for one of the Hungerford family, almost certainly Sir George of Cadenham (whose wife was Frances, daughter of Aubrey's old friend, Charles Seymour), a large and small armorial for the Mariots of Whitchurch (Thomas Mariot, or Mariet, was also a friend of Aubrey), and the Hacket gift plate (see No. 14). Gore's other bookplates include an allegorical armorial by Michael Burghers, the earliest English example in this style; an armorial by the unknown Joseph Browne, which is a slavish copy of the Faithorne but of single arms; and a plate by the engraver of the arms of Edward Waterhouse which is frontispiece to Waterhouse's *Discourse and Defence of Arms and Armory*, 1660. He also had engravings made to ornament his books, and so treasured these and his bookplates that he detailed them in his will, dated 20th July, 1683, expressing a desire that the copper plates might be 'transmitted to Posterity'. His will is reprinted in full in 'The Last Will of Thomas Gore, the Antiquary' by the Rev. Canon J. E. Jackson, FSA. (Wiltshire Archaeological Magazine, XIV, 1873) and the passage relating to the coppers is quoted in *The Ex Libris Journal* for August 1903. Gore's library was dispersed in the Montagu sale at Lackham, near Chippenham, in 1815–16.

VI ET VIRTVTE

13

14 John Hacket, Bishop of Lichfield and Coventry

John Hacket (1592–1670), the son of Andrew Hacket, a rich tailor and senior burgess of Westminster, was educated there and at Trinity College, Cambridge, where he afterwards became a popular tutor. Ordained in 1618, he was much esteemed as a preacher and speaker, both for his incisive delivery and tact; later chaplain to James I, he became archdeacon of Bedford in 1631 and was Bishop of Coventry and Lichfield from 1661, devoting himself energetically in the latter to rebuilding the Cathedral. His skill as a writer is seen in Latin translation and in his excellent biography of Archbishop Williams, but he was also a dedicated parish priest and a brave man—being undeterred, for instance, when a soldier levelled a gun to his chest in church for using the Book of Common Prayer. He left his books to Cambridge University Library, and this bookplate by Faithorne (see also No. 13) was engraved to mark the gift. The Hacket plate occurs in two states, the retouched one showing more work to the chin, and vertical lines under the right nostril. The same portrait in large size was engraved also by Faithorne and used as frontispiece to Hacket's *Sermons,* 1675.

15 Andrew Barker of Fairford

A notably early example of the Early Armorial style, which became very popular between 1698 and 1720. Andrew Barker was the son of a Bristol merchant, and came of the ancient family of Barker, alias Coverall, of Coverall (Cowerhall) and Hopton Castles in Shropshire. He purchased the manor of Fairford from Lord Tracy about the time of the Restoration, and procured a charter for a weekly Thursday market at Fairford in 1668. He married Elizabeth, daughter of William Robinson of Cheshunt in Hertfordshire, and the Visitation of Gloucester records that he was living in 1682, *aetatis* 52. The bookplate probably dates from about this time. The arms are Barker quartering Goldstone and Titteley, and the only print recently seen is cut round to the shape of the arms. Barker gave £100 for paving and seating the body of Fairford Church, and the money was used for this purpose in 1703, but the date of his death is not apparent. He was succeeded by his son Samuel, who was high sheriff of the county in 1691 and died in 1708.

16 (Sir Edward Bysshe)

This bookplate shows the arms of Edward Bysshe, later Sir Edward (c.1615–1679), Garter King of Arms, as borne by him before his father's death in 1655; arms: quarterly dimidiated, showing two quarterings and half the label, 1. Bysshe; 2. Clare, impaling Greene. The first son of Edward Bysshe of Burstow in Surrey, where his ancestors were lords of the manor, he was called to the Bar at Lincoln's Inn. He married Margaret, the daughter of John Greene, Serjeant-at-law, and her brother John Greene of Naverstock in Essex, who died in 1659, had a similar bookplate engraved by the same hand and very similar in its composition; only one print of this has recently been seen, in a bookplate collection at the Dundee Street Public Library in Edinburgh. One assumes that both plates were engraved at about the same time, and since the Greene plate shows no label it must have been engraved after the death of his father in 1653, which indicates a date between 1653 and 1655 for these bookplates. Bysshe, who was made Garter about 1643, after Sir John Borough followed the king to Oxford, was forced to leave office in 1660, but with difficulty obtained the office of Clarenceux. Wood, however, spoke harshly of his later activities.

17 Sir Henry Hunloke, Bart.

Sir Henry Hunloke (d.1715) succeeded his father as 2nd Baronet in 1648, and—as the inscription grandly declares—married Catherine, only daughter and heiress of Francis Tyrwhit of Kettelby in Lincolnshire. She bore him seven sons and six daughters, but some died young. Sir Henry enjoyed the title and estate for sixty-seven years and was succeeded by his third son, Sir Thomas-Windsor Hunloke. This is one of about ten bookplates by the engraver of Blome's *Guillim,* 1679, which are different engravings from the arms there shown, and all are rare. The Viner Collection has a print with inscription, and another with it cut off, and of the latter Viner notes that it was one of six that Lister of Oldham had when working for Sutton of Manchester before he himself became a dealer; all six were cut in similar fashion and were in that state in the books from which they were removed, which suggests that his successor perhaps used it as a bookplate later. The Franks Collection print is not the bookplate, but merely a cut from the 1679 *Guillim* (see also No. 18).

W. Faithorne Sculp

Ex dono Ioannis Hacket Lichfieldens.
et Couentriens Episcopi: 1670.

14

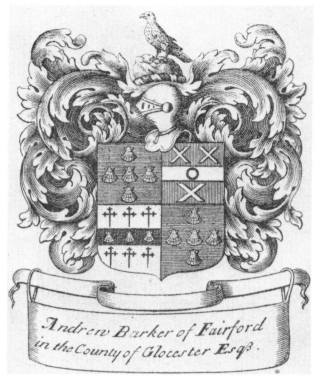

Andrew Barker of Fairford
in the County of Glocester Esq.

15

PRVDENS SIMPLICITAS

16

Sᵗ Henry Hunloke of Wingerworth in Derbyshire Barᵗ In ÿ Escocheon of
pretence is ÿ Armes of Katherine his Lady, who was sole daughter & heyr
of Francis Tyrwhit of Kettleby in Lincolnshire Esqᵗ ÿ last of ÿ Eldest
branch of ÿᵗ great & antient family.

17

18 Sir Robert Southwell, Knight

Like the preceding Hunloke plate this is by the engraver of Blome's *Guillim,* 1679, who also engraved an armorial for Samuel Pepys (see note to No. 11). A most interesting association copy containing the bookplate illustrated was recently offered for sale by Traylen of Guildford (Cat. 87, 1977): a copy of the first issue of the first edition of Pepys' *The state of the Navy,* 1690, with Pepys' autograph corrections. From the Scott Library, it contained this bookplate, and a manuscript note inserted read: 'This Copy on Fine Paper, was no doubt a Present from Samuel Pepys Esqr. Secretary of the Admiralty, to Sir Robert Southwell, Clerk of the Privy Councell, whose arms have been preserved when rebound in its present state'. Sir Robert Southwell (1635–1702) was made one of the Clerks of the Privy Council in 1664, and knighted a year later; he resigned his post as Clerk in 1679. A friend of Evelyn, he became in 1690 President of the Royal Society, a year after his appointment as Commissioner for Customs. He was buried at Henbury in Gloucestershire beside his wife Elizabeth, daughter of Sir Edward Dering of Surrenden Dering in Kent, 'a very pretty woman' Pepys said. (Her grandfather's bookplate is No. 6).

19 Winchester Cathedral

The only bookplate with the signature of Duchaine, Fincham suggests it dates from c.1680, though it may well be a little later. Apparently the earliest British *ex-libris* to depict a particular scene, no other is known with a pictorial subject in the traditional Early Armorial frame, and probably no other bookplate of comparable date is still in use, as this is.

20 (Sir Samuel Grimston)

This quaint woodcut armorial occurred in books given by Sir Samuel Grimston to St. Albans Grammar School. It shows a combination of the arms of the city of St. Albans and the motto of the Bacon family, which was adopted by the Grimstons. Sir Samuel (1643–1700) was a politician, and succeeded his father to the baronetcy in 1685. He was MP for St. Albans for many years, except during the reign of James II, who was said to have disliked him very much. Early woodcut and type metal armorials—very often difficult to distinguish from each other—are not common, but in addition to the Bacon plate, shown as frontispiece, and the Courtenay of Tremeer (No.3), there are Early Armorials for the Digby family (two different examples), Ralph Farthing, LL.B., Vicar of Ottery St. Mary, Francis Nash of Wallingford, Berks, and the Revd Mr Ben. King. Among about thirty Jacobean examples are several relating to the Guernsey families of Beauvoir, Bonamy and Carey; some early woodcut armorials also appear to have been impressed by hand. The plate shown here, with the additional typographic inscription 'ST. ALBAN'S', was reprinted in Victorian times in black and in red, and prints of both are in the Franks Collection.

21 Jacob Asselin

A very early cypher plate dating from about 1690. Franks noted that Asselin's signature, with the date 1689, was written in ink on the cover of the book from which his print came; and, according to a note on the back, the example shown here came from a book published in 1680. Cypher bookplates of the eighteenth century are not uncommon, but most are unidentifiable, and so not much sought after.

22 The Society for Propagating the Gospell

Illustrated and discussed in Allen's *American Book-plates,* 1895, this plate is nevertheless English work and was engraved for books sent out by the Society to establish parish libraries. It was the work of William Jackson (see p. 10), for the Society's account book has entries in 1703 and 1704 recording payments to him for engraving the Society's seal for printing; one of these was the bookplate (see A. K. Pincott's article, 'Oxford bookplates by William Jackson' in *The Bookplate Society Newsletter* for June, 1974). Dr Thomas Bray (1656–1730) was responsible for the establishment of thirty-nine parish libraries in the American colonies (as he was for many in this country), and use of the bookplates was fairly extensive. At least three states are known. In the first, two sailors are aboard the ship of the Society—which the missionary's weight would surely sink—and the natives on shore have black bodies; the sun's face and rays are very sharp and black, the rays short. In the second the bodies of the Indians are in outline, as are the sailors, who are increased by one; the sun's rays enter the motto ribbon, and the flag, almost black before, has just a few horizontal lines. In the third there is an extra Indian behind the trees; there are four sailors, their bodies black, the sun's rays penetrate the top masts, and the flag shows a cross. Shown here is the third state.

Sr. Robert Southwell Knight, one of the Clerkes
attending his Majesty King Charles the Second
in his most Honourable Privy Councell &cª

18

Lib: Eccles: Catª: Winton

19

MEDIOC-RIA FIRMA

20

JACOB·ASSELIN·

21

The Gift of the Society for propagating
the Gospell in Foreign parts 1704

22

23 Simon Scroope, Esqr.

The eldest of three sons of Simon Scroope, 6th of Danby (1615–1691), who married Mary, daughter of Michael Wharton of Beverley, Simon Scroope, 7th of Danby (1666–1723), whose bookplate this is, married firstly Mary, the daughter of Robert Constable, 3rd Viscount Dunbar; she died in February 1694–5 without issue; he then married Frances, daughter of Ralph Sheldon of Beoly in Worcestershire (whose bookplate is No. 10). By her, Scroope left at his death two sons and three daughters. Though there is a degree of complexity about the various Scroope bookplates—which will be detailed below—one can say that the plate illustrated is the larger of two which Scroope used; his smaller plate has single arms, occurs in the Brighton Collection, and reads 'Simon Scroop [sic] of Danby Esqr.'. His sister's bookplate, also in that collection, reads 'Mrs. Margaret Scroope' and shows the arms of Scroope quartering Tibetot, Badlesmere and Fitz Bernard (the address 'Mrs.' was a common courtesy title at the time for mature unmarried ladies). Though Scroope's large armorial is not in the Brighton Collection there is little doubt that it emanates from the workshop of William Jackson (see p. 10), and the Scroope plates so far described are in themselves some evidence of the diverse hands at work there. It is also worthy of note that the example of the large plate in the Franks Collection appears to have been used as a bookplate, though it is a late print. The complexity referred to above arises from the existence of a second and variant copper of the large Early Armorial. The story of this can be fully investigated in *The Ex Libris Journal* for June and August 1899, and involves the strange vicissitudes of the copper(s) of the armorial (experience incidentally shows that even today there are few things as apparently vulnerable as coppers and wood-blocks). The author of the 'Book Notice' in the above *Journal* for June of that year records of the large plate that 'about twenty years ago the plate, known to be at Danby, was looked for but could not be found. Shortly after, Mr. Scrope [the spelling of the family name having altered by this time] and his daughters were in town, and went one day to the family lawyer to look over some old deeds, etc., and there came upon the missing copper. Miss Margaret Scrope (the family genealogist) was so delighted that she took possession of it, with the intention of carrying it back to Danby. On the way back to their hotel in a cab they called at various shops. The next day they returned home, and on arriving Miss Margaret was horrified to find the plate had again disappeared. No end of trouble was taken to find the plate at the hotel, the lawyer's office, cabs, shops, etc., through the police, but all without effect. All hope of ever finding it seemed gone. In 1895–6, wanting it for his 'Armorial Book-plates', Mr Metcalfe offered to advertise in a few likely papers for the missing plate, but suggested that it might be as well to have another hunt at Danby in boxes of papers from the lawyer's about the peerage case. This was done, and in one case, in a loft in the roof, the plate was again found, to the great delight of the family'. As a result, the copper they found was reprinted in J. H. Metcalfe's *A great historical peerage, the earldom of Wilts,* 1899. The correct answer to this careless and cautionary tale of the lost copper seems almost certainly to have been provided by James Hayes in the August number of the above *Journal*: the copper found at Danby must surely have been there all the time, and the copper lost in London must have been a second one. It was a version of the large armorial, but probably a later variant, for Hayes possessed a print of one in use as a bookplate in a copy of Heylin's *Help to History,* 1773. Though his print was cut down in size to fit this particular book, it was seen to differ in its motto. Unfortunately the motto scroll was also damaged in the cutting down, but part of the motto reading '*Esp* [overlapped] *tend Grace*' was left, and this bears no relation to the Mainwaring motto, '*Devant si je puis*', which appears on the large original Scroope plate. One would be grateful to know of any prints of the variant in existence today.

DEVANT SI IE.PUIS

SIMON SCROOPE, OF DANBY SUPER YORE, IN COM. EBOR. ESQ. 1698. quarters as his Complete Atchievment, by right of Descent from Heirs General, these several Coats of Arms, viz.

1. *Scroope*, of Bolton; Baron. 2. *Tibetot*, of Langar; Baron. 3. *Badlesmere*, of Leeds-Castle, Baron. 4. *Fitz-Bernard*, of Kingsdown; Baron. 5. *Clare*, Steward of the Forest of Essex; Baron. 6. *Gifford*, Earl of Buckingham. 7. *S.Hillary*, a Noble Family. 8. *Constb*, Earl of Gloucester. 9. *Fitz-Hamon*, Earl of Carboil. 10. *Marshall*, Earl of Pembroke. 11. *Strongbow*, Earl of Pembroke. 12. *Mac-Morogh*, King of Leinster. 13. *Lacy*, Earl of Lincoln. 14. *Fitz-John*, Constable of Chester. 15. *Nigel*, Baron of Halton. 16. *Lizures*, a Noble Family. 17. *Quincy*, Earl of Lincoln. 18. *Bellamont*, Earl of Leicester. 19. *Waleran*, Earl of Mellent. 20. *Waher or Guader*, Earl of Norfolk. 21. *Fitz-Osborn*, Earle of Hereford. 22. *Grantmesnel*, of Hinkley; Baron. 23. *Chester*, Earl. 24. *Lupus*, Earl of Chester. 25. *Leofric*, Earl of Mercia. 26. *Fitz-Maurice-Fitz-Girald*, Justice of Ireland. 27. *Conyers*, of Danby. 28. *Scrope*, as before.

23

24 Sir John Aubrey, Baronet

The arms of the Aubrey bookplate are Aubrey quartering Mansel, Bassett and South, and it was engraved for Sir John, the 2nd Baronet (d.1700), who married firstly Margaret, daughter of Sir John Lowther, Bart., who bore his son and successor, and then Mary, daughter and coheir of William Lewis of The Van, in the county of Glamorgan, and Boarstall and Brill, in the county of Buckingham, widow of William Jephson who died in 1691. Sir John died from a fall from his horse, and his son, Sir John (1680–1743), adopted his father's bookplate and used it, apparently, in two states: first retaining the 1698 date but omitting the escutcheon of pretence, then re-dated 1717. A smaller version of 1698 date occurs in the Brighton Collection, but it may never have been used as an *ex-libris*.

25 William Fitz-Gerald, Lord Bishop of Clonfert

Though generally described as Jacobean, this is really a transitional bookplate and is also reminiscent of a larger and more handsome plate belonging to Gilbert Sheldon, Archbishop of Canterbury, who died in 1677. The son of Dr John Fitzgerald, Dean of Cork, William Fitz-gerald (d. 1702) was born in that city; he became Dean of Cloyne, and was consecrated Bishop of Clonfert in 1691. He was twice married: firstly in 1688 to Letitia Cole, the daughter of Sir John Cole of Newland, 1st Baronet, and secondly to Mary, widow of Boyle Maynard Esq., and 2nd daughter of Sir Henry Tynte of Ballinairy. The arms shown on the bookplate are Fitzgerald impaling Cole.

26 John Sayer, Esq.

This bookplate belonged to John Sayer (d. 1712), who held the Manor of Hounslow. This and the site of the hospital were sold by the Povey family in 1671 to James Smith and Henry Meuse, Esquires, and the following year were conveyed to Henry Sayer, Esq., Drysalter, of London and Biddlesden (or Bitlesden) in Buckingham-shire. He was still living in 1681, but died soon after, and was succeeded by his son John Sayer, then still a minor, who sold the Manor of Hounslow in 1705 to Whitelock Bulstrode. Sayer was murdered in 1712 by John Notley, an attorney, who—according to the *Victoria County History*—'had intrigued with his wife'. He was succeeded by his son Henry Sayer, who seems an even less attractive character than his father (who had destroyed a figure of Christ at Biddlesden Church in 1704), for he demolished evidence of the site of the ancient Abbey, destroyed the old St. Margaret's Chapel and desecrated its churchyard— for he told Browne Willis (see his *History and antiquities of Buckingham*) that he had 'several thousand human bones removed and thrown away, as he gloried in, to level ground, together with the rubbish, with great indecency'. He did, however, build the present parish church at Biddlesden. Henry (d. c.1755) used his father's bookplate, with its inscription amended to read 'Henry Sayer of Bidlesden in the County of Bucks'. This armorial is a particularly interesting example of the variety of treat-ment of the Early Armorial style in the plates of the Brighton Collection, notably in its mantling and the inscription tablet.

27 William Rogers, Esqr.

The elder son and heir of Richard Rogers of the Upper House, Dowdeswell, William Rogers (1657–1734), of Dowdeswell House, in Gloucestershire, formerly of Filberts in the Parish of Bray, Berkshire, was educated at Oriel College, Oxford and Lincoln's Inn, of which he became a barrister-at-law in 1685. He was treasurer of Lincoln's Inn in 1715, became Senior Master in the High Court of Chancery, and was eventually threatened with the Fleet Prison and forced to resign this post for speculating with suitors' funds. He never married. In an article in *The Times* of 28th November, 1959 there is an entertaining account of his portrait, which had been left some little time before in the library of the Chancery Masters by someone who thought they might like to purchase it. Rogers' bookplate occurs in several variants. It is known cut round, which generally suggests use by a later member of a family; a print is recorded in the Marshall Sale Catalogue with the date altered in manu-script to 1766; and there is a nineteenth-century reprint.

Sʳ Iohn Aubrey of Lantrithyd in the
County of Glamorgan Baronet and of
Boareſtall in the County of Bucks 1698

24

William Fitz-Gerald Lord Biſhop
of Clonfert 1698.

25

Iohn Sayer of Hownslow in the
County of Midd: Esqʳ 1700.

26

William Rogers,
of Dowdeswell, in the County
of Glocester Esqʳ: 1700

27

[39]

28 Charles, Earl of Dorset

Charles Sackville, 6th Earl of Dorset (1638–1706), succeeded his father in 1677, and in right of his mother succeeded to the estates of the Earl of Middlesex. Created a Knight of the Garter in 1691, his second wife was Mary, daughter of James, 3rd Earl of Northampton, and niece of Bishop Henry Compton (see No. 31). Sackville was a poet whose life was early somewhat dissipated, and at one time he took under his wing Nell Gwynne who is said to have called him her Charles I. Dr Johnson described his verse as 'gay, vigorous and airey', and he showed a kindly concern for other poets, for he recognised the youthful talent of Prior and assisted his education, and also financially assisted Dryden. His bookplate shows the typical arrangement of large Early Armorials with supporters; the earlier form of the style without supporters—to about 1700—is shown by the Aubrey plate (No. 24), and the later large Early Armorial without supporters by the Jodrell plate (No. 33).

29 Sir Peter Killigrew, Knight and Baronet

The Killigrews were an ancient Cornish family, and acquired the Arwennick estate through marriage with an heiress in the reign of Richard II. Sir Peter Killigrew (d. 1704) was the son of Sir Peter Killigrew, knight, who was known as 'Sir Peter the Post' on account of his faithfulness in taking messages to Charles I during the Civil War, and succeeded his uncle Sir William as 2nd Baronet in 1665. He married Frances, daughter of Sir Roger Twisden of East Peckham in Kent, and by her had one son and two daughters. His son George was killed in a tavern in Penryn by a Captain Walter Vincent, who, though acquitted, took the affair so much to heart that he sank under the affliction. On Sir Peter's death the title became extinct. This ex-libris shows in smaller size the work of the engraver of the Jodrell plate (see No. 33).

30 Anthony, Earle of Kent

The Grey family used an interesting group of bookplates, and shown here is the smaller of two armorials of identical design for Anthony, 11th Earl of Kent (d. 1702), engraved in the year of his death. He succeeded in 1651 his father, Henry, the 10th Earl—whose wife, incidentally, survived him forty-seven years. Both sizes of this bookplate are in the Brighton Collection, as is a version of the smaller with its inscription re-engraved, but with the same date, for his successor and only son Henry, the 12th Earl (d. 1741), later created Marquess, and in 1710 Duke of Kent. As Duke he used four finely engraved bookplates: large and small armorials dated 1713 and 1733. The smaller of the earlier of these shows Grey quartering Lucas, with Crewe on an escutcheon—his first wife being Jemima, daughter and coheir of Thomas, 2nd Baron Crewe of Steine (the earlier of her two plates is shown at No. 50). The 1733 plates both show Grey impaling Bentinck—his second wife, whom he married in 1728, being Sophia, daughter of Hans William, 1st Earl of Portland. The Duke's son, Anthony, Earl of Harold, who died in 1723, had a bookplate dated 1717, and his wife Mary one dated a year later.

31 Henry Compton, Lord Bishop of London

A fine example of an episcopal Early Armorial. These took several forms, sometimes eschewing the mantling for a wreath of palms, sometimes showing neither, but often having the crossed crozier and key and almost invariably ensigned with the episcopal mitre. A number of early episcopal ex-libris are illustrated in W. Griggs' 147 Examples of Armorial Book Plates, 1892. Henry Compton (1632–1713) was sixth son of the 2nd Earl of Northampton. Bishop of London from 1675 to 1712, he signed the invitation to William of Orange to accept the Crown of England in 1688, and crowned William III and Mary at Westminster in 1689, since Archbishop Sancroft of Canterbury had refused to subscribe the oath of allegiance.

32 Thomas Knatchbull, Esqr.

Thomas Knatchbull was son of Sir Thomas Knatchbull, 3rd Bart. (d. c. 1712), who succeeded in 1696 and married Mary, daughter of Sir Edward Dering, 2nd Bart. The Knatchbulls had been at Mersham Hatch since it was purchased by Richard Knatchbull in 1485. Mantle plates of this period are not common, though they enjoyed a small popularity later, but another good early example, also in the Brighton Collection, is the plate of Sir John Wentworth, Baronet.

TOUS IOURS LOYAL

The Right Hon.ble Charles Earl of Dorset and Middlesex
Knight of the most Noble Order of the Garter

28

Sr. Peter Killigrew of
Arwenack in Cornwall
Knight and Baronet

29

The Right Hon.ble Anthony Earle
of Kent: 1702

30

Henry Compton Lord Bishop
of London 1701

31

Thomas Knatchbull Esqr. third Son of
Sr. Thomas Knatchbull of Mershamhatch
in the County of Kent Baronet: 1702

32

33 Paul Jodrell, Esqr.

Paul Jodrell (1646–1728), of Duffield in Derbyshire, was the son of Symon Jodrell of Lichfield, who died before 17th May, 1707. As Clerk to the House of Commons, Jodrell was obviously much respected, for though Richard Onslow, irreverently called 'stiff Dick' by the Tories, was made Speaker in Queen Anne's third Parliament, some would have preferred Sir Peter King or Paul Jodrell, and it was suggested that the latter was the most competent adviser in matters of precedent and procedure. He married Jane, eldest daughter of Thomas Rolles of Lewknor in Oxfordshire, Esquire, at St. James', Clerkenwell on 8th January, 1673, and she died at the age of seventy-eight in 1727, the year before her husband's death; both are buried at Lewknor. Jodrell's bookplate is amongst the most handsome of the large Early Armorials, both for its balance and fine mantling and for the artistic advantage of its single arms. A small version of the plate, clearly engraved by the same hand, also exists. Both sizes are known in nineteenth-century reprints, and a reproduction in an intermediate size but based upon the larger one was used by Neville Paul Jodrell of the Inner Temple, barrister-at-law, probably towards the end of the nineteenth-century. Paul Jodrell's first son, Paul, barrister-at-law, married Judith. daughter and coheiress of Gilbert Sheldon, of the family of Archbishop Sheldon, whose bookplate is illustrated in Griggs' *Examples*, 2nd Series. Jodrell's grandson, Paul, was solicitor-general to Frederick, Prince of Wales, and seemed set for a distinguished legal career, but he died in 1751 aged about thirty-six.

Paul Jodrell of Duffield in y County of Derby Esq. Clerk of y Hon.ble House of Commous

33

34 New College, Oxford

Oxford and Cambridge college bookplates might be expected to give useful reference to developments of bookplate style, but librarians tended to reprint Early Armorial and Jacobean plates long after they ceased in use elsewhere, and specific gifts or bequests were often marked by book labels—some printed centuries after the donation (see the author's *Early Printed Book Labels*). This Early Armorial was the first plate used by New College and shows the arms and motto of its founder, William of Wykeham, son of a carpenter and the first of his family to bear arms, who became Bishop of Winchester in 1368. The early New College plates are all listed by Henderson Smith in *The Ex Libris Journal* for June, 1902. Hamilton, quoting Warren, describes the plate as showing Wykeham's arms impaling those of the See of Winchester, but this is not so. The other New College bookplates include a similar undated example, but with the mitre turned slightly to the right, which continued in use printed from the worn plate as late as 1844; two states of a Jacobean design, one with 'MANERS' in the motto, the other with 'MANNERS'; a rare Chippendale signed by S. Nash, with two shields, the arms of the second being Eyre; and a simple armorial first used in 1894. The plate now used is a process block of the plate illustrated with the inscription and part of its tablet removed. (See also No. 36).

35 Thomas Penn

Thomas Penn (1702–1775) was son of the Quaker founder of Pennsylvania, and with his brothers succeeded his father as hereditary proprietors of the province. Born at Kensington while his parents were visiting England, he married in 1751 Lady Juliana Fermor, daughter of the Earl of Pomfret. He used his father's bookplate with re-engraved inscription and the shading of the three roundels on the fess removed. In its original state this *ex-libris* is much sought after, and is one of very few of which a forgery exists. The genuine plate is shown in Warren's *Guide to the Study of Book-plates,* but Allen in *American Book-plates* illustrates the forgery in error. The fake is easy to identify, for the uneven shading of the roundels of the original is marked, the lines almost merging at points, whereas in the fraudulent copy their shading is regular and there is a dot at the centre. The inscription reads 'William Penn Esqr. Proprietor of Pensylvania [sic]: 1703', and the engraving is English work. William Penn (1644–1718), having decided that freedom from persecution for his co-religionists lay in America, obtained by letters patent grants of East New Jersey and Pennsylvania in 1682.

36 Trinity Hall, Cambridge

This and the bookplate beside it are among the earliest examples of the Jacobean style, and show by comparison with No. 34 how it co-existed with the Early Armorial even at this early date. Like many Jacobeans it eschews the crest, though the College has one, and it shows the fish-scale ornament typical of the style. It incorrectly shows the bordure engrailed, and unlike most Jacobean plates it was superseded by an Early Armorial, by Cole of London from a design by a scholar, John Bunce; the inscription of the latter reads 'Trinity Hall in ye University of Cambridge 1724'. Our illustration (and probably also the Mason armorial at its side) was the work of William Jackson, a London engraver who was responsible for over forty Oxford and Cambridge college *ex-libris* at the turn of the eighteenth century; he seems to have worked in Cambridge between 1700 and 1702 and in Oxford 1702 to 1704. However, it was not until 1706 that the Bursar's accounts showed £5 12s 6d. (£5.62½p) paid for the 'Copper Plate of the College Arms, Prints & pasting ym on'.

37 Dame Anna Margaretta Mason

Probably by the same engraver, or at least from the same workshop as No. 36, this is among the earliest of ladies' bookplates. Printed book labels had been used in a small way by ladies in the previous century, but after the earliest recorded woman's bookplate—the gift plate of the Dowager Countess of Bath, 1671 (a number of examples of which occur in books in the library of Trinity College, Dublin)—there are no others until Dame Alice Brownlowe's two dated armorials of 1698, after which they modestly established themselves fairly quickly. The Jacobean style seems perfectly to ornament an armorial lozenge (proper to unmarried ladies and widows). Dame Anna was the widow of Sir Richard Mason, Knight, who, as the inscription tells us, was 'Late Clerke Comtroler of the Green Cloath to King Charles and King Iames the Second'; she was the daughter of Sir James Long of Draycot Cerne in Wiltshire.

34

35

36

37

38 Mr. George Craufurd

The genealogist and historian George Craufurd (or Crawfurd) was son of Thomas Crawfurd of Cartsburn and his wife Jean Semple. Born on 20th June, 1684, he married Margaret, daughter of James Anderson the author of *Diplomata Scotiæ*, and died at Glasgow in 1748. Some of his manuscripts were in the Advocates' Library (now transferred to the National Library of Scotland), and all his books have on the title-page an inscription reading 'George Craufurd is owner hereof'. He was the author of *Genealogical History of the Royal House of Stewart*, 1710, *The Peerage of Scotland,* and *Lives and Character of the Crown Officers of Scotland,* 1726, and was employed by Simon Fraser to investigate his claim to the barony of Lovat; but though Craufurd's researches are said to have aided his success he was not paid for his work and indignantly called Fraser one of the greatest scoundrels in the world (Fraser's bookplate is No. 43). Little is known of Archibald Burden, the engraver, but he was son of James Burden and his wife Margaret Drummond who was said to be a daughter of James, Earl of Perth. *Alexander Nisbet's Heraldic Plates*, ed. Andrew Ross, 1892, gives this information under the Burden of Feddal genealogy, where he is described as 'Goldsmith and Engraver in Edinburgh'. Since, however, his name doesn't appear in the list of the craft of goldsmiths of Edinburgh, he was probably principally a goldsmith's engraver, albeit a poor one. This and the four following illustrations show the style and standard of early Scottish armorial bookplate work. (See John Orr's article on Burden in *The Ex Libris Journal* for February 1896.)

39 Birnie of Broomhill

Like the preceding plate this is the work of Burden; it occurs in several states, and though they are too complex to be detailed here there is a thorough account of them in J. Henderson Smith's notes with his bookplate collection at the National Library of Scotland. The bookplate belonged to John Birnie, who was born at Caerlaverock on 29th December, 1674, was apprenticed to a writer to the Signet in Edinburgh, and married in 1702 Elizabeth, the daughter of Alexander Frogg, merchant in Edinburgh. She died aged thirty-nine in 1716, leaving eight children. A larger armorial for John Birnie by Robert Wood, without supporters and engraved originally for Nisbet's *System of Heraldry* (see the notes on Sir James Primerose's bookplate which follow, and the author's article referred to there) was used as a bookplate; there are prints in the Franks and Crouch Collections, and Henderson Smith notes that it occurred in a copy of L'Estrange's *Fables of Aesop,* 1692, which also had Birnie's signature in it. There is a list of Birnie's library in 1728 in BM. MS.28,850, and a record of the family in Turnbull's *Account of the Families of Birnie, etc.,* Edinburgh, 1838.

40 Mr. John Balvaird M.D.

This extremely rare armorial is difficult to date on account of its individuality, but its heraldic style suggests that it is certainly the earliest of the four plates here shown. It is undoubtedly Scottish work. A print, then in the possession of Miss E. Davidson, was illustrated in W. Griggs' *147 Examples of Armorial Book Plates*, 1892, and it occurs in the Crouch Collection, with a manuscript note on the back suggesting that Balvaird was Chaplain to the Archbishop of St. Andrews in the seventeenth century.

41 Sir Hew Dalrymple, Baronet

Sir Hew Dalrymple, third son of James, 1st Viscount Stair, was born in 1652; he was elected in 1690 to the Scottish parliament for the burgh of New Galloway in Kirkcudbrightshire, and in 1698 was created a Baronet of Nova Scotia and nominated by William III Lord President of the Court of Session, an office vacant since the death of his father three years earlier. He retained this office until he died in 1737, and Lord Woodhouselee said of him that 'If he inherited not the distinguished talents of his father, the Viscount of Stair, and his elder brother, the secretary, [he] was free from that turbulent ambition and crafty policy which marked the characters of both; and with sufficient knowledge of the laws was a man of unimpeached integrity, and of great private worth and amiable manners'. His elder brother John, the 1st Earl, used an Early Armorial bookplate, and his younger brother, Sir David of Hailes, created a baronet in 1700, a Jacobean in its early form, both plates of English workmanship and probably engraved by William Jackson (see p. 10).

38

39

40

41

42 Sir James Primerose

Alexander Nisbet, the heraldic writer, published the first volume of his *System of Heraldry* in 1722, the arms twelve to a plate, but it was a mere shadow of what he had intended, for writing of illustrations for his proposed 'Heraldry' in 1699 he stated: 'I have already a considerable Number of Plates . . . the Nobility every one of them on a Plate by themselves . . . many of the Gentry by two's on one plate'. He had planned to publish by subscription, the money to go to the engravers and the plates to be restored to the owners when the book was published. The proposals, however, hung fire and a promised Parliament Grant in Aid remained unpaid until cancelled by the Union, so Nisbet had to abandon his scheme; the 'Heraldry' was published on a modest scale, and the copper plates were presumably returned. Two collections of prints of them are known, and the combined total of plates is eighty-four. Several of them were used by their owners as bookplates in spite of their large size. Dr. J. Henderson Smith, who made a study of the armorials, notes of the Primerose plate that 'use as a bookplate is evidenced by a book in the possession of Mr John Orr, which contains the plate together with the autograph of Sr. Ja. Primerose himself', and G. H. Viner had the plate in a copy of *The Acts & Orders of the Meeting of the Estates of the Kingdom of Scotland,* etc., 1690, pasted on the verso of the title-page. A list of other plates in the series which occur as *ex-libris* may be found in an article by the author, 'A problem for the bookplate collector', in *The Private Library* for Autumn 1973. Sir James Primerose of Carrington (d. 1706), second son of Sir William Primerose, was MP for Edinburghshire in 1702. This armorial must pre-date his creation as Viscount Primerose on 30th November, 1703. He married Lady Eleanor Campbell, youngest daughter of James, 2nd Earl of Loudoun; she later married John, 2nd Earl of Stair, and died in 1759.

FIDE · ET · FIDUCIA

Sʳ James Primerose of Carington Barronet

Rᵒ Wood. sculp

42

43 Simon Lord Fraser of Lovat

Illustrated here is the second of two states of this plate; the first differs in reading 'Cheif' and 'Fraser's' in the inscription. A pleasant example of an armorial on a mantle, its greater interest lies in its owner. The life of Simon, 12th Baron Lovat (?1667–1747) was packed with such Jacobite and personal intrigue as would be impossible to summarise here. The death of Hugh, Lord Lovat in 1696 brought the inheritance to Simon's father, as heir male, and Simon tried to marry by force his cousin's daughter. Failing in this he compelled her mother to marry him, taking a clergyman to her room at night to wed them and causing bagpipes to be blown to drown her cries. Proceedings were taken against him and he was condemned to be executed, but he evaded capture. Later adventures led to imprisonment in France, escape to London and arrest, and a full pardon in 1715. In succeeding years he several times pressed his claim to the title Lord Lovat, and was finally successful in 1733. However, his involvement in the Rebellion of 1745 led to arrest, and he was brought to London and beheaded on Tower Hill in 1747. (See note to No. 38.) Mantle plates enjoyed small favour over a long period, and in the absence of other evidence are most easily dated by examination of the ornamentation or manner of the armorial frame.

44 The Honble. Ann North

This beautiful little armorial is by Simon Gribelin (1661–1733). Born at Blois, he studied engraving in Paris and came to England in 1680; though he was little noticed for twenty years, his engravings after the Raphael cartoons, completed in 1707, were admired and led to increased work; but he failed to recapture the manner of the masters he copied. However, he ornamented many books with pleasant engravings, and eleven bookplates he made (including No. 49) are listed by Fincham. Others, unknown to Fincham, include a pictorial for Ro(ber)t Baillie, MD, the anonymous armorial for Richard Boyle, Earl of Burlington (who died 1753), and anonymous Jacobean plates for Floyer or Slayer and the Hon. Russell Robartes (the last of which occurs in a second signed state). The Hon. Ann North was daughter of Dudley, 4th Baron North and Anne, daughter and coheiress of Sir Charles Montagu, Kt.; she married Robert Foley of Stourbridge. The bookplate was also used by a later member of the family, for the Christian name is often seen amended in manuscript to 'Aud' (as here), presumably Audrey, and the print in the Franks Collection has the name cut off.

45 Dr. Timothy Goodwyn, Lord Arch Bishop of Cashel

Timothy Goodwyn (c. 1670–1729)—whose name is elsewhere given as Godwin or Godwyn—was born at Norwich and began his education at the nonconformist academy of Samuel Cradock at Geesings in Suffolk. At first intended for a medical career, he entered St. Edmund's Hall, Oxford, and graduated MA in 1697; he was domestic chaplain to Charles, Duke of Shrewsbury, and after travelling abroad with him went to Ireland in his company in October 1713. The following year Goodwyn was made Bishop of Kilmore and Ardagh, and he was translated to the Archbishopric of Cashel in 1727. The arms of the bookplate are those of the See of Cashel impaling Goodwyn with Anderson(?) quartering Alleyne on an escutcheon. There are many interesting ecclesiastical bookplates, and a series of them, including many Irish ones, is illustrated in W. Griggs' *147 Examples of Armorial Book Plates,* 2nd Series, 1892.

46 (Peregrine Bertie)

This exceedingly rare bookplate shows the arms of Bertie with an escutcheon of pretence, Hungerford quartering Dayrell, in right of his wife Elizabeth, the daughter and heiress of John Hungerford of Doctors' Commons, a descendant of the Hungerfords of Cadenham (a family for which William Faithorne engraved a very fine bookplate in the seventeenth century); she was the widow of John Fisher of London, merchant, and died in 1731. Peregrine Bertie (d. 1743), was the son of Peregrine Bertie of Long Sutton in Lincolnshire, descended from the second son of the 1st Lord Willoughby d'Eresby. They were married at St. Paul's Cathedral on 8th November 1720, when he was described as of Low Layton in Essex. They resided at Layton and were buried there. An engraving of Bertie by E. Finden is in the British Museum (see the *Catalogue of Engraved British Portraits,* 1908–25), based on a miniature. The bookplate was engraved by G. Davis, who is otherwise apparently unknown, and yet crude though his workmanship is his design is remarkably ambitious for one who apparently left no other signed bookplate.

E SUIS PREST

SINE SANGUINE VICTOR

The R.t Hon.ble Simon Lord Fraser of Lovat,
Chief of the Ancient Clan of the Fraser's,
Governour of Inverneſs &c.

43

The Hon.ble Dud.e North

44

D.r Timothy Goodwyn
Lord
Arch Bishop of Cashel

45

46

47 Sir Francis Fust, Baronet

An example of a bookplate with misleading date, which indicates in this instance the creation of the baronetcy and not the date of the engraving. In fact it cannot have been engraved before 1728, in which year Sir Francis succeeded as 5th Baronet on the death of his half-brother Sir Edward. This is the largest of three bookplates he used; the others are of more usual size, one with quarterly Fust arms impaling Tooker, the other—which is incidentally the rarest of the three—with the single Fust arms. There are, however, two variants of the large plate, for it is also known printed in red, and occurs in black without the motto above the crest (both are exceedingly rare, but extant prints are in the de Tabley Collection). Sir Francis married in 1724 Fanny, daughter of Nicholas Tooker, merchant of the city of Bristol, and died in 1769. The forty quarterings are all named, and Henry Jenner, writing on the Fust lineage in *The Ex Libris Journal,* suggests there is good reason to believe that when Sir Francis could not find a real ancestor he invented one and that his assertion that he descended from the associate of Schoeffer at Mainz is fanciful. Perhaps no other Jacobean bookplate is so overloaded with arms, and it is also unique in its identification by name of all the quarterings. A note signed 'C.S.B' in *Gentlemen's Magazine,* March, 1823, states, 'I lately had in my possession a copy of Wither's *Emblems,* printed in 1635, which contained two different book plates for the same owner, one at each end of the Book, a peculiarity I have only observed in this instance'. These were the Fust plates, one of the small armorials at the front, the larger at the back. There was also in the Marshall Collection a copy of *The Character of Queen Elizabeth,* 1693, with two Fust bookplates. Such usage may, therefore, have been Fust's custom, as it was Pepys' (see notes on Nos. 11 & 12). For fuller details of the Fust plates and genealogy see *The Ex Libris Journal,* August–October 1892, and Warren's *A Guide to the Study of Book-plates.* There is a chapter on 'Arbitrary dates, and doubtful plates' in Hamilton's *Dated Book-plates,* and the problem is also discussed in Hardy's *Book-plates,* 1st edition, pp.34–37, 2nd edition, pp.43–47.

48 Arthur Onslow

The elder son of Foot Onslow, Arthur Onslow (1691–1768) was educated at Winchester and Wadham College, Oxford, though he took no degree, and in 1713 he was called to the bar at the Middle Temple. He was the third of his family to occupy the office of Speaker of the House of Commons, which post he held for thirty-three years, 1728–1761. By all accounts a man of rare public zeal and unimpeachable probity, he was highly esteemed by all parties, and Sir Robert Walpole found him no pliant political tool. In the 1727 general election he was returned both for Guildford and for Surrey, and continued to represent the county until his retirement. In 1720 he married Anne, the daughter of John Bridges of Thames Ditton, and by her had a son, George, who became 1st Earl of Onslow, and a daughter who died unmarried. His bookplate, the original copper for which may be seen on display at Clandon Park near Guildford, the family seat, shows the Speaker's insignia. Prints of it are in many collections, for the Clandon Library, which Onslow formed, was sold by Sotheby's in 1885, and nineteenth-century reprints also occur, printed in red, brown or black. There is also a rare early state of it without the name, an example of which occurred in the Marshall Sale in 1906. Its engraver, the first B. Cole of London, was probably Benjamin Cole whom Ambrose Heal records as being at London House Yard, St. Paul's Churchyard in 1725 and 1729 (see 'The trade cards of engravers', *The Print Collectors' Quarterly,* July 1927). The plate is, however, more notable as the only *ex-libris* design by William Kent (1684–1748), the painter, sculptor, architect and landscape-gardener. Born in Yorkshire, William Kent ran away to London about 1704 after an apprenticeship to a coach-painter. On arriving there his winning manners quickly gained him popularity and such was his promise that friends paid towards a period of study in Rome, which he visited in all three times. It was there in 1716 that he met Lord Burlington, who brought him back to England and made an apartment available in his house for the rest of Kent's life. Kent had little success with portraiture and illustrations, but found his metier in ornamental design and, by rescuing nature from the shears and the compass, in landscape-gardening; indeed, he became something of an all-round oracle of taste in his day, according to Walpole.

47

48

49 Sir Philip Sydenham

No Englishman until Victorian times used as many bookplates as Sydenham, for whom eleven plates in twenty-three varieties are known. The 3rd Baronet, he succeeded his father in 1696 and died unmarried in 1739, when the baronetcy became extinct. A reason accounting for several plates is his changing his crest and motto three times, but only a real liking for *ex-libris* can explain them all. The first were large and small Early Armorials, the earliest 1699 state of the former noting that he was 'of Brimpton in Sommerset & M.A. of ye Univercity of Cambridge'; later states mention his residing also at Hackness in Yorkshire and his fellowship of the Royal Society. His 1699 bookpile, a very early example of the style, is a poor armorial, but like several of the plates mentioned above declares that he was then in his twenty-third year. His fourth bookplate, shown here, is by Simon Gribelin (for details of whom see No. 44), who engraved three more plates for him: a crest and monogram 'P.S' and two crests, one reading 'Sir Philip Sydenham', the other with 'Baronet' added. Next comes a Jacobean quartering the Stourton arms, followed by one reading 'Ye Waunges. 1727', later altered by St. Barbe Sydenham; another Jacobean is dated 1735, and his last plate, with ram and crucifixes, is in two states, the latter dated 1738. For details see *The Ex Libris Journal* for November 1899 and February 1902, where the states are fully listed.

50 Jemima Dutchess of Kent. 1710

Other bookplates of this family have already been noted (see No. 30), and it seems curious that Henry, Duke of Kent's first bookplates are dated three years later than his dukedom, than this plate for his first wife, and a year later than her second Jacobean plate, dated 1712; perhaps he was finally persuaded to use one by his installation as Knight of the Garter in 1713. Highly esteemed by both George I and George II, the Duke carried St. Edward's staff at the latter's coronation. After Jemima's death he married in 1728 Sophia, daughter of the 1st Earl of Portland. Note here the quaint spelling of his wife's title, and more importantly how Jacobean bookplate design was amended to accommodate two shields accolé.

51 Henrietta Countess of Pomfret

Also with two shields accolé, but transitional in its hint of the Chippendale style, this is one of three *ex-libris* for Henrietta Fermor, Countess of Pomfret. The daughter and heiress of John, Baron Jeffreys of Wem, she was grand-daughter of Judge Jeffreys. In 1720 she married Thomas Fermor, 2nd Baron Leominster, who the following year was created Earl of Pomfret; he held office as Master of the Horse to Queen Caroline, and his wife was Lady of the Bedchamber until her retirement from public life at the Queen's death in 1737. Her other bookplates are a Jacobean armorial trophy dated 1733, also seen printed in red-brown, and a large Chippendale pictorial armorial by Samuel Wale (see note to No. 88). A variant of the plate illustrated has the Herbert and Vere quarterings wrongly tinctured. *The correspondence between Frances, Countess of Hartford and Henrietta Louisa, Countess of Pomfret,* 1805, is an interesting record of the Countess's later life.

52 The Revd. Mr. Saml. Guise

Samuel Guise (1681–c. 1735), son of Thomas Guise of Burcester (Bicester) in Oxfordshire was educated at Gloucester Hall, Oxford. He became master of the Grammar School at High Wycombe in 1707 (remaining there until 1750), Vicar of Thame in 1711, chaplain to Philip, Duke of Wharton in 1719, and was presented to the living of Chipping Wycombe twice, in 1711 and 1724. This unusual plate is among a small series of early eighteenth-century bookplates cut on type metal, pewter, or sometimes wood, several of which—including perhaps this example—are ascribable to Francis Hoffman, whose cuts adorn many books of the period (see No. 219). For an account of Hoffman see Stanley Morison's *The English Newspaper,* 1932.

53 Saml. Bracebridge

The son of Abraham Bracebridge of Atherstone in Warwickshire, Bracebridge was educated at Brasenose College, Oxford, and was called to the bar at Inner Temple in June 1699. He was MP for Tamworth from 1710 to 1722, and served as Treasurer at Inner Temple from November 1733 to November 1734. The particular significance of the bookplate's precise date is not apparent from Inner Temple records. Three of his sons were later admitted to the Inn, and Samuel Bracebridge died before 19th November 1735, having been confined to bed for some time.

MIHI

DUX

DEUS

Sr Philip Sydenham   S: Gribelin sculp:

49

IEMIMA DUTCHESS
OF KENT.
MDCCX.

50

The Right Honble Henrietta Countess of
Pomfret Lady of the Bed Chamber to the Queen

51

The Revd Mr Saml GUISE
Vicar of CHIPPING WICOMBE BUCKS.

52

INNER TEMPLE

PRODESSE JUVABIT

Saml BRACEBRIDGE TREASURER
Feb 2d 1733. 4 o'Clock

53

54 Henrietta Cavendish Holles

Described in Horace Walpole's *Catalogue of Engravers*, 1794, as a 'Plate to put in Lady Oxford's books', this *ex-libris* by George Vertue is unique in the phraseology of its inscription, which indicates the plate was used only for books which were gifts. The printed inscription reads 'Henrietta Cavendish Holles Oxford and Mortimer Given me by', and a print in the author's collection is typical in its manuscript addition 'my Lord June 1732'. Considering that the Countess was the only daughter and heiress of John Holles, 4th Earl of Clare and subsequently Duke of Newcastle, and that much of her fortune of over half a million pounds was spent by her husband in the enhancement of his father's library, her modesty in recording his gifts of books to her is rather touching. The bookplate was probably engraved about the year 1730, for examples of that date are extant, but it had been her custom similarly to record such gifts in manuscript before the plate was engraved, for a copy of the second edition of Swift's *Miscellanies in Prose and Verse*, 1713, has a manuscript inscription 'Henrietta Cavendish Holles Harley, Given by my Lord May 1720', and other inscriptions seen record early gifts from her mother; they are also, incidentally, rather pleasant pieces of calligraphy. Though no other British bookplate contains a similar donatory inscription, a copy of William King's *The Art of Cookery, In Imitation of Horace's Art of Poetry. With some Letters to Dr. Lister, and Others: Occasion'd principally by the Title of a Book publish'd by the Doctor, being the works of Apicius Coelius, Concerning the Soups and Sauces of the Antients,* 1708, contains a manuscript inscription by Selina, Countess of Huntingdon (whose subsequent and coarsely-engraved armorial bookplate is familiar to collectors), 'Given me By my Dear Lord 1728'. A quaint bibliophilic conceit of Lady Oxford was the mysterious 'Daer Tuo', sometimes found written in books containing her plate. Spelt backwards this gives 'Read Out', and probably indicated that she had read the work in its entirety. Her husband, Edward Harley, 2nd Earl of Oxford, was the friend of the most famous men of letters of his day, which friendship the Countess did not share with him, for she disliked most of his friends and 'hated' Pope, though she was fond of Lady Mary Wortley Montagu. George Vertue (1684–1756) was born in the parish of St. Martin-in-the-Fields, London. After a disturbed apprenticeship, he worked seven years with Michael Van der Gucht (who engraved only one bookplate, an armorial for Sir William Fleming in 1716), and in 1709 began to work for himself. He designed the Oxford almanacs for many years, is said to have engraved over 500 portraits, and had a high reputation as an antiquary; he was official engraver to the Society of Antiquaries from 1717 to his death, travelling about England to find the subjects for his engravings and drawings, sometimes in the company of his great patron, Lord Oxford. Another interest was his research into the lives of artists, his notebooks on which were later used by Walpole for his *Anecdotes of Painting in England*, 1780. Vertue's five other bookplates are listed by Fincham.

55 (John Holland)

William Hogarth (1697–1764), the delineator of fallen nature and its vain pomps and vanities, engraved—in more formal vein—three bookplates, the most elaborate of which is this *ex-libris* for John Holland. Hardly any record survives of Holland, though from Horace Walpole's *Anecdotes of Painting* we learn that he was a herald painter. Of the four states of the engraving, two were used as bookplates: the first has seven fleurs-de-lis and a lion rampant guardant on the shield, and the other shows a slightly smaller lion and eight fleurs-de-lis. An example of the second in the Wilmarth Lewis Collection has 'John Holland No. 185' in manuscript beneath the plate, and the Victoria and Albert Museum impression has a similar inscription, which indicates that Holland numbered some of his books—though most examples of the plate are cut close. The date of its engraving is unknown. Hogarth's second bookplate belonged to the almost equally obscure George Lambart (1700–1765), who shared Hogarth's devotion to the theatre and as a landscape painter was considered by Samuel Ireland 'our English Poussin', which was a ludicrous comparison. Ireland also recalls that Lambart was 'deficient at drawing the human figure' and frequently called in Hogarth to help out. He was perhaps of the family of Lambart (or Lambert) of Banstead in Surrey, to which the arms pertain: gules three narcissus flowers argent; a mount vert with a centaur passant, regardant, girt with laurel wreath and holding bow and arrow gules. The supporters are Painting and Music, and the engraving dates from c. 1725. Similarly delicate and Jacobean in style is the anonymous Paulet armorial, the third bookplate, which occurs like the others in the Franks Collection (though under Powlett) and was first ascribed to Hogarth by Franks himself. Though its date is unknown, it perhaps belonged to Charles, 3rd Duke of Bolton (1685–1754), who succeeded in 1722 and appears in Hogarth's painting 'The Beggar's Opera', 1728, making eyes at Lavinia Fenton as Polly Peachum; indeed, she soon became his mistress, but he did not marry her until 1751. The supporters on this plate are Peace and Justice. For fuller details of these engravings see Ronald Paulson's *Hogarth's Graphic Works*, 1965.

Henrietta Cavendish Holles
Oxford and Mortimer.
Given me by my Lord June 1732

54

55

[57]

56 (George I)

The largest of four bookplates engraved by John Pine (1690–1756) for George I's gift of books to Cambridge University. This gift comprised 28,965 volumes and 1,790 manuscripts, the library of John Moore, Bishop of Ely, which the king purchased after the bishop's death. It was Viscount Townshend, Secretary of State, who suggested the gift, as acknowledgement of the University's loyalty to the king—in contrast with Oxford which was strongly Jacobite in its sympathies. The king's 'munificence', and his sending soon afterwards a troop of horse into Oxford, gave rise to two well-known epigrams. Dr Joseph Trapp of Oxford wrote:

> King George, observing with judicious eyes,
> The state of both his Universities,
> To one he sends a regiment;—For why?
> That *learned* body wanted *loyalty*;
> To th'other books he gave, as well discerning
> How much that *loyal* body wanted *learning*.

To this, Sir William Browne, founder of the prizes for odes and epigrams at Cambridge, retorted:

> The King to Oxford sent his troop of horse,
> For Tories own no *argument* but *force*:
> With equal care, to Cambridge books he sent,
> For Whigs allow no *force* but *argument*.

The books were received in 1715, but it was not until 1734 that they were suitably housed in rooms prepared for them, and Pine's bookplates were apparently commissioned by John Taylor, MA, of St. John's College, Librarian 1731–4. A letter from Pine (at Aldersgate Street, London, 29th August 1736), to the Vice-Chancellor, Dr John Adams, offers to make the king's face 'more like'. The receipted bill for the engravings, dated 8th July 1737, indicates that 28,200 copies of the plates were printed in all: 2,200 of the largest size, 6,000 of the next, 7,000 of the next and 13,000 of the smallest. The total cost of the engraving was £12 12s 0d (£12.60), and for the printing £25 5s 6d (£25.27½). Of the four sizes, the three largest are identical in design; the smallest omits Minerva and Apollo, the sun, clouds and pyramid. The largest and smallest plates are signed 'J. Pine', and the others 'J.P', but these medium sizes also occur in more recent prints with the initials 'J.B'. These are the initials of John Baldrey, a Cambridge engraver in the late eighteenth century, who improved and partly re-cut the original coppers when, due to rebinding, there was need for more prints of the bookplates. Pine also engraved *ex-libris* for Gray's Inn Library (No. 94) and Dr John Burton. He kept a print-shop in St. Martin's Lane, and was a close friend of Hogarth; he appears as the friar in Hogarth's 'Calais Gate'. Among his finest works are the engravings from the House of Lords' tapestry of the 'Destruction of the Spanish Armada', and his engravings of the text and illustration for an edition of Horace. He died at the College of Arms, of which he was in his latter days Bluemantle.

56

[59]

57 John Wiltshire, Bath

Though this plate's engraver, J. Skinner of Bath, was undistinguished and is largely forgotten, his designs are interesting in showing something of the development of *ex-libris* style during the 1730–55 period. His first signed plate is a plain armorial for Musgrave of Eden-Hall, 1732; his most ambitious is here shown. It is based on a drawing by Ross, and is Skinner's only plate known to be after another's design. Like several plates on foregoing pages, its subject includes allegory. Hardy wrote of it: 'Shakespeare stands on the right, and listens, with pleased expression, to the music of a rustic piper, whose head appears at the back of the cippus, whilst, on the left, Pope weighs the eloquence of an orator, whose head and up-raised hand also appear from behind the cippus. A medallion of Augustus is . . . above. Lying on the plat-form are a globe and books and many emblems of the painter's and musician's art, and amongst these sits Cupid thinking, perhaps, with which he will play next'. Hardy suggested the bookplate may have belonged to that John Wiltshire who, some twenty years later, when Gainsborough moved to Bath, was not only the local carrier but a man of taste, who became the artist's friend and insisted on carrying free all pictures he wanted sent to London—but in the absence of other evidence this remains conjecture. Skinner also engraved an allegorical bookplate for the famed Dr William Oliver, best remem-bered as the inventor of the 'Bath Oliver' biscuit, and another of his designs follows (No. 72).

58 William Hoare

Some families used bookplates over several generations, and amongst the most interesting was the Hoare family of Stourhead, whose plates are shown and discussed in an article by the author in *The Bookplate Society Newsletter*, June 1978. This *ex-libris* belonged to William Hoare (c. 1716–1752), nephew of Henry who purchased Stour-head, and son of Henry's elder brother Richard by his second marriage to Mary Bolton; she was daughter and coheiress of William Bolton, Esq., of Charterhouse Yard in the City of London, which accounts for the arms: Hoare impaling Bolton. William's father didn't enter the family's banking business except to borrow from it (he was owing £49,000 in 1702), but like his son was a merchant in London and Bury St. Edmunds. There was much intermarriage, as the pedigree appended to the above article shows, and William was no exception, for his wife Martha Cornelisen—who bore him four children —was daughter and coheiress of Henry Cornelisen of Braxted and grand-daughter of Henry Hoare of Stour-head, her mother being his elder daughter Jane. William died aged thirty-six, and Martha died in 1777. Other notable plates of the family include the Early Armorial of 'Henry Hoare, Goldsmith in London 1704', his many posthumous gift plates, and pictorials for Frances Ann Hoare (see No. 103), Sophia Merrik Hoare, Charles Hoare, the Stourhead Library, and H. A. Acland. The design shown here also occurs on a plate with the arms and crest of Antonius Allen (see the Franks Collection No. 354), but it is a crude copy.

59 (John Boswell, M.D)

John Boswell of Auchinleck (c. 1708–1780), twin son of James Boswell and Lady Elizabeth, daughter of the Earl of Kincardine, graduated in medicine at Leyden in 1736; he became a Fellow of the Royal College of Surgeons in 1748, and was later Censor of the College. He married Annie, daughter of Robert Cramond, Esq., of Auldbar in Forfarshire before 1740. Uncle to Johnson's Boswell, he is twice mentioned in his nephew's great work, once when Dr Johnson's setting books in order amid clouds of dust reminded Boswell of his uncle having referred to Johnson as 'a robust genius born to grapple with whole libraries'. John Boswell was an able physician, but was also eccentric. He left the Kirk and joined the Glassite (Sandemanian) sect, but found himself excommunicated for whoring. A keen mason, he was Depute Master of the Canongate Lodge in Edinburgh in 1759, the year his famous nephew was admitted. The earlier of his two plates is shown, an anonymous design with confused arms. The first quarter is, of course, Boswell, the galley in base probably referring to Sinclair, Earl of Orkney; the second quarter is Bruce, the third Abernethy, and the last is unidentifiable. Its subject is described on page 130 of *The Ex Libris Journal* for 1893: 'A beetling cliff overlooks the broad ocean, upon which are seen full-rigged ships; from a jutting rock "half-way down hangs one that gathers samphire", while upon a foot-path runs a young man guided by Father Time upwards towards a cornu-copia overflowing with good things'. There are prints in black and in brown in the Viner Collection. His second bookplate was a Chippendale design, likewise with incorrect arms; though its sinister supporter appertains to Boswell, the dexter is the rod and serpent of Aesculapius.

57

58

59

60 Tho. Shaw

This neat little design is by Michael Burghers (?1653–1727), and is signed in ligature. Fincham lists ten bookplates by Burghers, and to these can be added an anonymous Rawlinson plate showing a flying cupid with pendant shield, and the Shaw bookpile. Burghers came to England about 1673, settled in Oxford and became engraver to the University. Thomas Shaw (1694–1751), son of Gabriel Shaw, a shearman dyer of Kendal in Westmorland, graduated BA from Queen's College, Oxford in 1716 and four years later went as chaplain to the English factory at Algiers. In thirteen years there he spent much time exploring northern Africa, and his loitering to inspect curiosities led him into some danger. He returned to England in 1733, and was elected FRS a year later; in 1738 he published his excellent *Travels or Observations relating to several parts of Barbary and the Levant*. A scholar, antiquary and natural historian, he became principal of St. Edmund Hall, Oxford.

61 (White Kennett)

White Kennett (1660–1728) was son of Basil Kennett, incumbent of Postling and Dymchurch in Kent, who married Mary, daughter of Thomas White of Dover— which accounts for his name. After holding several livings he became vice-principal of St. Edmund's Hall, Oxford, Archdeacon of Huntingdon, Dean of Peterborough, and was consecrated Bishop of the same in 1718. Early a firm Tory, his change of side led to his being called 'Weathercock Kennett', and he became unpopular with Jacobites and Tories. A gun smashed his skull in an early accident, causing him to wear a velvet patch on his forehead, and some idea of his disfavour is shown by the fact that on a painted altarpiece of the Last Supper in Whitechapel Parish Church, Judas Iscariot was made to resemble Kennett and given a black patch on his forehead. Kennett published many works, and was interested also in antiquarian and genealogical matters. This is his third *ex-libris*. His first was a less ornate bookpile with motto, which must date from before 1708, and the second is an Early Armorial as Dean, therefore dating from 1708–18. He was thrice married, but the earlier plates show the single Kennett arms with a label for difference, and that illustrated impales the arms of the See with those of his family.

62 Gabriel Neve

Bookplate usage by men of the Inns of Court was established in the first decade of the eighteenth century, and a study of its continuance and development would throw useful light on bookplate history. Few used bookpiles, but among them was Gabriel Neve (1711–1773) of Dane Court in Thanet, who was admitted to the Inner Temple in October 1730. He was son and heir of Gabriel Neve of St. Michael's Cornhill, and married Sarah, eldest daughter of Peter Bridger of Dane Court. He 'died at his chambers in the King's Bench Walke, and was carryed out to be buried at Wilmington near Dartford in Kent'. The arms are Neve impaling Bridger, and he also used a second bookpile of the same design.

63 Saml. Wegg, Esqr.

The son of George Wegg of Colchester, Samuel Wegg (1723–1802) was born in that town, and after six years at school there spent a year at Bury under Mr Kinsman. He was admitted pensioner at St. John's College, Cambridge in 1740, but entered Gray's Inn the next year and was called to the Bar in 1746. As well as becoming treasurer of the Inn he occupied the same office for many years for the Royal Society and was a governor of the Hudson's Bay Company. He used three *ex-libris*. The first was a label dated 1734 (see the author's *Early Printed Book Labels,* 1976); the second was a Chippendale armorial with the arms of Lehook on an escutcheon; the third was the bookpile illustrated, with the arms of Wegg quartering Cowper. His mother was Anna Maria Cowper, and his wife—whom he married in 1745—was Elizabeth, elder daughter and coheir of Benjamin Lehook of the City of London, factor, and of Acton, where Wegg himself died.

64 John Thomas Troy, D.D.

Though never common, bookpiles were favoured by a number of Irishmen, including John Thomas Troy (1739–1823). Troy was born near Dublin and at fifteen went to Rome, where he joined the Dominican order in 1756. In 1776 he became Bishop of Ossory, and in 1784 was translated to the archbishopric of Dublin. He used three different bookplates, one of them in two states, but all are basically similar in design. The first two were as Bishop of Ossory, and on the second copper the Troy arms have been corrected in their field from argent to azure and a crescent is added for difference. The second was then amended on his translation to Dublin, the arms being changed to those of the archbishopric and the crescent omitted. The fourth, shown here, is a different but similar plate with 'D.D.' added to the inscription.

60

W.H: DE BURGO St PETRI. M.DCCXX.

61

GABRIEL NEVE
INTERIOR TEMPLI

62

SAMl WEGG ESQR.

63

LAUDAT TENTAT VINCIT

John Thomas Troy
D:D
DUBLIN

64

65 Frans. Columbine, Esqr.

Amongst the largest and most handsome of Chippendale *ex-libris,* this was the second plate used by Francis Columbine (c. 1680–1746), for over thirty years earlier he commissioned an Early Armorial inscribed 'Francis Columbine, Esqr., Colonel of Foot, 1708'. He was for many years in the Eighth Regiment of Foot, and served under John, Duke of Marlborough, being doubtless present at Blenheim and Ramillies. His efforts in the latter may have earned him the lieutenant-colonelcy of the Tenth, to which he was appointed in the same year, 1706—and to which the earlier bookplate alludes. He was promoted to major-general in 1735, and rewarded with colonelcy of the Tenth, or North Lincolnshire Regiment of Foot, two years later. Since he was advanced to the rank of lieutenant-general on 2nd July, 1739, our illustration must date between then and 1746, for he died at Hillingdon in Middlesex on 16th September of that year. He married Ann, the daughter of Streynsham Master, Judge Advocate and Commissary of Musters at Gibraltar, whose Jacobean bookplate is familiar to collectors, and was himself for a year from 1738 Governor of Gibraltar. There is an engraved portrait of Columbine and his wife by J. Faber Junior, based on Highmore's portrait, in the British Museum Print Room. (See *The Ex Libris Journal,* January 1893, for fuller details of his military life.)

66 Joseph Banks, Esqr.

Sir Joseph Banks (1743–1820), President of the Royal Society for forty-two years, was son of William Banks of Revesby Abbey in Lincolnshire, and his wife Sarah, daughter of William Bate. Educated at Harrow and Eton, he was at first a poor student, but his life changed when, after bathing with friends in the Thames and then finding himself alone, a solitary walk home revealed to him the fascination of flowers. His love of botany increased while at Christ Church, Oxford, and his father's death in his first year there, 1761, left him with ample money. Elected a Fellow of the Royal Society in 1766, he went the same year to Newfoundland to collect plants, and on his return became a friend of Solander, who later became his librarian. Banks joined Cook's expedition round the world in the 'Endeavour' in 1768; and his endurance of the hazardous adventures of the voyage show astonishing dedication; thirty of the party never came back, seven being buried in Batavia and twenty-three at sea. The expedition ended in 1771, and the following year Banks visited Iceland. Elected President of the Royal Society in 1778, he was created a baronet in 1781, and CB in 1795. At his death his library and botanical collections were left to the British Museum. Banks' armorial bookplate provided the pattern for a pair of loving cups, c. 1760, made for him in China in the reign of the Ch'ien-lung emperor, and these were shown in the 'British Heraldry' exhibition at the British Museum in 1978. In fact, quite a number of bookplates served to provide the arms shown on porcelain during a long period, and in D. S. Howard's *Chinese Armorial Porcelain,* 1974, a section is devoted to recording bookplates which were so used.

67 Lancelot Brown

Like the Banks plate, this shows the attractiveness of Chippendale armorials where ornamentation has not run riot, for though there are some fine elaborate early examples in the style, it is generally true to say that ambitious later designs show a lack of regard for compositional harmony by an excess of pictorial accretions. Lancelot Brown (1715–1783), known as 'Capability' Brown, was born at Kirkharle in Northumberland, and went to the village school at Cambo. After working as a gardener first at Kirkharle, then at Wotton, in 1740 he went to Stowe, where he met William Kent (see note to No. 48). His genius in landscaping gardens showed itself early, and won him a wide patronage, his works including the gardens at Kew, Nuneham Courtenay, Petworth and Blenheim. His work as an architect was competent, but his houses show a greater skill and sensitivity in their interiors than their exteriors. High Sheriff of Huntingdonshire in 1770, he lived the life of a country gentleman and had more than enough money to be comfortable. His portrait by Nathaniel Dance was engraved by J. K. Sherwin, who also engraved a handful of bookplates, but our illustration was not one of them and was engraved years before Sherwin took up this kind of work.

COLUMBINE MASTER

FRAN.ˢ COLUMBINE ESQ.ᴿ
LIEU.ᵀ GEN.ᴸ OF ALL HIS MAJ.ˢ
FOR.ˢ & COL.ᴸ OF A REGIMENT.

65

Joseph Banks Esq.ʳ

66

NUNQUAM MINUS SOLUS QUAM CUM SOLUS

Lancelot Brown

67

68 R. Bigland

This is a most interesting stock pattern among bookplates of the period. Signed by H. Copland, its design includes six busy cherubs, and the little essay in husbandry is explained by the biblical reference in the lower frame, 'Deut: 8th. 7,8,9,10': 'The Lord thy God bringeth thee into a good land . . . a land of wheat and barley, and vines, and fig trees, and pomegranates; a land of oil olive and honey; a land wherein thou shalt eat bread without scarceness'. This is the third state; the first and second have just the surname and vary in the engraving of the arches and ears of grain. Elsewhere there are small adaptations of this pattern: William Gordon's plate by Mordecai shows a fishing scene in the lower compartment; Samuel Norris's, signed 'I.H', has no motto but a floral spray in that compartment; and the unsigned Charles Thomas Coggan and C. Eve plates show the design reversed. None of them includes the biblical reference, and the Eve bookplate also occurs printed in green and in brown. Ralph Bigland (1711–1784) was born at Stepney, the son of Richard Bigland and his wife, Mary, daughter of Ralph Errington. His father died in 1724, and in letters of the 1740s Ralph is described as 'cheesemonger'; he was perhaps a factor importing Dutch cheeses, for he visited the Low Countries about this time. In 1737 he married Ann Wilkins of Frocester, who died in 1738 after giving him a son, Richard, and there was no issue of a second marriage he made in 1760. He collected inscriptions and material for a history of Gloucestershire, and by 1757 became a herald. First Bluemantle Pursuivant, he became Somerset Herald (to which the bookplate alludes) in 1759, Norroy King of Arms in 1773, Clarenceux the next year, and Garter in 1780. For his life and work see *Transactions of the Bristol and Gloucestershire Archaeological Society,* Vol. 75, 1956.

69 Bryan Edwards, Esqr.

Bryan Edwards (1743–1800), who became a rich West Indian merchant, was born at Westbury, Wiltshire. His father died in 1756, leaving his family poor, but his widow had two wealthy brothers in the West Indies, one of whom, Zachary Bayly of Jamaica, took the family under his wing. Edwards moved to a French boarding school in Bristol, where he learned to love books, but when his younger uncle Nathaniel (whose Chippendale bookplate is in the Franks Collection) came to England the boy went to live with him in London. They didn't agree, however, and Bryan went to Jamaica to finish his education. Later he succeeded to his uncle's business and became important in the colonial society of the island. He married Martha Phipps in 1774, returned permanently to England in 1792 and four years later was elected MP for Grampound in Cornwall. An anti-abolitionist, he was recognised as a powerful adversary by Wilberforce, and he published works on the slave trade and colonial history. His bookplate by Ashby of Russel Court in London shows the Chippendale style at its best, entirely free from the heaviness which mars so many examples; and he also used a crest plate.

70 W. Stratford, Esqr.

This very rare plate recalls the munificence of William Stratford (1679–1753), son of a shoemaker of Northampton of that name, who must, however, have possessed a sizeable business, for at his death in 1685 he left his widow and children with goods valued at £304. William took the degree of LLD from Pembroke Hall, Cambridge; from 1714 to 1726 he was secretary to Francis Gastrell, Bishop of Chester, and apparently wrote additions to Gastrell's *Notitia of the Diocese of Carlisle,* which gave a lamentable account of the poverty of many parishes. Though never ordained, Stratford was a lawyer and bachelor with a real concern for the Church, and in 1721 he became Commissary of the Archdeaconry of Richmond, Yorkshire. His monument by Roubillac at Lancaster, where he was buried, reports that 'His Conduct was influenced by the Dictates of Conscience A rational Faith in his Redeemer and unaffected Devotion to God; Hence it became his Delight to do good and to distribute', and a tablet in All Saints', Northampton, erected in 1831, gives details of local bequests. An article on him by Caine and Collingwood in *Transactions of the Cumberland & Westmorland Antiquarian & Archaeological Society,* New Series, Vol. XXVI, gives an account of his life and details his gifts and bequests. His long and detailed will runs to eleven foolscap pages and lists several bequests of books. The largest, and the one to which the bookplate perhaps refers, was to the Archdeaconry of Richmond itself. Here £300 was to be spent on New Testaments, and other books specifically detailed, including *Whole Duty of Man,* two works by Gastrell, including *Christian Institutes,* Archbishop Sharp's *Sermons,* etc. He directed that these were to be bought at the shops of 'Mr Manly, bookseller, near ludgate, and Mr. Innys in Pater Noster Row'. Another of his gifts is recorded by a printed book label with an ornamental border; it reads, 'The GIFT of WILLIAM STRATFORD Esq., Doctor of Laws, late Commissary of RICHMOND'.

68

69

70

71 Richd. Mill

One of four bookplates by Mountaine of Winchester for the Mill family of Camois Court. The first, with baronet's badge, belonged to Sir Richard, the 5th Bart., who married Margaret, daughter of Robert Knollys of Grove Place, and died 1760. His four sons all in turn succeeded him, and three had *ex-libris* by Mountaine. Richard, the eldest—whose plate, with label for cadency, is shown— married in 1760 Dorothy, daughter and heir of Richard Warren of Redcliffe in Somerset; he lived at Mottisfont in Hampshire, and died 1770. The next, John Hoby, who died 1780, used an entirely different Chippendale by another engraver. Henry's plate occurs in two states: one with a mullet for cadency in the third quarter, the rarer with it in the second; he was a clergyman, and died 1781. The plate of the last son, Charles, who died 1792, has a martlet for cadency. The series of bookplates engraved by Richard Mountaine and William Haskoll have an unmistakably delicate line and ornament, and details of them with a check-list can be found in *The Ex Libris Journal* for January and February 1907.

72 The Revd. J. Dobson

The very different series by J. Skinner of Bath (see No. 57) concludes, so far as signed and dated examples are concerned, with this plate, the arms of which seem to belong to Dobson of Lynn, and another of the same pattern and year for Morris Bowen. Though these reveal Skinner's skill on the wane, they show the freedom from restraint he found in this style, and contrast with the mean line of many of his Jacobean plates. They also, with the Mountaine-Haskoll series, and that of Milton referred to below (see No. 75)—all of them west country engravers —reflect the increase of bookplate engraving in centres away from London, Cambridge and Oxford, which dominated in the early years of the century. For details of Skinner's work see *The Ex Libris Journal* for July and October 1908. (See also p. 10.)

73 Chas. Nalson Cole, Esqr.

Charles Nalson Cole (1723–1804), son of Charles Cole, rector of North Crowley in Buckinghamshire, graduated BA from St. John's College, Cambridge in 1743, and was called to the Bar at the Inner Temple. Registrar of the Bedford Level Corporation, he published an account of its laws, an edition of Dugdale's *History of Imbanking and Drayning of divers Fenns and Marshes*, 1772, and an edition of Soame Jenyn's works. Though a tradition of designs larger and more elaborate than usual was early established, some owners showed a preference for very small plates. Perhaps the first—and most unusual—was the Early Armorial for Richard Bateman of Hartington dated 1697, the arms of which are only 14mm. high, but plates of the size shown here become more familiar in the eighteenth century.

74 Coplestone Warre Bampfylde

Coplestone Warre Bampfylde (c. 1720–1791) of Hester-combe in Somerset, only son of John Bampfylde, MP for Devonshire and of an old Devonshire family, matriculated from St. John's College, Oxford in 1738. He was an amateur artist who became popular as a landscape painter towards the end of the century, and was honorary exhibitor at the Royal Academy from 1763 to 1783. Benazech, Canot and Vivares engraved after his work, the last copying two of his views of Stourhead in Wiltshire, where the Hoare family lived (see note to No. 58). He was also sometime a colonel in the Somersetshire militia.

75 John Tyler

Though Fincham notes that William Milton (d. 1790) was of London, much of his working life must have been spent in Bristol, where many of his bookplate clients lived, some in West Indian trade and some with homes in those islands. Though an almost forgotten engraver, his style is individual and there is an account of his bookplate work in *The Ex Libris Journal* for May, June and August/ September 1908. The last of these details his will, proved in London on 24th August 1790; he died in the parish of St. Paul's, Covent Garden. John Tyler (1736–1810) was born at St. Mary-le-Port in Bristol, the son of Richard Tyler. His father died early, leaving his fifteen-year-old son sole male survivor of his branch of the family. He was in the South Gloucestershire militia, serving from 1760 for several years as cornet in the 10th Dragoons, and by 1780 was referred to as Captain Tyler. In the Redland Green Chapel at Bristol is a memorial tablet to him with the arms of Tyler impaling Chatfield. (See A. K. Pincott's article on him, *The Bookplate Society Newsletter*, No. 7, September 1974.) The design of the bookplate, with a dog and dead hart at the base of the shield, is a stock pattern which Milton used for several other plates, including those of Edward Brice, William Buller, Martin Byam, William Hart, John Le Mesurier of Alderney (see note to No. 85), and a member of the family of Wheathill or Colman (anonymous). Another of his stock patterns depicts merchandise and shipping (see No. 86).

Rich.ᵈ Mill
MOTTISFONT.

R. Mountaine Winton

71

The Revᵈ J. Dobson A.M

1753

Skin.ʸ Sculpᵗ

72

DEUM · COLE ·
Cha.ˢ Nalson Cole esq.ʳ
Inner Temple

73

JOHN TYLER Nᵒ

75

Coplestone Warre Bampfylde

74

76 David Hume, Esqr.

The design and fine, rather finicky engraved line of this plate is typical of Scottish Chippendales of this period. It belonged to David Hume (1711–1776), the historian and philosopher, and is one of two virtually identical plates he used; these differ in several details, but are most easily differentiated by the 'H' of the surname, which in the other is shorter on the right upstroke and curls back. Hume, the second son of Joseph Hume of Ninewells, Berwickshire, was brought up under the care of his mother, his father dying while he was an infant. He early had a passion for literature, and several years spent in France shaped the plan of his future life, which was so full and distinguished that an attempt to summarise it here would be absurd. He was, however, a real individualist in his approach to historical writing, for he began his great history with Charles I and worked back to the ancient Britons. A decided dandy, and pompous in manner, he was also a confirmed sceptic—and it served him right when after falling in a bog he was rescued by an ancient dame only on condition that he first repeated the Lord's Prayer; but Dr Johnson said of him that he was 'cheerful, obliging, instructive, and charitable to the poor'. There is a short account of him in an article by W. Bolton on 'The Homes and the Humes' in *The Ex Libris Journal* for September, October and December 1899.

77 Miss Anna Maria Blackman

Anna Maria Blackman was the second daughter of Rowland Blackman (whose Jacobean bookplate reads 'Roland Blackman of the Middle Temple Esq.'), who had estates in Antigua and married Priscilla, the daughter of Robert Warren, MD of Barbados; he died in 1780. Anna Maria, who seems never to have married, was named after her father's sister Anna Maria, who married before 1748 George Hannay, Esq., of Barbados—too early for the bookplate to have belonged to her. There is a pedigree of the family and details of their wills in V. L. Oliver's *The History of the Island of Antigua,* 1894, Vol. 1. The Blackman bookplates, and the Baijer which follows, are listed in Oliver's *West Indian Bookplates,* reprinted from *Caribbeana,* 1914, which is an excellent guide and checklist of *ex-libris* relating to those islands, though it includes plates of owners whose connections with the West Indies were somewhat tenuous. The plate shown is amongst the most pleasing of Chippendale ladies' plates; another state has a short first 's' in 'Miss', and it also occurs with 'Miss' erased. Only one other plate by J Brooke of Fetter Lane is recorded: a Chippendale of similar date for John Spencer Esqr.

78 John Otto Baÿer Esqr.

Crest plates first came into regular use about the middle of the eighteenth century but were commoner in the next century, particularly in the Victorian 'die-sinker' style, uninspired enough when it showed a full armorial let alone when this was eschewed for a mere crest. Chippendale examples, in contrast, are generally worthier, and none is more impressive than this one. John Otto Baijer, or Baÿer, belonged to a family of Dutch origin with estates in Antigua; a pedigree of the family may be found in *The History of the Island of Antigua,* referred to above. There were two of those names, first cousins of Dutch stock. One, a captain in the 38th Regiment, was sometime of Ham Common in Surrey and died in Antigua in 1817 aged 66. The other, a colonel of militia, lived some years at St. Thomas, near Exeter, and died there in 1790 aged 67. The same crest, with arms, is on a 1727 tomb in St. John's churchyard, Antigua. See *Caribbeana,* Vol. 2, p. 289.

79 Pat: Blair. M.D. Cork

While most Scottish Chippendales are marked by a fussy line, Irish plates in the same style are generally of somewhat crude engraving, as may be seen from the illustrations in H. F. Burke's *Examples of Irish Bookplates,* 1894. This is most interesting in that it illustrates examples apparently gathered by an Irish collector of the 1750–60 period, but disappointing in that there is no text. A singular feature of Irish Chippendales is a little series engraved on wood or type metal (as there had been of English Jacobean armorials; see No. 52). This includes *ex-libris* for Thomas Farrell, John Grogan Knox, John Ormsby, Esq., of Cammin, Sligo, Col. Roberts 1st Horse and Robert Scott, MD. Though engraved on copper, this plate for Patrick Blair—who obtained his MD at Edinburgh in 1738—has a similar naïveté. Medical plates and book labels are very varied and repay study. There are collections at the Royal College of Surgeons, the Royal College of Physicians and the Wellcome Institute in London, and there are lengthy check-lists by MacDowel Cosgrave in fourteen issues of *The Ex Libris Journal* for 1901 and 1902.

76

Miss Anna Maria Blackman

J. Brooke fecit Fetter Lane.

77

MANU FORTI

John Otho Baijer Esq.

78

PAT : BLAIR . M D.
CORK

79

80 James Gibbs, Architect

James Gibbs (1682–1754), the architect, was son of Peter Gibbs, a merchant of Footdeesmire near Aberdeen, and his second wife, Isabel Farquhar. Educated in Aberdeen, he then travelled abroad, where in Holland he met John Erskine, 11th Earl of Mar, who assisted his architectural studies and became his patron. When Gibbs' brother became fatally ill in 1709 he returned to Scotland, and after settling his affairs travelled to London, where he enjoyed the further patronage of the 2nd Duke of Argyll and of the Earl of Oxford. He published *A Book of Architecture,* 1728, *Rules for Drawing the several Parts of Architecture in a More exact and easy manner than has been hitherto practised, by which all Fractions, in dividing the principal Numbers and their Parts, are avoided,* 1732, and *Bibliotheca Radcliviana,* 1747. He designed St. Mary-le-Strand, which shows the influence of Wren, then St. Peter's, Vere Street and his most famous work, St. Martin-in-the-Fields. In addition to several distinguished monuments, he designed parts of the Senate House and of King's College, Cambridge, the quadrangle of St. Bartholomew's Hospital and the Radcliffe Camera at Oxford, and to the last of these he left at his death his printed books, and drawings, etc. The bookplate occurs in his books there, and, since some of them were sold towards the end of the last century to Blackwells of Oxford, copies of the plate have found their way into collections. Dated 1736, this *ex-libris* is one of only two recorded by Bernard Baron. The other is a curious and exceedingly rare pictorial, of which a print occurs in the Summers Collection. The upper part of the design is a rectangular engraving of the 'SOUTH-WEST VIEW, OF THE PARISH-CHURCH OF ECTON IN NORTH-AMPTONSHIRE', with Baron's signature and the date 1753 in the lower right-hand corner; beneath are the arms of the Palmer family (who, with their relations the Whalleys, held the living from 1640 to 1849), suspended from the motto scroll on which is a cloth bearing the inscription, 'In Usum Rectorum et Incumbentium Ecclesiae de Ecton, Johannes Palmer Patronii, D.D.D. MDCCLII' [sic]. The view of the church is based on a drawing by J. Shipley, and occurs engraved in much larger size (not of course as a bookplate) with a portrait of John Palmer by Baron, after Hogarth, in the lower part (see BM. Prints & Drawings: 1842-8-6-397; 1863-1-10-75 & 76; 1868-8-22-1650).

81 Public Record Office

This very unusual bookplate for the Public Record Office, then housed in the Tower of London, was engraved by J. Mynde, who worked in London around the middle of the eighteenth century, chiefly in the undistinguished illustration of books. It dates from about 1760–70 and occurs in two states, the second having more shading and cross-hatching than the first; but very few copies apparently survive in the Public Record Office. Five other bookplates with Mynde's signature are known: Chippendale designs for Elliot Bishop of Middle Temple, Sir Peter Thompson, Thomas Toller, VDM, an anonymous Jacobean for the Royal Society, and an anonymous Chippendale portrait for Edward Rowe Mores, the antiquary, based on R. Van Bleeck's painting; a smaller copy of Mynde's portrait of Mores was later engraved by an unknown hand.

82 Robert Bloomfield

Grotesque heraldry is uncommon on British bookplates, but this example engagingly recalls the most popular work of Robert Bloomfield (1766–1823), the poverty-stricken poet and shoemaker, *The Farmer's Boy,* published in 1800. Hardy, in his *Book-plates,* explained the composition in this way: 'A farmer on cow-back does duty as a crest, two ploughmen act as supporters, whilst the bearings on the shield represent every variety of agricultural implement, every occupant of a farmyard ordinarily met with, with the farmer's boy himself, in an attitude suggestive of his having done full justice to the fare provided at a harvest-home—not conducted on total abstinence principles . . . the whole—even to its motto, 'A Fig for the Heralds'—is most characteristic of Bloomfield'. Walter Hamilton, writing in *The Ex Libris Journal* for May 1893, and reviewing Hardy's book, takes him to task on his interpretation of the design, pointing out that 'Bloomfield . . . was a shoemaker by trade, and in the first quarter of the dexter shield he deploys the instruments of the trade, such as awls, a last, a bench, and leather-cutting knives; whilst the sinister half of the shield is occupied by the figure of a man dancing in slippers, with a cobbler's leather apron on; in his right hand he holds a cobbler's shoe strap, and in his left a cobbler's hammer'. The bookplate was engraved by W. Jackson of Gutter Lane, Cheapside, and is the only one known with his signature. An earlier version of this subject for Robert Bloomfield, differently handled, without supporters, and anonymous, is illustrated on page 59 of *The Ex Libris Journal* for April, 1899. It is a poorer engraving, but rarer than the plate here illustrated.

80

81

82

83 Wm. Skinner, Esqr.

Apart from military trophies, several of which follow, specifically military pictorials are rare. This plate, with its figure pointing to a fortification, with pick, shovel and wheelbarrow, suggests the building of forts, and probably belonged to William Skinner (1700–1780), son of Thomas Skinner, merchant of St. Kitts, and great-grandson of William Skynner, mayor of Hull, Yorkshire in 1665. An engineer, he began work at the ordnance office at the Tower of London in 1719. He built fortifications in Gibraltar, where he became chief engineer in 1741 and director in 1746, worked on the same in Scotland, and in 1749 began building Fort George from his own designs, of which Wolfe spoke highly. In 1755 he advised in Ireland, and two years later became chief engineer of Great Britain and was commissioned in the Army, in which he reached the rank of lieutenant-general. The bookplate occurs in two states, the other inscribed 'W. SKINNER', and there is a print in the Franks Collection with the design reversed and the cannon and cannonballs only drawn in, which suggests it was a preliminary design. Another plate showing a fortification, for John Bullock, also known in an anonymous state, shows soldiers before what may be a representation of Quebec, at the siege of which it has been suggested that Bullock served under Wolfe.

84 Capt. Wm. Locker

Son of John Locker, Commissioner of Bankrupts and Clerk of the Leathersellers Company, William Locker (1731–1800) often went for his father to the Tower with gifts to relieve Highland soldiers confined after the Rebellion. He entered the Navy and in the American War commanded the 'Lowestoft' on the Jamaican Station, with Nelson as 2nd Lieutenant. He was a close friend of Nelson, who wrote to him in 1799: 'I have been your scholar. It is you who taught me to board a Frenchman by your conduct when in the 'Experiment'. It is you who always said 'Lay a Frenchman close and you will beat him', and my only merit in my profession is being a good scholar. Our friendship will never end but with my life'. For fuller details see Augustine Birrell's *Frederick Locker-Lampson*, 1920, where thirteen family bookplates are shown. Locker married in 1770 Lucy, the daughter of Admiral William Parry, and in 1792 was appointed Lieutenant-General of Greenwich Hospital. The *ex-libris* occurs printed in blue and in black and is signed by W. Darling of Great Newport Street (fl. 1760–1790). Twenty-seven bookplates signed by Darling are listed by Fincham, but there are several others, and his urn plate for James Tobin follows (No. 98).

85 John Le Mesurier

The Le Mesuriers and their bookplates over several generations are recorded in an article by Edith Carey in *The Ex Libris Journal* for November 1897. Lieutenant-General John Le Mesurier (1781–1843) came of an old Guernsey family whose Alderney connection began with his great-grandfather, John Le Mesurier. He married in 1704 Ann, sister and heiress of George Andros, of whom an ancestor was in 1683 granted by letters patent the island of Alderney for 99 years for a rent of thirteen shillings per year. On Andros' death in 1721 government of the island reverted to Mrs Le Mesurier and her family. Her son Henry in 1736 built the 'Old Harbour', but finding the island folk lawless released the patent to his younger brother John (who incidentally used two bookplates, the earlier a Chippendale by Milton). He obtained a further lease, and died in 1793. His son Peter then became Governor, and at his death in 1803, John—of the bookplate—succeeded him. His *ex-libris* was engraved by Silvester (who made another for Frederick Le Mesurier of the Guernsey branch), and gives a view of the harbour before the breakwater was built. He married Martha, daughter and coheiress of Peter Perchard, Lord Mayor of London, and was the last hereditary Governor, resigning his patent to the Crown in 1825.

86 James Laroche, Junr. Esqr.

William Milton of Bristol and London (see No. 75) engraved a series of Chippendale bookplates depicting merchandise and shipping scenes, and the Laroche plate is a typical example. It is listed in Oliver's *West Indian Bookplates,* reprinted from *Caribbeana,* 1914. James Laroche, Junior (c. 1734–1805) was the grandson of Peter Crothaire, of the Province of Bordeaux, who came to England with George, Prince of Denmark, and at his desire changed his name to Laroche, and was nephew of James Laroche, alderman and merchant of Bristol. He lived at Over, in Almondsbury in Gloucestershire, was MP for Bodmin and was created baronet in 1776. He married in 1764 Elizabeth Rachel Anne, daughter and heiress of William Yeamans, Esq., of Antigua, widow of Mr Archbold; they had no children, and at his death the baronetcy became extinct. Note Milton's signature down the rudder of the West Indiaman in dock, and the owner's initials on the stern of the small boat. The series of shipping plates also includes examples for a member of the Carey family, Samuel Gomond (a merchant, whose several labels give the address '38 Prince's-Street, Bristol), Benjamin Stevenson (the Franks print of which seems to be an altered plate) and John Stevenson. The rather different John Gresley plate by Milton is printed in red.

83

84

John Le Mesurier,
GOVERNOR OF ALDERNEY.

*La première chose qu'on doit faire quand on a emprunté un
Livre, c'est de le lire, afin de pouvoir le rendre plutôt*
Menagiana Vol.4.

85

86

87 The Royal Hospital (Dublin)

The practical result of concern for the problems of old and homeless soldiers of the Irish Army, the Dublin Royal Hospital was, like Chelsea Hospital, based on Les Invalides. A site was chosen in Phoenix Park, and building was financed by small deductions from army pay, with the idea of giving accommodation for 300 pensioners. The architect was William Robinson, Irish Surveyor General, and building was almost complete in 1684, though the tower was not finished as proposed until 1701. (For an account of its building and history see Nathaniel Burton's *The Royal Hospital, Kilmainham, Dublin, 1843*). The bookplate, which occurs without manuscript inscription in the Franks Collection, was probably engraved not long before 1712, the year of the inscription recording Dr John Finglass' gift, and there is in the Simpson Collection a print similarly noting a gift from Mr Peter Ward in 1713. This is perhaps the earliest British bookplate in the trophy style, which comprises the arms of the owner, generally surrounded by a pile of arms, implements of war, trumpets, drums, banners, etc., and the two plates following give a glimpse of the subsequent history of the style, which can be more fully investigated with the aid of the check-lists of military trophy plates in *The Ex Libris Journal* for 1897 and 1898. (Non-military trophies—of musical instruments or agricultural implements, etc.—are much rarer). In the Viner Collection there is another early Irish trophy plate for Thomas Burgh, a later Surveyor General for Ireland, who died in 1730.

88 Thos. Dowdeswell, Esqr.

Thomas Dowdeswell (d. 1811) came of a family which had suffered for loyalty to Charles I in the Civil War, and was son of William Dowdeswell (1721–1775), whose Chippendale bookplate reads 'William Dowdeswell, Esqr., of Pull Court Worcester Shire'. William was a remarkable man. Educated at Westminster and Christ Church, Oxford, he went to Leyden and there met Wilkes. He made the grand tour of Europe, then entered parliament as member for Tewkesbury in 1747, the same year marrying Bridget, daughter of Sir William Codrington of Dodington. In 1765 he became Chancellor of the Exchequer, and on his taking office the king said, 'This is the first time, Mr Dowdeswell, I think, that you have served as a Minister. Lucky man, sir, lucky man—no words to eat'. He was the intimate friend of Edmund Burke. His son Thomas, who married in 1798 Magdalene, the daughter of Admiral Sir Thomas Pasley (her two armorial lozenge bookplates are in the Franks Collection, one reading 'Magdalene Dowdeswell', the other 'M.D'), was Colonel in the Guards and lost his sight in the American War. He was nevertheless a great lover of books, and formed the nucleus of the Pull Court Library; he also transformed the old Elizabethan manor house into a stuccoed Italian mansion! His bookplate is by Moses Mordecai, but it is based on a design by Samuel Wale (see note to No. 51), as is evidenced by two plates of identical composition for the 67th Regiment. One, dated 1763, is signed 'S. Wale del. I Taylor Sculp.', and is as the Dowdeswell but has 'LXVII Regt.' in the oval for the arms, and an inscription beneath, 'Bellona ceased let Science take the Field To keep your conquests; Pallas lend a Shield'. On the other, which is undated, the design is reversed, the engraving is signed 'S. Wale Del. B. Green Scul.', the oval contains only 'LXVII', and beneath is the inscription 'Britain's Cause fought, stand up in Wit's Defence. And twine with martial Wreaths, a Wreath from Sense'. Moses Mordecai worked with J. Levi in Goodman's Fields in the East End of London just after the middle of the eighteenth century, and a trade card gives his address as 35 Houndsditch, near Bishopsgate Street; but he later worked as a goldsmith in Fore Street, Exeter, where he had a jeweller's shop in 1792, and he was still alive in 1807.

89 William Strickland

The first son of Sir William Strickland, 5th Bart. and Elizabeth Letitia, the daughter of Sir Rowland Winn, Bart. of Nostel, William Strickland of Boynton (1753–1834) married in 1778 Henrietta, daughter and coheiress of Nathaniel Cholmley, of Whitby and Howsham—hence the impaled arms of his bookplate, which is dated 1789 on the ribbon. He succeeded his father in 1808, and like him was actively engaged in improving his estate and livestock, though experiments with South Down sheep failed. He worked similarly at Reighton and Carnaby, where the family had large estates and where Sir William is said to have built the school. In 1808, on becoming baronet, he had a new bookplate engraved, a print of which is in the Franks Collection; and the design of his earlier plate, shown here, was later used by his nephew, Edward Rowland Strickland, son of his younger brother Walter. A similar but simplified version of the same basic composition, with the arms on a spade shield, was engraved by the same artist for John Ganton Legard.

The Gift of the Revd Doct.^r John Finglass To the Royal Hospitall 1712

87

Thos Dowdeswell Esqr Pull Court Worcestershire.

88

89

90 Earl of Aylesford

Heneage Finch, 4th Earl of Aylesford (1751–1812), was educated at Westminster and Corpus Christi College, Oxford; he was MP first for Castle Rising and then for Maidstone from 1772 until his father's death in 1777. A friend of Horace Walpole and Fellow of the Royal Society, he also collected Rembrandt etchings and painted and engraved as an amateur; he received tuition as an artist from John Baptist Melchiar, and was sufficiently successful to be an honorary exhibitor at the Royal Academy. There is an article on Finch's engravings in Volume XI of *The Print Collectors' Quarterly*, by A. P. Oppé. Most of his subjects are architectural and landscape scenes, but there is a group of five pictorial bookplates, and these are also listed in A. K. Pincott's article 'Bookplates by the Earl of Aylesford' in *The Bookplate Society Newsletter*, No. 18, June 1977. Four of them were apparently for the Earl's own use, and the only one familiar to collectors is illustrated here. The second has scrolls with Greek inscriptions, with his title under a butterfly on a twig; the third is an open book, standing on books above a label with his title; and the fourth is a closed book on other books, without inscription. The fifth bookplate shows an open scroll on closed books, and was known by Oppé in two early states, one without inscription, the other with 'Viscount Lewisham' on the scroll. A presumably later state has the inscription 'Lord Viscount Lewisham', and the final state or reproduction reads 'Earl of Dartford'; this must date from after 1801 when he took the senior title. George, Viscount Lewisham was cousin of Heneage Finch and married one of Finch's sisters in 1782. All the *ex-libris* except the final state of the last probably date from the 1780s. The suggestion often made that the Finch bookplate shown here was the work of Piranesi is erroneous, and probably arises from the reference to the Aylesford sale at Christie, Manson and Woods in *The Athenaeum* for 28th April, 1888, where it is stated that 'the Aylesford bookplate was engraved by Piranesi, perhaps the only one he executed'.

91 Messrs. Sharp, London

The sons of Dr. Thomas Sharp, Archdeacon of Northumberland, and grandsons of John Sharp, Archbishop of York, the brothers Granville, James and William lived in London. Granville (1735–1813), the ninth and youngest son of the family, was of such diverse scholarly and philanthropic activities as would be impossible to detail here, but he was preoccupied with the laws of personal liberty, and, through the Somerset Case, personally instigated the first decisive step towards the emancipation of slaves: the judges' decision 'that as soon as any slave sets foot upon English territory, he becomes free'. This pictorial bookplate was used by the brothers together for their music books, and it is a most unusual design, with its ecclesiastical interior and organ screen. It was designed by Granville, who had a talent for drawing, and was engraved by a young artist of his acquaintance who is unfortunately not named in Prince Hoare's *The Memoirs of Granville Sharp*, 1820. The inscription round the picture, beginning 'It becometh well the Just to sing praises to our God', recalls the famous Sunday evening sacred music concerts which these three musical brothers organised. They held these gatherings at William's and James' houses (Granville was unmarried, and lived with them), and on a barge on the Thames, which attracted a distinguished audience including the king himself. James was an iron merchant, and William (d. 1810) was the notable surgeon of London and Fulham, who became an assistant surgeon at St. Bartholomew's Hospital in 1755. William himself used a quaint and fanciful Chippendale *ex-libris* which shows three cherubs about to perform an operation on a fourth, while a fifth looks on, which occurs printed in red and in black. The same design in reverse was engraved by Yates for John Walford, Surgeon, Chelmsford, in 1754, and a different but allied design of more gruesome aspect, with a cadaver and a skeleton in a cupboard, was used by Matthew Turner, a Liverpool surgeon.

EARL. OF. AYLESFORD.
PACKINGTON. WARWICKS.

90

91

92 The Revd. John Eade

As the arms of this plate relate to Eade of Saxmundham, this bookplate must have belonged to John Eade (c. 1734–1811), son of Thomas Eade, a farmer of that place, and the label for difference indicates that John was the eldest son. Born at Saxmundham, he was at school at Dedham under Mr Grimwood, and went to Emmanuel College, Cambridge, from which he graduated BA in 1756. He was ordained at Norwich in 1762, and became curate of Roydon in Suffolk. He was vicar of Tannington from 1772 to 1811, and rector of Cotton from 1793 to 1811, in which year he died. The inscription of his bookplate was later amended to read 'John Eade', perhaps for his son; and the same design occurs reversed in a very poorly engraved bookplate for John Crane, a print of which is in the Viner Collection.

93 Sir John Smith, Bart.

Son of Henry Smith of Ratcliffe Highway and afterwards of New Windsor, Berkshire, and Mary, daughter of John Hill of Wapping, Middlesex, Sir John Smith (1744–1807) was high sheriff of Dorset in 1772. He inherited as an infant the large estates of his kinsman, Alderman Sir William Smith, Knight of the City of London and of Sydling St. Nicholas in Dorset, and was created baronet in 1774. He married first Elizabeth, daughter and sole heir of Robert Curtis of Wilsthorpe in Lincolnshire, who bore him three children and died in 1796; and secondly Anna Eleanora, daughter of Thomas Morland of Lamberhurst in Kent, who died without issue. Sir John used three bookplates, all as baronet. The first, a wood-engraved non-military trophy plate—showing musical instruments, a telescope, dividers, etc.—with a typographic inscription, occurs in two states. One is inscribed 'Sir John Smith, Bart.', the other has 'Sydling House, Dorset' added. The next is a library interior with an antique bust and the arms on a mantle by Hughes (shown here), whom Fincham lists as R. B. Hughes (see No. 120), presumably on the evidence of the Lanham bookplate, though he is not to be confused with Robert Ball Hughes, the sculptor. The third plate is by W. Darling of Great Newport Street (see also No. 98); it shows a rather unconvincingly placed pile of books, the arms in a spade shield being on the nearside of the front upright book in the first state, and on a napkin below in the second. All three plates show the same arms, the escutcheon of pretence bearing the Curtis arms, thus relating to Sir John's first marriage. Fincham lists twenty-seven bookplates by Darling, but there are also pictorials for Uriah Bristow and John Collins.

94 Grays Inn Library

This bookplate was engraved by John Pine (see No. 56). The records of Gray's Inn inform us that on 24th November 1750 it was 'Ordered that the arms of the Society be engraved by Mr Pyne and that the words Gray's Inn Library be also engraved at the bottom of the arms and that 2,000 of them be printed off and fixed in the books in the Library'. It was not until 1752/3 that Pine was paid £3 13s od (£3.65) for the prints. Castle suggested that the engraving was after a design by Gravelot, which seems possible; and the original plate remained in use until about 1900, when—again according to Castle—Moring made a modern print which is smaller in size but adheres to the old design (fuller details of the commission were doubtless lost with the destruction of the Inn's records in the Second World War). For an account of the bookplates of the Inns of Court see P. C. Beddingham's articles in *The Bookplate Society Newsletter* for September—March 1977–8.

95 Rev. W. T. Bree, M.A.

The Bree family's association with Allesley in Warwickshire has been long. Right of presentation to the living was sold in 1746 to Dr Thomas Bree, a Warwick physician, it is said in order to pay electioneering expenses. The then rector, Benjamin Marshall, died in 1749 and Dr Bree or his executors appointed his younger son Thomas to the living, the patronage being bequeathed to him. From then there were Bree rectors until 1917, and the living is still in the family. Thomas died in 1778, and was buried at Hatton, Warwickshire, from where the family came, and his elder son Thomas succeeded him. He died unmarried in 1808, and his younger brother William became rector. This William was the father of the Rev William Thomas Bree (c. 1785–1863), whose bookplate is shown, and Castle notes that his father etched it for him. W. T. Bree married Helena Maria, daughter of Joseph Boultbee of Springfield House, Warwick, and was rector of Allesley from his father's death in 1823. Details of the family's wills and monumental inscriptions are in *Visitation of England and Wales, Notes*, Vol. 3, 1898, where the bookplate is also illustrated printed from the original copper, and there are loose examples of the bookplate about which must date from this printing. The Franks Collection print, however, is an inferior photographic reproduction. Dr J. S. Pearson reported a state reading 'Allesley Rectory', but this I have not seen.

92

SIR JOHN SMITH, BAR.ᵗ F.R.S.
SYDLING Sᵗ NICHOLAS, DORSET

93

GRAYS INN
LIBRARY.

94

REV. W. T. BREE M.A.

Allesley

95

96 Heath Crump

In the second half of the eighteenth century there arose a vogue for designs of a monumental character, often funereal in aspect, sometimes comprising just an urn, elsewhere a cippus or pyramid—and several are shown here. The plate of Heath Crump occurs in the Franks Collection with its inscription cut off, under Crompe, and though its owner remains elusive the arms and crest seem to be those of Crompe (or Crumpe) of Stonelinch, Sussex. The arms are given in Horsfield's *History and Antiquities of the County of Sussex*, and there is a note that 'the family of Crumpe of Maidstone, Kent, are also reported, in 1634, to be . . . the owners of Stonelinch Manor. They afterwards removed to Hastings, where they were mayors, and . . . were buried at Bexhill'. The design of this bookplate is virtually identical to that of the plates of James Gildart, St. John's College, Cambridge and Johnson Gildart, Liverpool. James Gildart was admitted pensioner at St. John's College, Cambridge in 1796, and graduated BA in 1801, in which year he was made deacon and licensed curate of St. Anne's, Richmond, co. Lancs. This suggests the approximate date of these three plates, all of which are most rare.

97 Revd. Sidenham Teast Wylde

The son of Samuel Wylde, of Walcot in Somerset, Sidenham Teast Wylde (c. 1756–1826) matriculated from Pembroke College, Oxford in 1774 and graduated BA in 1778. He was rector of Burrington in Somerset from 1795 and of Ubley in the same county from 1805 until his death. The print of this plate in the Franks Collection, like the one above, is mutilated and catalogued under Wellard. The escutcheon of pretence is for Newman.

98 Jas. Tobin

This bookplate is by W. Darling of Great Newport Street (see also No. 84), but nearly always occurs with the signature cut off or mutilated. There are two states, the second with a martlet as crest on the lid of the urn, and the inscription of this state was later amended in manuscript to read 'GEO: TOBIN'. It was, however, originally the bookplate of James Tobin (1737–1817), a merchant, who married the daughter of a rich West Indian sugar planter named Webbe. His sons George and John were born in Salisbury in 1768 and 1770, and about 1775 James Tobin and his wife went to Nevis in the West Indies, leaving the children behind to be educated. Tobin returned to England in 1783, and settled at Redland near Bristol. George, his son (1768–1838), who used the amended plate, entered the Navy in 1780 and was present at action in the West Indies. From 1791–3 he was in the 'Providence' with Captain William Bligh in voyage to Tahiti and the West Indies. He thus missed service with Nelson, who later spoke well of him and said that if he had been with him he would long since have been captain; he was made a commander in 1798, advanced to captain in 1802, and became a rear-admiral in 1837. His brother John was a dramatist, author of *The Honey Moon*, and another brother, James Webbe Tobin, was acquainted with Lamb and Coleridge.

99 Revd. Christr. Harvey, D.D.

The Rev Christopher Harvey, DD (d. 1796) was the son of the Rev William Harvey of Bargy Castle in County Wexford and his second wife, Dorothea, daughter and heiress of Christopher Champney, Esq., of Kyle. He married Rachel, the daughter of Lorenzo Nickson, Esq., of Munny in County Wicklow, who bore him a son and two daughters. He was incumbent of Rathdowney in the diocese of Ossory, and of Ross in County Cork, and prebendary of Edermine in the diocese of Ferns, but inherited only the estates brought into the family by his mother. His bookplate occurs in two states, the difference being in the spelling of the surname, which in the other—and earlier—is spelt 'HERVEY'. In the present century the same design was used for the bookplate of 'Alfredus Guilelmus Bradshaw Mack', who gave his collection of old Irish silver to the Dublin Museum. There is a very useful check-list of bookplates in the urn style in *The Ex Libris Journal* for 1899.

96

97

98

99

100 Robt. Robinson

Thomas Holloway (1748–1827) illustrated publications of Bowyer, Boydell and Macklin and did some painting and crayon drawing, but is best remembered as the engraver of Raphael's cartoons, which took him many years. Two other bookplates are signed by him: an allegorical for Charles Hoare (see Nos. 58, 103), an early state of which is in the Viner Collection; and a pictorial for Rowland Hill, AM, who being denied ordination built Surrey Chapel and preached in dissenting chapels. This may have led to his knowing Holloway, who was a Baptist, as was Robert Robinson (1735–1790), the minister and hymnologist. The youngest child of Michael Robinson, a ne'er-do-well exciseman, with whom his mother eloped, Robinson was educated at Swaffham and Scarning. Too poor to study for the Anglican ministry, he was apprenticed to a hair-dresser; he preferred, however, books and spiritual matters and—drawn by Whitefield—began preaching at Mildenhall. In 1759 he went to Stone Yard Baptist Chapel at Cambridge, where his preaching was very popular; the meeting flourished, a new meeting house was built in 1764, and he remained there for life. He went to live at Chesterton in 1773 with his wife, nine children and aged mother, and there actively farmed almost 200 acres, dealt in corn and coals and managed the ferry. He was succeeded as minister by the even more remarkable Robert Hall. (See *The Victoria County History. Cambridgeshire,* Vol. 3, 1959; and G. W. Hughes' *With Freedom Fired,* 1955.)

101 Sir Thomas Gage, Bart.

There is a good pedigree of the Gages of Hengrave in *The History and Antiquities of Suffolk. Thingoe Hundred,* 1838, by John Gage, youngest brother of Sir Thomas (1781–1820), 7th Bart. They were the sons of Sir Thomas, 6th Bart. and his first wife, Charlotte, daughter of Thomas Fitzherbert, Esq., of Swinnerton, and Thomas succeeded his father in 1798. He married in 1809 Lady Mary Anne, daughter of Valentine, Earl of Kenmare, by whom he had two sons, and at his early death was buried at the Chiésa del Gesù in Rome. His handsome bookplate occurs in two states: the less imposing has the pictorial in a single line border, close above and at the sides but extended below to include the inscription; the state here shown has the additional inscription 'Drawn by Signeira. Engraved by Bartolozzi, Lisbon. 1805'. This is probably a misprint, intended to read 'Sequeira', a Portuguese designer popular at the time. Francesco Bartolozzi (1727–1825) enjoyed enormous popularity, but engraved only about twelve bookplates; the influence, however, of his work and that of pupils and followers like Sherwin and Henshaw (see No. 102) was considerable.

102 W. F. Gason, Clare Hall, Camb.

Venn's *Alumni Cantabrigienses* lists Walter Fletcher Gason and notes that the family was of Tipperary, but he is not found in Burke's *Landed Gentry* or *Irish Family Records,* 1976. The Gasons, believed to be of French Huguenot origin, lived at Ickham in Kent but settled in Ireland in 1640 when Richard Gason went over with Cromwell's army. W. F. Gason was admitted pensioner at Clare College, Cambridge in 1768 and graduated BA in 1773, which dates this and his similar but larger bookplate for us—as does the brief life of its engraver. William Henshaw (c. 1753–1775) was nephew of the bookplate engraver William Stephens and worked under him at Cambridge, many of his plates being for university men there. In 1773 he went to London and worked as a pupil of Bartolozzi. His *ex-libris* for Samuel Heywood is similar in design and size to the smaller Gason plate but is in an oval leaf border; and another for John Jackson of Trinity College (which has the arms of Sheldon) is like the larger Gason plate but reversed, with a cornucopia instead of books.

103 Fras. Ann Hoare

The very interesting series of bookplates of the Hoare family has already been mentioned (see No. 58). This example belonged to Frances Ann (c. 1736–1800), the daughter of Richard Acland, merchant of London, and she married Sir Richard Hoare, 1st. Bart., in 1761 as his second wife. She bore him four sons and two daughters; Charles (see No. 100) was her son, and her daughter Henrietta Ann (who used a pictorial bookplate depicting Minerva) married Sir Thomas Dyke Acland, 9th Bart., her mother's first cousin once removed. Mrs L. Nevill Jackson, in an article in the January 1906 issue of *The Connoisseur,* suggests this *ex-libris* is probably from a design by Angelica Kauffman. The bust is a portrait of Frances Ann Hoare, and may still be seen at Stourhead.

104 Wilson

Pictorial plates with no arms and either a surname, as here, or just Christian and surname are nearly always unidentifiable in the absence of other evidence. This steel-engraved plate is, however, not only very attractive but shows the last flowering of the pictorial bookplate before the heavy awkwardness which undistinguishes so much mid-Victorian *ex-libris* design. The work of T. Dick of Edinburgh, it may well be thirty or forty years earlier than the Greg plate by Dick which Fincham dates c. 1870, for Dick was active in the 1830s.

Rob.ᵗ Robinson,

– Chesterton .–

100

Drawn by Siqueira.   Engraved by Bartolozzi. Lisbon. 1805.

Sir Thomas Gage Barᵗ Hengrave Hall. Suffolk.

101

102

103

104

105 Geo. Losh

This is one of few bookplates ascribable to Thomas Bewick (1753–1828), the greatest English wood-engraver. Son of a farmer and tenant-collier, his *Memoir,* written late in life and published in 1862, beguilingly portrays his early history and the development of his spontaneous talent, and gives an unrivalled view of a craftsman of the time at work. Apprenticed to Ralph Beilby, he became after a brief stay in London his partner for twenty years. His first major work, *A General History of Quadrupeds,* 1790, was an immediate success and, like his even more popular *History of British Birds,* went into many editions. Such was his genius, and the truth of his response to nature, that many have found the natural world realised with a new vividness in his engravings, the acute observation on a minute scale of which has passionate intensity. Most vignette bookplates of his time—casually ascribed to Bewick in the past—were by his pupils, including Luke Clennell (see No. 106). George Losh (1766–1846) came of a family established at Woodside near Carlisle since the time of Henry VIII, and was son of John Losh. The third of four brothers, all eminent locally, he married in 1798 Frances Wilkinson, settled in Newcastle, and engaged in commerce and manufacturing. His work included the production of alkali, ship and insurance broking, merchanting, and proprietorship of the Newcastle Fire Office and Water Company. He moved to Saltwellside in 1803. See R. Welford's *Men of Mark 'twixt Tyne and Tweed,* 1895.

106 Wm. Nicholson

Also son of a farmer, Luke Clennell (1781–1840) was born at Ulgham near Morpeth. His seven year apprenticeship with Bewick, begun in 1797, coincided with work on the *British Birds,* tail-pieces for which he engraved. In 1804 he moved to London, where he worked in wood-engraving but after 1810 turned to painting in water-colour. However, after engaging on a large picture of a dinner of allied sovereigns at the Guildhall his mind gave way in 1817, and he never recovered his reason. William Nicholson (1784–1844), the portrait painter, was born at Newcastle, but by 1820 was settled in Edinburgh where he was a founder of the Royal Scottish Academy. He worked in water-colour, etched, and engraved some of his own works. The water-colour on which this engraving is based is in the Laing Gallery at Newcastle, with a larger one which was engraved—presumably as a trade-card—for A. Cunningham.

107 Thomas Deane, Architect, Cork

This grandly ruinous and overgrown subject makes a fine bookplate for Sir Thomas Deane (1792–1871), the architect. His father, also a builder, died early, but with his mother's aid Thomas remarkably extended his father's business and became Mayor of Cork in 1830, in which year he was knighted. Taking up architecture he joined Benjamin Woodward, and his own son later joined them. His taste was classical, and he was responsible for many buildings in his native city, including the Bank of Ireland, the Queen's College and the classic portico of the Court House. Other works of the partnership included the University Museum at Oxford and the Venetian addition to Trinity College, Dublin. Deane's bookplate was engraved by William Brocas (c. 1794–1868), third son of Henry Brocas, the landscape painter. William Brocas is best remembered for his portraits, but he also etched after Hogarth's engravings and caricatures for James Sidebotham. He designed one other bookplate, for the 'Classical and English School, No. 1, Upper Mount Street, Merrion Square, 182–', which was engraved by Alpenny. Guy Dawber (see No. 150) became assistant to Sir Thomas's son, Sir Thomas Newenham Deane.

108 John Headlam, M.A.

John Headlam (1769–1854), son of Thomas Emerson Headlam of Gilmonby Hall, Yorks, was rector of Wycliffe, Archdeacon of Richmond and Chancellor of the Diocese of Ripon. This *ex-libris,* copied from an earlier one he had used, is by Bewick's pupil Mark Lambert of Newcastle-upon-Tyne, whose bookplates are recorded by J. Vinycomb, with a check-list, in issues of *The Ex Libris Journal* for 1895. The first plate of this design, 'John Headlam M.A', occurs in two states, differing in the 'H' of the surname, and another variety has no 'M.A'; Arthur C. Headlam and Horace Headlam reproduced the early plate with new inscriptions; the different, later engraving shown here was subsequently copied for Maurice Headlam.

109 G. C. Bainbridge

A self-taught animal painter, Samuel Howitt (1756–1822) became a drawing-master; for a time he was at Dr Goodenough's academy at Ealing, and he married Rowlandson's sister. Though Redgrave and others record that he lived some time in Bengal, this was not the case, though he worked up some of Captain Williamson's drawings for *Oriental Field Sports,* 1807, as well as publishing other books of engravings of animals and hunting subjects. This pleasant example of his work is one of three bookplates he engraved. The others are a design with books and a cloud above, partly obscuring a shield, for Robert Barnett, and a landscape pictorial for William Edkins. The Marshall Collection contained six impressions of this plate, 'chiefly different states, including a fine proof before letters', but probably only two of the states were used as bookplates. The first reads 'Wm. Edkins. PAINTER, 37, Bridge Street. BRISTOL'; the second, also found printed in sepia, reads 'WILLIAM EDKINS'.

105

106

107

108

109

110 Sir Ashton Lever

This and the plates following show spade shield and festoon *ex-libris,* which became popular towards the end of the eighteenth century. Sir Ashton Lever (1729–1788) was the eldest son of Sir James Darcy Lever and Dorothy, daughter of the Rev William Ashton. Educated at Manchester Grammar School and Corpus Christi College, Oxford, he was an ardent sportsman and collector; stuffed and live birds, fossils, shells and all kinds of collectables fascinated him, and in 1774 he was induced to move his museum, which he named the Holophusikon, to London. Here he filled sixteen rooms in Leicester House with curiosities, viewable at a fee of 5s 3d (26p) per person, but the outlay of his money later forced him to sell his collection to a Mr James Parkinson, and it was finally dispersed in 1806. He married in 1746 Frances, daughter of James Baylay, but there were no children of the marriage; and he was knighted in 1778, which dates this bookplate within ten years. Fanny Burney in her diary records a visit to Lever's museum in July 1778, where she spent a Saturday morning 'extremely well' and heard a thousand names which were new to her; she also lists some of the things on display (see *The Early Diary of Fanny Burney,* ed. Ellis, 1907).

111 Thomas Stanley Massey

The Stanleys of Hooton in Cheshire were of ancient lineage, and the baronetcy was created in 1662. This is the bookplate of Sir Thomas, 7th Baronet. His father, Sir John, 6th Bart., was the second adopted heir of Sir William Massey of Puddington in Cheshire, and assumed —as did his younger brother Thomas, a clergyman—the additional surname of Massey. The arms of Salvin are impaled, for Sir Thomas married Catharine, daughter of William Salvin, Esq., of Croxdale in Co. Durham, and the plate shows the label of an eldest son. This explains Massey as the second and final surname, for under the terms of the 5th Baronet's will Sir John took the further surname of Stanley to become Sir John Stanley-Massey-Stanley, and presumably Sir Thomas did the same when he succeeded. He had five sons and a daughter, but enjoyed the baronetcy only a very short time, for he died three months later in February 1795. In the frilly border to the arms of this and the Lever plate are vestiges of the Chippendale ornament which preceded the spade shield.

112 Sir Thomas Bankes J'Anson, Baronet

The Rev Sir Thomas Bankes J'Anson (or I'Anson), 5th Bart. (1724–1799), was the son of Sir Thomas J'Anson of New Bound in Kent, who held office as Gentleman Porter of the Tower of London. Born at Montpelier in France, he was educated at University College, Oxford, from which he graduated BA in 1748, and became rector of Corfe Castle and prebendary of the church of Wells. His son, the Rev Sir John Bankes J'Anson, who also became rector of Corfe Castle, died in the same year. An account of the family is given in an article entitled 'Doubtful Baronetcies' in *The Herald and Genealogist,* Vol. IV, pp. 280–2, and there is a good pedigree in *History of the I'Anson Family* by Bryan I'Anson, 1915.

113 The Revd. Sir John Cullum, Bart.

The Rev Sir John Cullum of Hardwick House, Suffolk, 6th Baronet (1733–1784), was eldest son of Sir John, the 5th Baronet and his wife Susannah, daughter and co-heiress of Sir Thomas Gery, Kt. Educated at Bury Grammar School and Catharine Hall, Cambridge, where he won a bachelor's prize for the best dissertation in Latin prose, he became rector of Hawsted in 1762, and in 1774 was instituted to the living of Great Thurlow. An amiable man and keen antiquary, popular among the leading men of his time, he spent much of his life writing 'The History and Antiquities of Hawstead and Hardwick in the County of Suffolk', published in 1784 in *Bibliotheca Topographica Britannica,* and later separately. He married in 1765 Peggy, only daughter of Daniel Bisson of Westham in Sussex, whose arms are impaled on the bookplate. He was buried, as directed in his will, under a great stone in the churchyard near the north door of Hawsted Church, doubtless in conformity with sentiments he expressed in his *History* showing his contempt for the vulgar superstition of refusing burial on the north side of the church. His father and mother used a book label dated 1760 (see the author's *Early Printed Book Labels,* 1976). The bookplate of his brother and successor, Sir Thomas Gery Cullum, 7th Bart., is interesting in that it is in the preceding Chippendale style, though it is a late and cumbersome example. In its first state it reads 'Thomas Gery Cullum', and shows the mark of cadency of a second son; after he succeeded the inscription was re-engraved—in rather inappropriate lettering—to read 'Sir Thos. Gery Cullum Bart. F.R.S'. He was of similar character to his brother, and an antiquary, but was also a medical man and pupil of the celebrated surgeons William and John Hunter; from 1771 to 1800 he was also Bath King of Arms (see *The History and Antiquities of Suffolk. Thingoe Hundred,* by John Gage, 1838). The plate shown here is an example of a spade shield armorial on a mantle.

VIGILANTIBUS FAUSTA OMNIA

Sir Ashton Lever.

110

Thomas Stanley Massey (PUDDINGTON:)

111

SIR THOMAS BANKES JANSON BARONET
OF CORFE CASTLE DORSET 1785

112

SUSTINEATUR

The Rev. Sir John Cullum Bar.
Hardwick House, Suffolk.
F.R.S. and F.S.A.

113

114 The Reverend G. S. G. Stonestreet, L.L.B.

This most unusual circular spade shield armorial belonged to George Stonestreet Griffin Stonestreet (1782–1857), the son of George Griffin, Esq., of Clapham in Surrey, Governor of the Phoenix Insurance Office. He took the name Stonestreet while still at school in 1794. From Merchant Taylors' he went to St. John's and then migrated to Jesus College, Cambridge from which he graduated LLB in 1807. Curate of Ewhurst in Sussex 1812–13, he became chaplain to the Duke of York and chaplain to the forces in 1814, and was with the Guards in the Waterloo Campaign. In 1817 he married Mary Elizabeth, daughter of Robert Shedden, merchant of London and Paulerspury Park, Northants., by whom he had issue. He died at Hastings.

115 Richard Johnson

One of four bookplates by J. Shepperd, an English engraver in Calcutta in the 1774–87 period, its inscription in Persian and Sanskrit reads: 'The Sword of War, the General Richard Johnson, eminent in the State, glorious in the Kingdom. A. H. 1194' (1780). Johnson arrived in India as a writer in 1770 and held a variety of posts, rising in 1788 to membership of the Board of Revenue, with a deliberative voice, and Accountant General, Board of Finance. He died in 1807 in Brighton. See *Fort William – India House Correspondence* (India Records Series) 1949. His plate, printed in brown or black, occurs in three states: the first has a Persian letter above the crest (and is shown here); the second lacks this; and in the third the names of Richard Johnson and the engraver have been removed. Shepperd's other bookplates were an elaborate stock-pattern pictorial for John Andrews' Circulating Library, Calcutta, 1774 (see *The Ex Libris Journal* for October 1891 and August 1894), an urn plate with Arabic inscription for Nathaniel Middleton, 1777, and a wreath and ribbon armorial, unsigned, for Thomas Boileau with a phonetic rendering of his name in Arabic script, dated 1781.

116 Mr. Willm. Sumner

William Sumner (1762–1796) was a banker in London, the second son of William Brightwell Sumner of Hatchlands (which he purchased in 1768 on his return from service in the East India Company in the time of Lord Clive) and Catherine, the daughter of John Holme, Esq., of Holme Hill, Cumberland. Several of the family used bookplates, including William's elder brother, George Holme Sumner, who had a festoon armorial, and his father, who used two Chippendales: one with the Holme impalement, the other recording 'The Bequest of my Brother, the Revd. Dr. Robt. Carey Sumner'.

117 Revd. W. Barrow, L.L.D.

The first of two states of this plate, signed by J. Thornthwaite (born c. 1740), an engraver and etcher in London; in the second state the signature is erased and the name is removed to take the place of 'ACADEMY, Soho Square' below, reading 'REVD. W. BARROW. L.L.D., S.A.S', with the same date. The famed Soho Academy opened at No. 1 Soho Square in 1717 and was run by Martin Clare, who wrote a textbook, *Youth's Introduction to Trade and Business,* 1720; in 1725–6 it moved to No. 8, and became known as Soho Academy. (See *Survey of London, Vol. XXXIII, The Parish of St. Anne, Soho,* 1966, for details of the school under Clare.) At his death in 1751, his partner Dr Barwis took over, and the school became noted for its Shakespeare performances; among actors who were boys at the school were Joseph Holman, John Liston and John Bannister, and the dramatist Thomas Morton also studied there. Thomas Rowlandson and J. M. W. Turner attended the school, as did the sons of James Boswell and Edmund Burke. Cuthbert Barwis was followed by his nephew, John; then Barrow ran the school from 1785 to 1799, when he was succeeded by Whitelock. Though numbers declined, (perhaps because of Barrow's stopping dramatic performances—the moral dangers of which discussed in his *Essay on Education,* 1804), the school was described, as late as 1801, as 'the *first* academy in London'. William Barrow (1754–1836) came of a Westmorland family; he was appointed archdeacon of Nottingham in 1830, and married Mrs E. A. Williams, who died childless.

118 Humphry Repton

Humphry Repton (1752–1818), son of John Repton an excise collector, was born at Bury and educated there, at Norwich and in Holland. He returned to learn the trade of calicoes and satin, but it seems not to have drawn him, for soon after his marriage in 1773 to Mary Clarke he became a general merchant in Norwich. The project failed, and he moved to Sustead in Norfolk, where he studied botany and gardening. After a brief stay in Ireland he settled at Hare Street, Romford in Essex, and following another failed business project he turned to landscape gardening to sustain his family. Since his wife bore him sixteen children it was expedient, and history records its magnificent success. His bookplate occurs in two states, the earlier lacking the horizontal sprigs to the wreath and other ornamental details. In his first gardening activity he was guided by Lancelot Brown (whose bookplate is No. 67), but he later discarded the formalism of Brown's work.

114

115

116

117

118

119 (Richard Ford)

On the bookplate of Richard Ford (1796–1858), the critic, traveller and author of *The Handbook for Travellers in Spain*, 1845, the name is not engraved; Ford signed all his bookplates beneath the arms, adding in special cases 'Heir Loom'. The plate is very delicately engraved with a design a little more individual and elaborate than most of its period, and John Leighton noted that it was taken from a popular seventeenth-century title-page ornament. Richard Ford was called to the bar but never practised, and in 1830 took his family to southern Spain, where they remained, making many tours, for four years before returning to England. He was a fine amateur artist, and some of David Roberts' illustrations of Spanish scenery and architecture were based on Ford's sketches. He was also a thorough connoisseur. The bookplate of his third wife, Mary Molesworth (1816–1910), sister of Sir William Molesworth, whom Ford married in 1851, is a lozenge plate in the Chippendale style inscribed 'Mary Ford of Pencarrow'; it was also a late commission, for it is dated 1894 (see *The Visitation of England and Wales*, Vol. 4, 1896).

120 Edward Gibbon, Esqr.

This unadorned and uninspired spade shield armorial by R. B. Hughes of London (fl. 1770–90) (see No. 93) for the historian Edward Gibbon (1737–1794) is largely of interest for its association. The arms have been a cause of slight controversy as to the right of Gibbon either to the arms of the Gibbons of Rolvenden or the Gibbons of West Cliffe, a younger branch of the family (see *The Ex Libris Journal* for May 1899). The plate is not at all uncommon, on account of the adventures of Gibbon's library. It was bought by Beckford and left in Lausanne; he gave it to a physician named Scholl, who sold it in 1830 to a bookseller who dispersed it. It is, nevertheless, suggested that half of it remained intact (see *Notes and Queries*, 5th Series, v.425, vii. 414).

121 Thomas Carlyle

Henry Thomas Wake of the Engineers Office, East and West India Docks, designed this bookplate for Thomas Carlyle (1795–1881), the historian and essayist. It was evidently one of several designs, for a letter—now in the Viner Collection—to Wake from Carlyle in Chelsea, dated 24th November 1853, indicates a preference for 'the one *first* sent, it has so beautiful a *monumental* character; and nothing of the "*caricature* human face", which in these latter specimens a diseased imagination (by aid of the wiverns, etc.) fashions for itself! We will stand by that first one, therefore; and, on the whole, if you have it at the right size, and know a good engraver, I will request you to have it engraved for me without further delay'. According to the note where the letter is quoted (see *The Ex Libris Journal,* December 1893), the bookplate was entrusted to Mr Thomas Moring to be engraved (see No. 173), but it is elsewhere suggested that H. P. Walker actually engraved it; and it was believed that 'the original copper is now in the South Kensington Museum'. The same design was later adapted for use by Carlyle's younger brother, John A. Carlyle, the physician (1801–1879).

122 Sir John Wolfe Barry, K.C.B.

Sir John Wolfe-Wolfe-Barry (1836–1918), the civil engineer, was son of Sir Charles Barry, architect of the Houses of Parliament. The inscription of the bookplate varies slightly because it was not until 1898 that he adopted the additional surname, but the plate cannot be more than a year earlier, for it was in 1879 that he was created KCB. He was the engineer of Earls Court Station, Barry Docks, Blackfriars Bridge, Kew Bridge, and (with Sir Horace Jones) Tower Bridge, etc. This design demonstrates how long and little changed the Victorian plain armorial continued, even while at the hands of Sherborn and others a renaissance was in progress.

123 Charles Kingsley

Charles Kingsley (1819–1875), the author of *The Water Babies* and clergyman extraordinary, used the dullest kind of Victorian 'die-sinker' bookplate, and this example may therefore typify the nadir of artistic armorial design for us. It has, however, like many thousands of similar plates of the period the merit of clear heraldry, which is of a different importance and makes many bookplates extremely useful to the genealogist. The print illustrated came from a book with a manuscript inscription reading 'Revd. Charles Kingsley, Eversley Rectory, 1849', and should, of course, never have been removed from it.

119

120

121

122

123

124 Joseph Rix

This unlikely gallimaufry, except in lumber rooms of dangerously irresponsible people, shows how cluttered and ungainly some mid-Victorian pictorial bookplates became, and lack of illustration of further examples will probably be forgiven. The design is, nevertheless, curiously evocative of its time and—for all its amateurishness—a little token of brotherly affection. Joseph Rix used four *ex-libris,* and this is the larger of two pictorial plates. The smaller, also dated 1857, is signed 'SWR' and is similar, but it has various alterations including an hourglass instead of a flower vase. The plate shown here has the inscription 'SWR Frat. Cariss', which identifies the designer as his brother S. Wilson Rix, who lived at Beccles in Norfolk and was local secretary of the Norfolk and Norwich Archaeological Society. S. W. Rix also designed a bookplate showing books and a lectern with the inscription 'BIBLIOTHECAE BECCLESIANAE CATALOGUS MDCCCXLVII'. Something more of Joseph Rix's history is evident from his two printed book labels, one reading 'Joseph Rix, F.L.S., F.R.C.S.E., L.S.A., St. Neot's Huntingdonshire', and the other with 'M.D' instead of 'F.L.S'. The latter must date from after 1860 when Rix became an MD of Aberdeen. He lived in the Market Square at St. Neot's, was medical officer of St. Neot's workhouse and district, and from the evidence of directories of the time seems to have died between 1876 and 1879. There are few such unusual inscriptions by designers or engravers of bookplates, but one or two others are noteworthy. A Chippendale armorial is signed by P. Simms and inscribed: 'P Simms sculpsit et dono dedit ob filiam unicam a morbo vindicatam', presumably a gift to the doctor who saved the life of the engraver's daughter; and some eighty years later Michell, an amateur engraver, inscribed three bookplates with declarations of gratitude, respect and love, including one for Captain F. T. Michell, RN which reads, 'Engraved as a token of the warmest affection by his brother Capt. C. C. Michell of the R. My. College'.

125 Jarrard Edw. Strickland

Jarrard (or Garrard) Edward Strickland (1782–1844) was 2nd son of Garrard Edward Strickland of Willitoft in Yorkshire, and Cecilia, daughter and in her issue heiress of William Towneley, of Towneley in Lancashire. He married in 1814 Annie, daughter of Francis Cholmeley of Brandsby in Yorkshire. Signed 'T.W', for Thomas Willement, this architectural armorial plate occurs in black or in sepia, and is one of a number of this period with ecclesiastical overtones. Several engraved *ex-libris* by the Jewitts (see Nos. 137, 138) are interesting in this way, as are James Bowker's by J. & J. Neale of the Strand and R. C. Brinton's, signed 'W.C.M. Sc. 1831'. In fact there was much quite interesting pictorial work in this period which has as yet been scarcely recorded at all.

124

125

126 (Christopher Sykes)

The only bookplate designed by Sir John Everett Millais (1829–1896), it shows St. Christopher carrying Christ across the water, and the canting arms denote the patronymic: argent, a chevron sable between three *sykes* or fountains. Christopher Sykes (1831–1898), second son of Sir Tatton Sykes, 4th Bart., was sometime MP for Beverley, the East Riding, and Buckrose Division East Riding; he never married. Millais was, of course, with Holman Hunt, a founder of the pre-Raphaelite movement and became President of the Royal Academy in 1896. The ingenious design and aptness of this little bookplate make one wish that Millais had engaged in more *ex-libris* work.

127 Mr Pollitt's Bookplate

Herbert Charles Pollitt, described by Oscar Wilde as 'gilt sunbeams masquerading in clothes', was at Trinity College, Cambridge in the early nineties, where he attracted much attention, not least for theatrical performances which included a scarf dance based on that of the American dancer, Loie Fuller. He was a great champion and friend of Aubrey Beardsley, who designed his bookplate, and there are four letters on the subject in Beardsley's correspondence (Ed. Henry Maas, 1971). Three relate to designing and printing the plate; the fourth, from the Hotel Foyot in Paris on 26th September 1897 asks: 'And how is my dear best friend? There is another wonderful book plate in the world. That makes two. Yours and another I have just made for a Miss Custance'. The Custance is illustrated in *The Studio*, Special Winter Number, 1898–9.

128 Sarah Nickson

Kate Greenaway's figures, with their characterless repose, are always immediately recognisable, and her ten known bookplate designs are illustrated and discussed by Keith Clark in *The Private Library*, Autumn 1975 (two further *ex-libris* referred to in Spielmann and Layard's *Kate Greenaway*, 1905, are yet untraced). Six of her ten plates were for members of the Locker-Lampson family, of which she became an intimate friend; others are for Lady Victoria Herbert, Vera Samuel (printed in colour by photogravure), Catherine Basilia Duff, and Sarah Nickson, whose bookplate, shown here, is among Kate Greenaway's more appealing designs.

129 E. Fitz-Gerald

The bookplate of Edward Fitzgerald (1809–1883), the poet and translator, famed for his *Rubaïyat of Omar Khayyam*. It was drawn for him by his life-long friend William Makepeace Thackeray (1811–1863), the novelist. The angel was meant to portray Mrs Brookfield, wife of William Henry Brookfield who was depicted as Frank Whitestock in Thackeray's *Curate's Walk*. Fitzgerald's letter of 19th March 1878, quoted by Castle, states that the *ex-libris* was 'done by Thackeray one day in Coram (Joram) Street in 1842. All wrong on her feet, so he said— I can see him now'. Thackeray had an early talent for drawing, which he studied in Paris; in addition to illustrations for publication he delighted in making caricatures to amuse children. Though this little plate lacks pretence to art, it is fascinating in its associations.

130 Frances Horner

Mrs J. F. Horner, nèe Frances Graham, was a close friend of the painter Sir Edward Burne-Jones (1833–1898), who designed this bookplate for her, probably in 1892. Several of his letters to her are quoted in his widow's *Memorials of Edward Burne-Jones*, 1904, and he wrote to Ruskin in 1883: 'To name every [picture] how could I remember? for instance, many a patient design went to adorning Frances' ways . . . Sirens for her girdle, Heavens & Paradises for her prayer-books, Virtues and Vices for her necklace-boxes'. The Marshall Catalogue records this as Burne-Jones' only bookplate design, but there is also a design of a vase of leaves and berries for Cicely Horner, illustrated in *Ars Decorativa* 4, Budapest 1976, and he allowed another design to be adapted as a bookplate for the Cambridge Musical Society. (His own book label is No. 252).

131 (H. G.) Seaman

This was designed by the illustrator Randolph Caldecott (1846–1886) for his friend H. G. Seaman of Chelford, Crewe. Caldecott was born in Chester, and until 1872 worked as a bank clerk; he then moved to London, where he drew for periodicals and became famous for his illustrated children's books, including *The House that Jack Built* and *Three Jovial Huntsmen*. The bookplate was drawn on the back of a postcard (see *The Ex Libris Journal* for May 1893), and Seaman wrote: 'I have just been reading the letter written in 1881, in which he sent it with a print from the block cut by his friend Mr. J. D. Cooper. In this he expressed himself much pleased with the excellence of the engraving . . . He had intended, with several other artists, friends of his and men of note, to make a study of this pretty art [bookplate designing] for its worthy revival, but alas, his hands were so full, and his life was so short, that I think mine was the only specimen he completed'.

126

Mr POLLITT'S BOOKPLATE.

127

SARAH NICKSON

128

E · FITZ · GERALD

129

E · LIBRIS · FRANCES · HORNER

130

VIVE PIUS MORIERE PIUS

BOOK OF PSALM

SEAMAN

131

[97]

132 William B. Scott

William Bell Scott (1811–1890) was son of the engraver Robert Scott, who gave him his first lessons in art. After further studies he helped his then invalid father in his work in Edinburgh, and concurrently began writing poetry. In 1837 he moved to London to live by art; he later organised art schools in the north, returning to London in 1864. His few *ex-libris* are little noticed now, but it was he who encouraged de Tabley to collect bookplates, and he designed a plate for him. His designs are emblematic scenes, and include three variant plates for Sir Walter Calverley Trevelyan of Nettlecombe, his kinsman Sir Charles Edward Trevelyan of Wallington, and the latter's second wife, Lady Eleanora, Henry Aylorde, George Burnett of Newcastle, H. Buxton Forman, Joseph Knight, Thomas Pigg of Newcastle, and two plates for himself. There are two varieties of his own larger plate, differing in the placing of the name and star; the smaller is circular and depicts the lamp. A letter from Scott to James Roberts Brown, dated 14th March 1890 notes: 'I have done several Ex Libris plates for my friends, but only for them. My own was first invented and etched by me as a title-page to [a] book of poems which I called *Poems by a Painter* . . . now out of print and very rare'. His father engraved a pictorial bookplate for Cupar Library about 1800.

133 E Dalziel

The wood-engraver and draughtsman Edward Dalziel (1817–1905), was educated at Newcastle-upon-Tyne, and followed his brother George to London—as their younger brothers John and Thomas were to do—to join in engraving, printing and publishing in the firm which bore their name. According to Gleeson White they probably learned their engraving from pupils of Bewick, and later, at Clipstone Street life class, Edward was a contemporary of Tenniel and Charles Keene (see No. 134). Three of the brothers are known to have used bookplates, which were no doubt their own work. Edward's, shown here, occurs in brown or blue; John's with similar ornament but of small seal shape has the monogram 'JD'; and Thomas', which is a quatrefoil on a square, with a monogram of his initial and surname, is printed in gold.

134 Charles Keene

This bookplate, in the printer's mark pounced style, is by Frederick Conway Montagu (1805–1891), a member of the Duke of Manchester's family. Montagu rarely signed his bookplates (some of which were probably cut on wood by William Harcourt Hooper), but G. H. Viner listed eighty examples by him. His younger brother, the Rev James Augustus Montagu, wrote the *Guide to the Study of Heraldry,* which Pickering published in 1840, and his sister Eleanora Louisa was also an author. The Keene *ex-libris* occurs in black, brown, light brown, and with the inscription bands and initials in red. Viner possessed two presumably preliminary designs by Montagu with monograms of C.S.K., the initials of the owner of this plate, Charles Samuel Keene (1823–1891), the humorous artist. Keene worked for *Punch* from 1851, for the *Illustrated London News* and *Once a Week.*

135 Birket Foster

Another pounced style plate by Montagu (see No. 134); a print of this occurs in the author's collection in a copy of *Poems of James Montgomery,* 1860, with the number 1009 in ink on the centre of the hunting horn. Montagu made three bookplates for Foster, the others being a full armorial and a large 'F' supporting a hunting horn. Myles Birket Foster (1825–1899), the painter and illustrator, was taught by the engraver Ebenezer Landells (with whom, incidentally, George Dalziel (see No. 133, above), was associated), and under him did his first work for *Punch* and the *Illustrated London News*; he began work on his own account in 1846. Montagu also made bookplate designs for Fanny, William and Miles Birket Foster, Junior.

136 Robert and Evelyn Benson

Laurence Housman (1865–1959), brother of the poet A. E. Housman, studied art at South Kensington and was prolific both as artist and writer. His few bookplate designs include one for A. W. Pollard ('A.W.P'), Hubert Bland, Hannah Brace and Robert and Evelyn Benson. The last, shown here, occurs in three varieties. The first is signed, printed from a wood-engraving, shows a lamp on the stern and has the greatest contrast of lights and darks; the second, also signed, is similar but weaker in its line and is perhaps a process reproduction; the third, unsigned, is quite different in its line and lacks the lamp, but has an additional outer border line. Housman drew for Harry Quilter's *Universal Review,* Pollard having introduced him to Quilter, and became in 1895 art critic of the *Manchester Guardian.* He took up women's suffrage, became a staunch pacifist, and wrote poetry and plays. His most popular successes were *The Little Flowers of St. Francis* and *Victoria Regina.*

132

133

134

135

136

137 Henry, 9th Baron Stafford

Sir Henry Valentine Stafford-Jerningham, 8th Bart. and 9th Baron Stafford (1802–1884), MP for Pontefract, 1830–34, had two plates engraved by Orlando Jewitt; the smaller is similar but has only the crests and knot. Orlando Jewitt (1799–1869), the wood-engraver, second child of Arthur Jewitt, was born at Chesterfield. The family moved where their father's work took him, and by 1815 were near Rotherham, where Orlando illustrated family publications including the *Northern Star, or Yorkshire Magazine*. He taught himself engraving, first in the Bewick manner, mediaeval and Gothic subjects; and moving to Duffield in 1818 engraved wild scenes for guidebooks, etc. His illustrations for *The Principles of Gothic Architecture*, etc., led to a move to Oxford and collaboration with Pugin. Several of the family joined him at Headington and became the firm of Orlando Jewitt. A check-list of the Jewitts' bookplates is in *The Bookplate Society Newsletter* for June 1977.

138 Llewellynn Jewitt and Elizabeth his wife

Llewellynn Jewitt (1816–1886), the antiquary, was sometime chief librarian at Plymouth, and edited the *Derby Telegraph* 1853–68. He was the youngest child of Arthur Jewitt, the topographer, and brother of Orlando (see No. 137). Though he engraved much, his few bookplates were for himself and friends. His own *ex-libris* dates from c. 1860. Others include plates for Thomas Bateman of Middleton in Derbyshire, his 'best-loved friend'; William Henry Goss, author of *The Life and Death of Llewellynn Jewitt*, 1889; William Hirst of Derby, a friend of fifty years; and John Fossik Lucas of Fenny Bentley, who co-operated as an antiquarian after Bateman's death.

139 Richard D'Oyly Carte

The greatest Victorian copper-engraver of bookplates, and inspirer of the revival of armorial bookplate design, was Charles William Sherborn (1831–1912). He is recorded in *A Sketch of the Life and Work of Charles William Sherborn*, 1912, by his son C. D. Sherborn, which includes a check-list by G. H. Viner of his *ex-libris*, which number more than 400 and are much sought after. Very few artists have worked, as Sherborn did, predominantly on bookplate design over thirty years; he was a founder member of the Society of Painter-Etchers, and was called 'The Little Master'. His 1898 plate for Richard D'Oyly Carte (1844–1901), the impresario who promoted Gilbert and Sullivan's operas, shows Sherborn's typical mantling, treatment of arms and usual and distinctive lettering; he often also incorporated pictorial elements, like the mask of comedy and symbols of music seen here.

140 (Everard Green)

George W. Eve (1855–1914) early in life entered the College of Arms, where his father had worked, and was author of *Decorative Heraldry*, 1897, and *Heraldry as Art*, 1907. His excellent bookplates, which are etched and eschew tinctures, number 250 and are listed in G. H. Viner's *A Descriptive Catalogue of Bookplates . . . by G. W. Eve*, 1916, and there is an article on his work in *The Ex Libris Journal* for December 1895. He married Mary Ellen, daughter of Dr Benjamin Hopewell of Chelsea, and latterly lived at Chiswick. This bookplate, which shows why he was considered second only to Sherborn (see No. 139), occurs in red or black, and was for Everard Green, Rouge Dragon Pursuivant of Arms.

141 Robert Clayton Swan

Robert Clayton Swan (1864–1929), eldest son of Robert Swan of Lincoln and his wife Lucy Clayton, was educated at Eton and Cambridge; he was Captain in the Lincolnshire Regiment and served in the Great War. He was married twice, firstly to Mildred, 2nd daughter of C. Perkins of Carham-on-Tweed. Allan Wyon (1843–1907), the medallist and seal-engraver who engraved this bookplate, was son of Benjamin Wyon, and his family had held office as Chief Engravers of HM Seals since 1812. He learnt engraving under his brother Joseph, travelled abroad, in 1873 became partner in the family firm, and compiled *The Great Seals of England*, 1887. Fincham lists about 100 bookplates by the Wyon family, but there were very many more. His son Allan G. Wyon continued the family tradition. There is an article on Wyon in *The Ex Libris Journal* for May 1901.

142 John Wynford, Baron St. Davids

John Wynford Philipps, 1st Viscount and 13th Bart. (1860–1938) was MP for Lanark 1888–94, for Pembrokeshire 1898–1908, and was Captain in the Pembroke Imperial Yeomanry. He married Norah, younger daughter of J. Gerstenberg of Stockleigh House, Regent's Park. He used four bookplates, this being the larger of two identical designs by Bernard Partridge. Sir Bernard Partridge (1861–1945) worked as an artist in various media and joined the staff of *Punch* in 1891. He designed very few bookplates, but they include one for Sir Henry Irving. The plate shown here cannot be earlier than 1908, when the Barony was created. The third and fourth bookplates, which show an identical design in two sizes by Acheson Batchelor, are very similar in composition to our illustration, but the sinister supporter differs, showing a muzzled bear, on account of his second marriage, in 1916, to Elizabeth Frances, Baroness Strange of Knokin, Hungerford and de Moleyns̄. Batchelor was working in London between 1910 and 1930.

137

138

Richard D'Oyly Carte

139

140

141

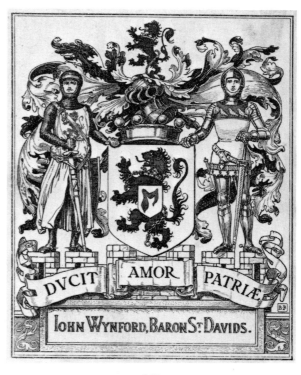

142

143 William Ewart Gladstone

The bookplate of the statesman William Ewart Gladstone (1809–1898) is typical of the style of its designer, T. Erat Harrison (1853–1917), who specialised in punning and rebus subjects. Trained at Mr Carey's Art School in Bloomsbury, and in Paris, he worked for a time with W. B. Richmond, and fourteen bookplates are listed in *The Ex Libris Journal* for August 1892. They are process blocks from drawings, this one by A. & C. Dawson of the Typographic Etching Company. This plate was a gift from Lord Northbourne on Gladstone's golden wedding. A note by Harrison in the *Journal* for January 1892 states that 'the kites and stones are a rebus on Gledstanes, the original form of the name (gled-kite), and it will be observed that the shield hangs on a holly bush, the reason for this being that the griffin of the crest issues from a wreath of holly leaves. The helmet is rather prominent, to show that Mr. Gladstone is still a commoner'. Harrison's bookplate for the Gladstone Memorial Prize was adapted from this design, and his other *ex-libris* include one of 1907 for John Ballinger, Librarian of the National Library of Wales.

144 Charles Dickens

The novelist Charles Dickens (1812–1870) used a crest plate, adopting without entitlement the crest granted to William Dickens in 1625 (see *Dickensian,* October 1922), and prints are much sought after. It is not, however, generally known that there were two different coppers for this. The earlier is shown here. Differences in line are many and minute, but the most obvious one is that the torse, or wreath of twisted silk, from which the crest issues, is in the later engraving more angular, especially at the end on the right. The second copper came into possession of Sotherans, the booksellers in Sackville Street, at the dispersal of Dickens' library, and may be seen on show in the shop. A label reading 'From the Library of CHARLES DICKENS, Gadshill Place, June, 1870'—which occurs in two settings, differing only in their lettering—was not used by Dickens himself; it records the month of his death, and Hamilton noted that the labels were placed in books by the auctioneers at the sale of his books (which suggests, incidentally, that his use of the crest plate was by no means comprehensive.)

145 Edmund William Gosse

The American artist, Edwin A. Abbey (1852–1911)—who also designed *ex-libris* for Brander Matthews and Austin Dobson—gave this bookplate to Gosse, who wrote of it: 'It represents a very fine gentleman of about 1610, walking in broad sunlight in a garden, reading a little book of verses'. Sir Edmund Gosse (1849–1928), the poet and author, could neither understand nor approve of book-plate collecting (see *Athenaeum*, 26th January 1894), but in his *Gossip in a Library,* 1891, he makes an amusing case for the usefulness of bookplates: 'There are many good bibliophiles who abide in the trenches, and never proclaim their loyalty by a book-plate. They are with us yet not of us . . . Such a man is liable to great temptations. He is brought face to face with that enemy of his species, the borrower, and dares not speak with him in the gate. If he had a book-plate he would say, "Oh! certainly I will lend you this volume, if it has not my book-plate in it; of course, one makes it a rule never to lend a book that has" '.

146 Granville Barker

Whether Sir Max Beerbohm (1872–1956), the cartoonist and author, made more bookplates is not apparent, but this example—if not among his more memorable pictorial observations—makes its point with a piquancy which will not be lost on the book collector. Harley Granville-Barker (1877–1946), the actor and producer, was a friend with whom the Beerbohms stayed, and the bookplate may have been a simple tribute to their amity.

147 W.E.H.

William Ernest Henley's bookplate is by William Nicholson, who also designed *ex-libris* for Elizabeth Valentine Fox, Phil May and himself. The poet Henley (1849–1903) always suffered precarious health, but wrote much; he was a friend of R. L. Stevenson, with whom he collaborated in four plays, and was depicted by him as Burly in the essay 'Talk and Talking' (Gosse, see No. 145, was Purcel in the same). Sir William Nicholson (1872–1949) discovered in his poster designs a personal style which he developed in the medium of woodcutting. He and James Pryde (for whom, incidentally, Craig made a bookplate) worked together as the Beggarstaff Brothers, and Nicholson married Pryde's sister. His *London Types* were accompanied by Henley's verses, and it was for him that Nicholson began the famous series of woodcut portraits.

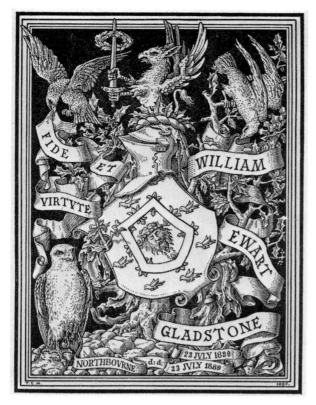

143

CHARLES DICKENS.

144

145

Granville Barker

146

Ex Libris

W.E.H.

147

148. Gleeson White

Allegory and symbolism, occasionally of a riotous and virtually unintelligible nature, enjoyed some popularity in later Victorian bookplate design, and Walter Hamilton in his *Dated Book-plates* writes some stern words on the subject, and comments: 'A book-plate which requires a column of explanation is apt to bore the uninitiated'. Not surprisingly, in view of its elaboration, he cites Gleeson White's *ex-libris* of 1890, engraved on wood by Charles Ricketts, but he ignores the fact that the interpretations of artist and owner vary. Ricketts writes thus of it: 'The tree of Creation (Igdrasil) springs from a swirl of water and flame which breaks into little gems; the flame, continuing, flows through the trunk of the tree, which branches on each side into composite boughs suggesting the different plant kingdoms. This central flame envelops the figure of man, placed in the midst of the tree in the act of awakening. The fruit on the eastern end of each bough represents in embryo the fish and water fowl, the reptile and creeping insects, the larger animals, and finally the creatures with wings. The rainbow shooting through the centre composition signifies the atmosphere; the two figures under one cloak in the lower part of the design represent night and day, i.e., the planets'. To this Gleeson White rejoins: 'The tree, whether under this particular shape of Igdrasil in Scandinavian mythology, or under that of the Tree of Knowledge in the Mosaic tradition, has always been a favourite symbol for Literature. It is therefore a felicitous choice as an emblem of knowledge, eternal, yet needing daily nourishment, and ALWAYS GROWING. In fact, the various interpretations of this mystical tree are as all-embracing as literature itself'. Whatever its interpretation, however, it is a fascinating composition and displays a rare imaginative power. Gleeson White (c. 1851–1898), after working in bookselling at Christchurch in Hampshire, moved to London and joined the staff of George Bell & Sons. He edited the Ex Libris Series of books, and was a founder and the first editor of the *Studio*; he died just after completing his text of the British section of the *Studio* Special 1898–9 Winter number, 'Modern bookplates and their designers', and himself designed a bookplate, showing a posy of flowers, for his daughter Cicely Rose Gleeson White (see note to No. 152) in 1891. Charles Ricketts (1866–1931) did much illustration for *The Dial*, a journal he founded with Charles Shannon in 1889, and for books from their Vale Press, founded in 1896. In addition to this *ex-libris* he designed a bookplate for John Morgan of Rubislaw House, Aberdeen, an architect and surveyor; its subject is mediaeval-architectural-allegorical, with angels engaged in construction work, framed in an inscription reading, 'THE HOUSE THE LORD BUILDS NOT WE VAINLY STRIVE TO BUILD IT'. The design contains Ricketts' monogram and is signed 'BS.sc'. This is used as the cover design in Keith Clark's *Bookplates of the Nineties*, published by James Wilson and The Bookplate Society in 1978.

ExLibris GLEESON WHITE

148

149 Frederic Leighton

Frederic, Baron Leighton of Stretton (1830–1896), was educated in London and on the Continent, devoting himself at an early age to painting. Made an RA in 1869 and President of the Royal Academy 1878–96, his most famous pictures include 'Hercules wrestling with Death', 'The Bath of Psyche', 'Perseus and Andromeda' and 'The Garden of the Hesperides'. He was raised to the peerage only the day before his death. This *ex-libris* dated 1894 is the larger of two for Leighton by Robert Anning Bell; it shows in fruit and flower the tree of knowledge of good and evil, with the serpent in its branches, a woman seated at the foot holding fruit from the tree while a young satyr crowned with its flowers pipes to her. The smaller design shows a meditative male scantily clad and perusing a book—a subject also used by the artist on his plate for Reginald L. Hine. Robert Anning Bell, RA (1863–1933), began his career as an architect, but after three years turned to art. He studied at the Royal Academy Schools, then briefly in Paris. Sometime Master of the Art Workers' Guild, he engaged —like a number of artists of his time—in a wide variety of work: oil and tempera painting, drawing for book illustration, coloured relief, stained glass and mosaic. Amongst his most famous mosaics are panels in the Houses of Parliament and the tympanum over the entrance to Westminster Cathedral. In view of the importance and influence of his work it seems extraordinary that he failed to find a place in the *Dictionary of National Biography*, nor has a monograph on him been published. He designed more than 85 bookplates, among them examples for Barry Pain, Cecilia Lady Glamis, mother of the Queen Mother (whose own bookplate is No. 188) and Fanny Dove Hamel Lister (see No. 151), one of two of his pupils whose bookplate designs are illustrated here. After several years Anning Bell took to numbering his bookplates, some of which occur in a number of sizes. Two are printed in colour, and for an interesting reason. One belonged to Theodore Mander, manufacturer of inks in Wolverhampton; the other is for Mander Brothers workpeople's library—a lending library run by the firm for its employees—printed in the colours of some of Mander Brothers' letterpress inks.

150 E. Guy Dawber

This bookplate was designed by Isabel B. Williamson, a pupil of Robert Anning Bell, and a print of it is in the Viner Collection. Sir Guy Dawber, RA (1861–1938) was born at King's Lynn, Norfolk and educated there. After being articled four years to William Adams, a Lynn architect, he became assistant in Dublin to Sir Thomas Newenham Deane (whose father's bookplate is No.107). A year later, political troubles having interrupted building, Dawber went to London and entered the office of Sir Ernest George, RA, at the same time attending the Royal Academy Schools. Sent by George in 1887 to work in Gloucestershire, his interests and talents were thereafter predominantly directed to domestic architecture in the Cotswolds, though he designed houses all over England. There is an account of his houses in the *Journal* of the Royal Institute of British Architects for 9th May, 1938. The author of several books, he was ever a fighter for rural England, and the distinctive character of his work has been described as a 'friendly gravity'. He was President of the RIBA 1925–7, RA 1935, and was knighted the following year. His wife was Mary, daughter of Alexander Eccles of Roby, Liverpool.

151 Leicester Nurses Home Norfolk & Norwich Hospital

Fanny Dove Hamel Lister (Mrs Calder) was born in Liverpool in 1864. An artist of the Liverpool School, she studied under Anning Bell (see No. 149), Augustus John and David Muirhead at the Liverpool School of Architecture and Applied Art. She was a painter, illustrator and stained glass and frieze designer, and exhibited from 1903 to 1922. As a designer of bookplates she seems scarcely to have been recorded, but she made a number of designs, for her plate for Thomas Duff Gordon is numbered 'IX 1896' (using a numbering scheme similar to her teacher's), and a plate of the previous year for Septimus Castle of Birkenhead occurs in two sizes. The arms of the plate shown here are those of the Earl of Leicester, of Holkham in Norfolk, and of the City of Norwich. Her own *ex-libris* by Anning Bell, designed in 1900, is illustrated in *The Ex Libris Journal* for July 1902.

EX LIBRIS

FREDERIC &
LEIGHTON

149

EX·LIBRIS: E·GVY·DAWBER

150

EX LIBRIS
LEICESTER
NVRSES HOME
NORFOLK & NOR
WICH HOSPITAL

151

152 Cicely Rose Gleeson White

This odd design nevertheless typifies its period, with the personifications of poetry and prose (helpfully named) rising from the trunks of trees behind a boat laden with books. It was the work of Harry Napper (d. 1930), who also designed bookplates in the 1890s for Alan Wright, Victor W. Burnand and an unnamed lady whose plate Labouchère illustrated in *Ladies' Book-plates*. Cicely Gleeson White was the daughter of Gleeson White, whose bookplate by Charles Ricketts is No. 148.

153 Eden Phillpotts

The eldest son of an officer in the Indian Army, Eden Phillpotts (1862–1960) was born in India, but came to England when his father died several years later. After leaving school he worked ten years in the Sun Fire office, unsuccessfully tried to become an actor, and then turned to writing. Here he won acclaim, and over many years was astonishingly prolific in his output. His bookplate was engraved on wood by Frank (later Sir Frank) Brangwyn (1867–1956), a man of like energy whose range as artist extends from enormous murals to bookplates, and Eden Phillpotts wrote the introduction to the Morland Press's *Bookplates by Frank Brangwyn, RA*, 1920. In this he gives his view of the ethos of the bookplate: 'What, then, should an ideal bookplate be? Emphatically not a picture of the master's crest, or his coat, his house or his library, but a line between his own personality and the treasures it adorns—a sign for other eyes, by which the possessor still holds for ever a sort of spiritual right in his volumes, that owners to come should recognise and respect'. The book illustrates sixty-nine of Brangwyn's *ex-libris*, most of them wood-engraved, some in several colours—and the colouring is unusual and sometimes rather violent. As Phillpotts comments, Brangwyn's 'distinctive quality of breadth and mass' is not lacking in them, and his designs certainly achieve the impact he sought—even if they are not to the taste of all of us.

154 William A. Bowie

James Guthrie (1874–1952), who designed this bookplate, is best remembered for his work at the Pear Tree Press between 1889 and 1951, but he was a key figure in certain areas of bookplate design during the first two decades of this century and edited *The Bookplate Magazine* and *The Bookplate*. Some of his publications, termed 'plate books', were printed on a rolling press from photographically etched plates; it was an intaglio method, and the process block for each print was separately coloured, which makes every page different from its counterparts in a limited edition. As Colin Franklin points out in an essay in the Spring 1976 issue of *The Private Library*—an issue devoted entirely to Guthrie—these plate books had their seed in bookplates, and some of his most unusual *ex-libris* were produced by his unique intaglio method. His interest in bookplates was shared by Pickford Waller, who also designed them, and for whom Guthrie made many personal plates. The quality of Guthrie's designs is extremely variable, for he was ever experimental and used several reproductive processes, but he was at his best in his romantic wood-engraved plates, such as those for Winifred Turner and Walter de la Mare. Among the publications on his bookplate work are *Eight Bookplates*, 1901, *A Little Book of Bookplates*, 1905, *James Guthrie, His Book of Bookplates*, 1907, *Some Bookplates*, 1909, *A Book of Intaglio Bookplates*, 1922, *Last Bookplates*, 1929, and *New Intaglio Bookplates*, 1934.

155 Clement K. Shorter

One of eleven known bookplate designs by Walter Crane (1845–1915), that most versatile artist, children's book illustrator and promoter of good design and craftsmanship. Ten of his bookplates are illustrated and described in Keith Clark's article in *The Private Library* for Summer 1975, and the eleventh is a plate for Adolf Cronbach. Most of the designs are signed by Crane's rebus, and his own plate illustrates a quatrain from *The Rubáiyat of Omar Khayyam*. Clement Shorter (1857–1926) chose another quatrain from the same work, for he was a founder member of the Omar Khayyam Club. He founded *The Sketch, The Sphere* and *The Tatler,* and for some years edited the *Illustrated London News*. He also either had a liking for personal bookplates or found them an attractive way of encouraging artists by personal commissions, for he used at least six other *ex-libris*, all of them pictorial. The designer of the first is unidentified, but was someone in *The Sphere* office; Phil May made a plate for him showing merry monks reading Rabelais; a design by C. Forestier was engraved by 'C.H.'; another is by Linley Sambourne, dated 1894; and Herbert Railton made two plates for him.

152

153

154

155

156 Denton Jenner-Fust

Though this has superficially the appearance of an etched bookplate, it is drawn and reproduced with an arbitrary plate-mark. Designed in 1935, it was the work of Frederick Landseer Maur Griggs, RA (1876–1938), whose fine etchings were inspired by the vision of Samuel Palmer's Shoreham years. The son of a baker-confectioner at Hitchin in Hertfordshire, Griggs remained there until he was twenty-eight; but it was at Campden in Gloucestershire that he truly found his artistic voice. He championed and sought to define and preserve a dream of old England, and, excluding early works, his fifty-seven etchings are the monument to a pastoral ideal which is abiding and authentic. His few *ex-libris*, designed over almost thirty years, show little of the power and insight of his etchings, but they have been—like the bookplates of a number of contemporaries—curiously disregarded. The earliest were two of 1906 for Fanny M. Elbourn and Isa Bell; later examples include designs for Janet Dodge, Mahlon Alanson Sands, Adrian Fortescue, CPRE, Joan Dorothy Townsend, Sidney Barnsley, Benjamin Martin Chandler and the plate shown here. There is an original drawing in the Viner Collection of a bookplate for F. L. Griggs himself, signed 'R.L.B.', but it was never printed or used.

157 W. D. S. Catalani

F. Rinder's *D. Y. Cameron: Catalogue of Etchings*, 1912, lists and illustrates in reduced size 30 bookplates etched by Sir David Young Cameron, RA (1865–1945), a year too early to list this 1913 plate. It is, however, recorded in A. M. Hind's *The Etchings of D. Y. Cameron*, 1924, from which it is apparent that the etcher's *ex-libris* work finished with five examples of the 1913-14 period. The plate shown here is a process reproduction of the much larger etching which Catalani also used. Cameron was the son of a Scottish minister, and after leaving commerce for art at the age of twenty he soon turned to etching; among 500 works in this medium his bookplates are small fry, but they are good designs with strongly-etched lines, interlaced initials or inscriptions in cartouches. There is an article by Haldane Macfall on Cameron's bookplates, with a check-list, in *Bookplate Annual* for 1925. His sister, Katharine Cameron (1874–1965), for whom he made a bookplate in 1895, herself etched several *ex-libris*, including two for her husband, Arthur Kay, but they are fussy and undistinguished.

158 Sidney Vere Pearson

Only two bookplates are recorded by Sir David Muirhead Bone (1876–1953): an armorial for Lincoln College, Oxford, and the plate shown here. A drypoint, eleven proofs of state iii are recorded, and state iv is the bookplate as used. Bone was born in a Glasgow suburb, son of the journalist David Drummond Bone. He studied drawing at the Glasgow School of Art evening school while an apprentice architect, and this combination profoundly affected his etched work when he later made art his career, for he thoroughly understood the architecture he depicted. He lived and etched some years abroad, was the first official artist appointed in the First World War, and was a Trustee of the National Gallery and the Tate. See Campbell Dodgson's *Etchings and Drypoints by Muirhead Bone. I. 1898-1907*, 1909 and *Later Drypoints of Muirhead Bone*, Print Collectors' Quarterly, 1922, and K. M. Guichard's *British Etchers 1850-1940*, 1977, for details of his etched work. His son, Stephen, also made a bookplate (See No. 177).

159 C. J. F. Knowles

Charles Julius Knowles (1840–1900) of Kensington Gore, London, was Legros' chief patron, and an extensive collector of paintings, drawings and etchings by Legros, Whistler and others. In *A Catalogue of the Etchings, Drypoints and Lithographs by Professor Alphonse Legros in the Collection of Frank E. Bliss*, 1923, it is noted that this plate is excessively rare. It is also a very typical subject. Alphonse Legros, RE (1837–1911) was a Frenchman who adopted England. He came here on the advice of Whistler, and taught etching, notably at the Slade. His portraits are important, and his figure subjects show the early influence of French peasant life and the Church. Bliss lists 704 etchings, and they include a bookplate for Leon Gambetta, though Wiggishoff's *Dictionnaire des Dessinateurs et Graveurs d'ex-libris Français* states that it was not used.

160 T. W. Dewar

David Strang's *William Strang. Catalogue of his Etchings and Engravings*, 1962 (a typescript), lists two bookplates by William Strang, RA (1859–1921), the chief pupil of Legros. Born at Dumbarton, Strang worked a year in shipbuilding after leaving school, and came to London in 1875. He studied six years at the Slade, becoming assistant master in the etching class in the latter part of the time. His portraits include some of the leading writers of his day. Only two etched bookplates by him are recorded, and David Strang lists them only by number. Of No. 1, shown here, there are three states: the first has 'W.S.' under the standing figure, there is a ¾″ (18mm) margin at the bottom of the plate, and the chin of the nearest kneeling figure is not drawn; in the second the chin is drawn, and a little shading is added on the lower scroll; and in the third the plate is cut (at the bottom line) to measure 3½ × 3″ (87 × 75mm). There were only two or three prints of each of the earlier states, and about six signed and a number unsigned of the third. Other modern etchers and engravers who did a little bookplate work include Stanley Anderson, Robert Austin, Robert Bryden, Martin Hardie, Sir Charles Holroyd, William Monk, Constance Mary Pott, Sydney Vacher, Joseph Webb and H. R. Wilkinson.

156

159

160

161 Ellen Terry

Edward Gordon Craig (1872–1966), the designer for the theatre and wood-engraver, was the son of Ellen Terry, and subsisted in his early adult years—as he fought for a better theatre—by engraving bookplates. His *Nothing or The Bookplate,* 1925 (re-issued 1931) tells the story of this. Though he could earn £8 a week in the theatre, he survived on the £2 or so which the making of *ex-libris* brought him. It was, however, no half-hearted work, for his ideas on design and their result were to be most beneficial in encouraging directness, a gentle wit and an uncluttering of composition. He considered this bookplate too big, and engraved it also in a smaller size more suited to his taste; but both have the addition of green, red and orange colour-blocks. If his work in this field has a weakness it is his preference for initials rather than names on his plates, for only friends could identify their ownership. There can be, however, no criticism of this design for Ellen Terry (1847–1928), the greatest actress of her day, for it is both named and has the delightful conceit of a map to direct the book home. He used colour in the majority of his bookplates, and profoundly influenced the *ex-libris* work of his friend Claud Lovat Fraser (see No. 165).

162 Rudyard Kipling

The story-teller and poet, Rudyard Kipling (1865–1936) was born in Bombay, the son of John Lockwood Kipling (1837–1911), sometime architectural sculptor in the Bombay School of Art, curator of the Museum at Lahore and designer of the Durbar Room at Osborne House. His bookplate, dated 1909 and signed with his father's initials, is redolent of colonial splendour and occurs in this and two other sizes in black and in brown. It is one of four *ex-libris* which John Lockwood Kipling is known to have designed. The second, a plate for himself, is shown facing p. 5 in *Rudyard Kipling the man his work and his world,* edited by John Gross, 1972. This is a portrait plate, in facsimile of sculptured relief, the figure in profile reading a book and smoking a pipe, with the motto 'FUMUS GLORIA MUNDI' in the smoke from the pipe. The third and fourth plates were for his grandchildren, John and Elsie Kipling. Rudyard Kipling himself designed a bookplate; it reads 'EX LIBRIS HUNTINGDON & DOROTHY BABCOCK' and is a punning pictorial. Mrs Babcock's maiden name was Doubleday, and this was inscribed on an earlier state of the plate. She also used a bookplate depicting the *Lusitania,* in which she and Kipling were fellow-passengers when the designs were made. There is a print of the Kipling plate for the Babcocks in the Viner Collection.

163 May Blackham Downs

This plate was engraved by Thomas Sturge Moore (1870–1944), the associate of Ricketts (see No. 148), Shannon and Lucien Pissarro (see No. 196). Ricketts and Shannon introduced him to the art of wood-engraving, but though the former became his teacher, Moore's work shows an independent spirit, and some of his *ex-libris* are very coarsely cut. They are, however, significant examples of their time, and include plates for Alexandra Helen Murray Baillie, Campbell Dodgson, W. S. Kennedy, George Harry Milsted, Sybil Pye, William A. Pye, Ethel Pye, Thomas L. Raymond, A. G. B. Russell, the poet W. B. Yeats and Mrs Yeats—and a drawing for their daughter Anne which was never printed. The *Bookplate Annual* for 1923 quotes Sturge Moore: 'My bookplates are in engraving on wood blocks. I specialise in my own designs. The cost is £20. I have been making bookplates for a dozen years'. There is an article on his *ex-libris* by A. J. Finberg in *Bookplate Annual,* 1922, and another on his engravings and book illustrations in *The Private Library* for Spring 1971.

164 G. F. Watts, R.A.

George Frederick Watts, RA (1817–1904) was born in London and studied at the Royal Academy Schools. He painted classical, allegorical and biblical subjects and portraits, sculpted, and made himself this *ex-libris.* It is illustrated in Wilfred Blunt's biography, *England's Michaelangelo,* 1975, where Watts is quoted as saying that he was more proud of this bookplate than any of his other pictures. He married Ellen Terry in 1864, but the marriage was dissolved.

165 R(alph) H(odgson)

Claud Lovat Fraser (1890–1921) first trained for a legal career, left to study art under Sickert, and then discovered his metier in design for the theatre, book illustration, textile design, posters and all kinds of graphic work. The quality and quantity of his work are astonishing for one who died so young and was plagued by ill-health. His bookplates are little known, but thirty-six were printed, mostly for friends, and a splendid little book of unused designs survives. They show in their line, composition and colouring the influence of his great friend Edward Gordon Craig (see No. 161), but have a spirit entirely their own. This *ex-libris* for Ralph Hodgson (1871–1962), the poet—several of whose works appeared in Fraser's *Flying Fame* series of booklets and broadsheets—dates from 1913 and was printed in fifty copies, each of them hand-coloured by the artist. Our illustration can, therefore, give no idea of the beauty of the design as used. Fraser used to refer to his bookplates and occasional sketches as his 'knitting', for they were undertaken in the evening as a relaxation after work, and there was much giving of them as gifts among his circle of friends. This included Haldane Macfall and Pickford Waller (see No. 183), whose work will be familiar to collectors. A study of Fraser's *ex-libris* is in preparation.

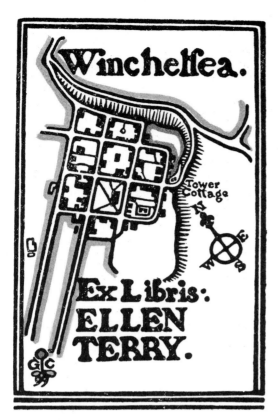

161

162

164

163

165

166 The Lady Agnes Durham

A popular way of commissioning a fine copper-engraved bookplate towards the end of the last century and in the earlier decades of the 1900s was through one of the high-class London stationers, and the Durham *ex-libris* is a lovely example of the quality of much of this work. Designed by Francis George House (1874–1946), who worked for Truslove and Hanson in Sloane Street, it was engraved by John Augustus Charles Harrison (1872–1955). The eldest son of Samuel Harrison, a Manchester line engraver, he joined Waterlows in 1890. Before 1900, however, he became a free-lance engraver, occupied chiefly with bookplate design. In 1910 he engraved for the Royal Mint the George V 'Sea Horse' high value stamp, and was later exclusively employed by Waterlows, where he gained international fame for stamp and banknote design. There are supplements and notices of House's designs for bookplates in *The Ex Libris Journal* for 1903, 1905, 1906, 1907 and 1908, and though it is not clear how fully he suggested composition to the engravers he employed it was probably to a greater degree than W. P. Barrett, who worked in a similar capacity for Messrs J. & E. Bumpus (see No. 167), for whom Harrison also worked earlier. House's initials occur on at least 132 bookplates. Lady Agnes Elizabeth Audrey Townshend (1870–1955), the daughter of John, 5th Marquess Townshend, married in 1903 James Andrew Cuninghame Durham of Cromer Grange and East Raynham House.

167 Sir David Lionel Goldsmid-Stern-Salomons, Bart.

Sir David Lionel Goldsmid-Stern-Salomons, Bart. (1851–1925), of Broomhill, Tunbridge Wells, succeeded his uncle in 1873 and assumed by Royal licence in 1899 the additional names and arms of Goldsmid and Stern. He married in 1882 Laura Julia, daughter of Baron Herman de Stern. This plate is one of four varieties which Robert Osmond engraved for him. The other three are much larger, and from one copper. In the first the centre and left hand crests are not tinctured; in the second (as here) they are; and the third is also a tinctured state with the inscription altered to 'of Broomhill, Kent, Baronet'. Robert Osmond (1874–1959) was born at Islington, the youngest son of Robert Osmond, a painter and grainer. On his fourteenth birthday he was apprenticed to William E. Corks, an engraver in Northampton Square, Clerkenwell, and in his early twenties was put in charge of Corks' West End branch in Carnaby Street. His extensive association with Messrs J. & E. Bumpus, the booksellers, began about 1905, and he did almost half of their bookplate work, in addition to that for House and independent commissions. All the Bumpus plates are signed 'W.P.B.', the initials of William Phillips Barrett (1861–1938), who was born at Christchurch in New Zealand; he certainly accepted and encouraged bookplate commissions for Bumpus, but there has been question whether he did much real designing. For a fuller account see Horace E. Jones' *Bookplates signed 'W.P.B.', 1896–1928*, 1978.

168 Arthur Henry Chetwynd Talbot

Graham Johnston (b. 1869), a native of Edinburgh, was the son of James M. Johnston, who was in printing. After studying in London he entered the firm of Scott and Ferguson, engravers and lithographers, and while with them was first employed by the Lyon Court in Edinburgh, to which he became heraldic engraver. Many of his designs in colour and monochrome enhance A. C. Fox-Davies' *Complete Guide to Heraldry,* and he seems to have employed more than one engraver to carry out work for him, though other compositions were reproduced from drawings. His *ex-libris*, which number 160, were reproduced over a long period in *The Ex Libris Journal*, and there is an article on him in the July 1902 issue. The Rev Arthur Henry Chetwynd Talbot (1855–1927) married in 1903 Eveline Mary, the daughter and coheir of Colonel C. J. Ashton of Little Onn Hall, Staffordshire.

169 Ignaz Jan Paderewski

This is another bookplate commissioned from Messrs Bumpus, engraved in 1908 by Charles Bird, RE. Though Bird did less than a tenth of the *ex-libris* engraving for the firm, this example shows an unusual and not unattractive composition, with its grand piano, portrait, and listing of favourite composers. It belonged, of course, to the famous Polish pianist and composer, Ignaz Jan Paderewski (1860–1941), the noted exponent of Chopin. Paderewski became premier of Poland in 1919, but opposition caused him to resign the following year, and in 1921 he resumed his musical career.

170 Mary Caroline Lawson

An amateur engraver, Mary Caroline Lawson remains obscure, but her life was short. In 1906 she was living at Clent Vicarage near Stourbridge; soon after 1911 she married, and a year later she died in India in a riding accident. The plate shown here is the smaller of two bookplates for herself, both dated 1906, but her total output numbers at least thirty *ex-libris*. They include five for members of her own family, four for the Grazebrook family, and one for Stanbrook Abbey.

166

167

168

169

170

171 Basil Charles Trappes-Lomax

Paul Vincent Woodroffe (1875–1954) was the son of Francis Woodroffe, who was in the Madras Civil Service. Educated at Stonyhurst and the Slade, he illustrated books, including *The Tempest, Froissart's Chronycles* and 1890s books of nursery rhymes, and designed stained-glass windows, including those for St. Patrick's Cathedral in New York. His few bookplate designs include this plate for Basil Charles Trappes-Lomax (1896–1963), the son of Richard Trappes-Lomax of Allsprings, Lancashire, and his wife Alice, the sister of the 13th Baron Stafford. Trappes-Lomax was a brigadier in the Royal Artillery, and as a hobby collected and studied *ex-libris*. He was sometime secretary of the Bookplate Exchange Club, and wrote an article on East Anglian bookplates which appeared in *East Anglian Magazine* for February 1956. His father's plate was also the work of Paul Woodroffe, and his wife Diana's was designed by Gerald Cobb, heraldic artist at the College of Arms for over fifty years, whose work is noted for its clear heraldry and good composition.

172 Audrey Gordon Gray

This bookplate depicting St. Audrey was designed by Kruger Gray for his future wife, Audrey Gordon, the daughter of the Rev John Henry Gray, sometime Archdeacon of Hong Kong. It dates from 1915, three years before their marriage, which explains the initials 'GK' at the side of the tankard which he often used to mark his work. George Edward Kruger Gray, FSA (1880–1943) was born in Kensington, the son of Edwin Charles Kruger, a merchant of St. Helier in Jersey, and added the surname Gray on his marriage. From the Bath School of Art he won a scholarship to the Royal College of Art, where he studied under Lethaby. He engaged in seal and coinage design, including the silver coinage for George V and George VI; he designed the George Medal (see No. 188), and also did stained-glass and heraldic work. His bookplates seem to number less than a dozen, but they include plates for Sir John Martin-Harvey, Henry Lawrence Bradfer Lawrence, Mildred Martineau, the Society of Antiquaries, Bristol University, St. John's College, Cambridge and Corpus Christi College, Oxford.

173 S. Baring-Gould

Thomas Moring published two books on his work: *Fifty Book-plates engraved on Copper* and *One Hundred Book-plates engraved on Wood,* both in limited editions in 1900, and many of his designs are pleasant of their kind. He particularly favoured the 'pounced' style, seen here, and monograms; and he was assisted for some time by the bookplate designer Harry Soane, though Soane did no engraving. Moring believed that 'public opinion has now been raised in favour of the more intelligent and artistic work, and the engraver has been put on his mettle and is encouraged by the fact that something good is appreciated', and his bookplates include a wood-engraved design for E. R. J. Gambier-Howe, the author of the *Catalogue of the Franks Collection,* and a design printed from two colour-blocks for himself. The armorial shown here was for Sabine Baring-Gould (1834–1924), the author and clergyman. He was born at Exeter, but due to ill-health was educated chiefly abroad. He married in 1868 Grace, the daughter of Joseph Taylor of Horbury, who bore him five sons and nine daughters, and on the death of his father in 1872 he succeeded to the family estate of Lew Trenchard in Devonshire, becoming incumbent there in 1881. A prolific writer on subjects including travel, myth, the lives of the saints and the West of England, his biography of R. S. Hawker, *The Vicar of Morwenstowe,* 1876, is very engrossing reading, even if it is inaccurate. Baring-Gould was also the author of 'Onward Christian Soldiers', and several other hymns.

174 Gilbert Murray

Edmund Hort New (1871–1931) was born at Evesham, the son of a solicitor. He studied at the Birmingham School of Art under E. R. Taylor and Arthur J. Gaskin (whose wife was a bookplate designer), and joined the teaching staff there. An exhibitor at the Royal Academy, he illustrated many books including several in the 'Highways and Byways' county series, Gilbert White's *The Natural History of Selborne* and Izaac Walton's *The Compleat Angler,* 1927. He lived and worked much of his life in Oxford, and was an Honorary MA of the University. His bookplates, which number about 120, have mostly an architectural character, many showing the frontage of houses; but he made an oval portrait design in 1897 for William Malin Roscoe, which was printed in three sizes and depicts William Roscoe (d. 1831). There is an article on New's bookplates, with a check-list, in the 1927 *Year Book* of the American Society of Bookplate Collectors and Designers. Gilbert Murray (1866–1957), the classical scholar, was born in Sydney, New South Wales, came to England at the age of eleven, and was Professor of Greek at Glasgow University from 1889 to 1899. He wrote many verse translations, at first to help his students. Made a Fellow of New College, Oxford in 1888, he returned there in 1905, and was Regius Professor of Greek at Oxford from 1908 to 1936.

BASIL CHARLES
TRAPPES·LOMAX

171

Audrey Gordon Gray.
Ano Dñi.

172

173

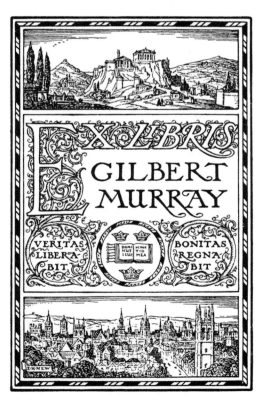

174

175 Gwyneth Lloyd Thomas

Gwyneth Lloyd Thomas (d. 1978) was a life fellow of Girton College, Cambridge and headmistress of Channing School, Highgate. Her bookplate is one of two engraved on wood by Eric Ravilious (1903–1942); the other, for Roger Bevan, also dates from 1932 and is illustrated in Severin's *Making a Bookplate*, 1949. Ravilious was born in Acton, the son of a coach-builder, and studied at the Eastbourne School of Art and the Royal College of Art, where he later became instructor in design. He was influenced by Alec Buckels, Paul Nash and more particularly Douglas Percy Bliss (see No. 176), and though he preferred the medium of water-colour his earliest professional works were book illustrations in wood-engraving, at which he also excelled. In 1926 he began a distinguished connection with the Golden Cockerel Press, but he also did work for the Curwen, Cresset and Nonesuch presses, as well as mural painting, lithography and advertising design. An official naval war artist, he was lost in a plane off Iceland in 1942.

176 W. D. H. McCullough

Douglas Percy Bliss (b. 1900) who engraved this bookplate on wood, was educated at Watson's College and the University of Edinburgh, and studied painting at the Royal College of Art. For eighteen years director of the Glasgow School of Art, he also wrote an important history of wood-engraving, and illustrated a dozen books, including *Border Ballads*, 1925 and *The Devil in Scotland,* 1934. His best work is in water-colour, though he has also painted in oils for many years; and he engraved until the early part of the Second World War, during which his blocks and tools were stolen when his home was bombed and left doorless. That unfortunately meant the end of his bookplate work, which numbered about fifty plates; among them are designs for Margaret. T Bliss, T. R. Bolam, Austin Reed, J. & R. Snedden, Archibald Stirling and Nancy Wright. The Liverpool Public Library has a number of his *ex-libris* in its collection. The bookplate illustrated, which was made for an old school-friend, shows the spirit of his work, the manner of his cutting on wood, and his treatment of lettering.

177 D. W. Bone, Mariner

Sir David Bone (1874–1959), master mariner and author, was the brother of Sir Muirhead Bone (see No. 158). Born in Glasgow, the ships and shipyards of the Clyde fascinated him. His first voyage was in 1891, and before he sat for his certificate as master mariner he had been round the world in the barque *Loch Ness*; he was commander in 1916 of the *Cameronia*, the flagship of the Anchor Line, and served in another *Cameronia* in 1939—but he tells his adventures best himself in *Merchantmen-at-Arms*, 1919, *Merchant Rearmed*, 1949 and his other books. He was knighted in 1946. His bookplate was made for him by his nephew Stephen Bone (1904–1958), the son of Sir Muirhead. Born at Chiswick, he lived as a child two years in Italy; he was at school at Bedales, then in 1920 went with his father on a European journey. In 1922 he entered the Slade, where he learnt much from Professor Tonks. He was engraving book illustrations from adolescence, and won a gold medal for wood-engraving in 1925; but though he continued engraving and also painted in oils most of his early professional work was in water-colour. Ever a traveller, he did well-composed and naturalistic topographical work, frequently exhibited at the Royal Academy, and did portraits. Later he was well known as art critic for the *Manchester Guardian* and for his broadcasts and appearances on television. He was, like Eric Ravilious, an official naval war artist in the Second World War.

178 Bank of England Library and Literary Association

John Farleigh (1900–1965) was a pupil of Noel Rooke. He engraved on wood for the Golden Cockerel Press and Shakespeare Press, and did the illustrations and cover for Shaw's *The Adventures of the Black Girl in Her Search for God*, 1932. In 1940 Macmillan published his autobiographical guide to engraving, *Graven Image*. Though principally a painter, engraver and illustrator, his work extended to the design of posters and textiles, and he did advertising work and murals. He apparently engraved few bookplates, but his 1933 William Maxwell plate is illustrated in *Bookplate Designers 1925-1975*, the catalogue of The Bookplate Society's 1976 exhibition; and others were for Jean Elizabeth Peace, Thomas Hudson Middleton and the design shown here.

179 Ellic Howe

This neat library interior design was engraved by John Buckland Wright (1897–1954), and is a modern interpretation of an engraving by Papillon. Born at Dunedin in New Zealand, Buckland Wright came to England as a child and was educated at Clifton, Rugby and Oxford, where he read History. He studied architecture, but determined to be an artist and went off to the Continent, where he lived for some years; and he spent ten years at Hayter's Atelier 17 in Paris, where he became his assistant. Many of his earlier books were published on the Continent, but he is best known in this country for his distinguished work for the Golden Cockerel Press between 1936 and 1954. There is an article and check-list by David Chambers of Buckland Wright's *ex-libris* in *The Private Library* for Autumn 1976. Engraved on wood or copper, they number thirty—and three more have been adapted from his book illustrations. Of very uneven quality, almost half of them were for continental clients, and perhaps the best of them is the copper-engraved mermaid and merman design for the Belgian bookplate artist, Mark Severin.

175

176

EX LIBRIS
D.W. BONE
Mariner.

177

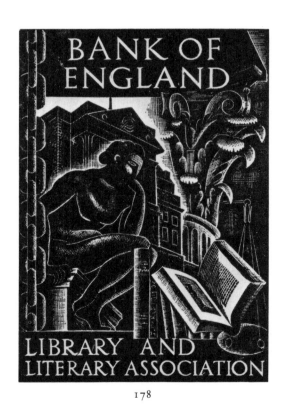

178

179

180 Robert Partridge

The illustrator Arthur Rackham (1867–1939) was born in London. He left school at the age of sixteen in frail health, voyaged to Australia, and returned to study at Lambeth School of Art in the evenings. He was soon selling work to magazines, and in the nineties developed his talent remarkably; but he established himself with his illustrations to Grimms' *Fairy Tales,* and many fine books followed, including *Rip Van Winkle*, 1905 and the magnificently-produced Christmas gift books. His colourings were delicate, but he revelled in the grotesque—as this bookplate for Robert Partridge demonstrates. It is printed on a pale green paper; and a design on cream paper for G. L. Lazarus shows an innocent child lying reading while two nasty-faced trees shake hand-like boughs behind him at the behest of mischievous goblins.

181 J. Ramsay MacDonald

James Ramsay MacDonald (1866–1937), the Labour leader and statesman, was born at Lossiemouth, the son of a labourer. He was prime minister in 1924 and from 1929 to 1935. His bookplate is signed by J. A. Adamson, and the author's print of it has 'Dec 1928' in manuscript beneath, but whether this indicates when it was made is not clear. Needless to say, a number of prime ministers have used *ex-libris*. Gladstone's is shown (No. 143); Disraeli used a die-sinker armorial; Clement Attlee had a small plate with a design based on the letters of his name; and Edward Heath has a Joan Hassall scraperboard design. Another plate relating to No. 10 Downing Street, and commissioned by MacDonald, is that of the Cabinet Library. Designed by Sir William Rothenstein and engraved by Robert Austin in 1931, it occurs in two sizes and depicts the front door. The idea of such a library came from MacDonald, who started the collection with three of his own books in January 1931, and invited past and present colleagues to contribute also. (See *John O'London's Weekly* for 4th February, 1938.)

182 Kevin O'Duffy

The bookplates of Jack Butler Yeats (1871–1957) really deserve to be thoroughly recorded, but it is yet to be done. Liam Miller, in his *The Dun Emer Press, Later the Cuala Press,* 1973, notes that a considerable number of bookplates were printed at the press, and that they were announced in early prospectuses. The majority of them were designed by Jack Yeats, and his plates for John Quinn, Lennox Robinson, and his sister Lily are reproduced in the book; but others were the work of his sister Elizabeth. The *ex-libris* for his friend Kevin O'Duffy shown here was occasioned by a remark he made to Yeats that though he loved books he was always kept too busy by work to have enough time to enjoy them—hence the workman leaving his home with a reluctant glance back towards the bookshelves. Yeats has signed his name on the top of the curtain, and the date on the top left window pane appears to be 1904. Another fine bookplate was for Madeline Jones. Yeats was born in London, the son of John Butler Yeats and younger brother of the poet William. When he was eight he was sent to his grandparents in Sligo, where he stayed eight years and found the subjects and inspiration for his later work as an artist. In 1888 he attended the Westminster School of Art, and made a living thereafter by his illustrations and paintings, for which he became justly famed; he had a retrospective exhibition at the National Gallery in London in 1942. There is an article on his *ex-libris* in *The Bookplate*, N.S.1, 1926.

183 Pickford Waller

Austin Osman Spare (1886–1956) was the son of a London policeman. He was producing powerful imaginative work by the age of fourteen, and in 1908 held an exhibition at the Bruton Gallery which was much noticed. George Bernard Shaw considered his work 'Too strong a meat for normal', and Augustus John thought his draughtsmanship unsurpassed. His subjects are grotesque, but extremely well composed. He illustrated *Earth Inferno*, 1905 and *A Book of Satyrs*, 1909, and later collaborated with Clifford Bax for the periodical *Golden Hind*. Though only four bookplates by him are recorded, there are probably more. One was for M. Robert Boss; another —depicting Pan, clothed and seated, playing his pipes, with a silhouette portrait below—was for Desmond Coke, author of *The Art of Silhouette*, 1913; and two were for Pickford Waller (who like Coke also had a bookplate by Lovat Fraser, and a great many others by Guthrie). The first of the Waller *ex-libris* is this design of 1905; the second shows a bust of Pan, armless, with thorny branches below, and dates from 1923.

"HOW MANY GOODLY CREATURES ARE THERE HERE?"
The Tempest

180

181

182

183

184 Edmund & Mary Davis

Sir Edmund Davis, the son of S. Davis, directed many mining concerns and was made a knight in 1927. A noted art collector, he presented a collection of works by modern British artists to the Luxembourg in 1915. His bookplate, a fine design drawn in the manner of an early woodcut, was the work of Edmund Dulac (1882–1953). The son of a cloth merchant, Dulac was born at Toulouse and studied art there and at the Academie Julian in Paris. Settling in London at the age of twenty-three (he was naturalized in 1912), he achieved notable success in the illustration of books. He also made masks, caricatures and straight portraits, and designed sets and costumes for the theatre, furniture and fittings, stamps and banknotes, and the King's medal for poetry. Indeed, he was a man of many parts, and his ability, for instance, to assimilate in his excellent book illustrations the character of the art of either east or west was impressive. Like Rex Whistler (see No. 187) he made a universal *ex-libris* for The Book Society, a design of a centaur-like female holding aloft a lighted torch, likewise signed with his initials.

185 To Aberdeen University from . . .
John Malcolm Bulloch

A capital 'N' or 'HN' in a rectangle often marks the bookplates of Harold Nelson, though he sometimes signed with his full name; and our illustration is a fairly typical example of his bookplate work, which began in 1893. Original drawings seen suggest that, like Edmund J. Sullivan, he made his drawings in large size and had them reduced for use as bookplates. Harold Edward Hughes Nelson (b. 1871) was born in Dorchester, and after working with a herald-painter and engraver he studied at the Lambeth School of Art. He illustrated books, including W. J. Thomas' *Early English Prose Romances*, and did much *ex-libris* design. Three books were published on the latter: *Harold Nelson: His Book of Bookplates*, 1904, *Harold E. H. Nelson*, 1910, and P. Hornung's *Bookplates by Harold Nelson*, 1923, and there were articles on his work in *The Ex Libris Journal* for April-May 1905 and *Bookplate Annual*, 1923. His compositions reflect, also, changing fashion in design from the 1890s onwards. In the introduction to his 1904 book he wrote: 'What should a book-plate be if not individual? I think that in many cases a simple symbolic figure with an appropriate border and inscription answers the purpose admirably; but it seldom satisfies, so many owners expecting to find in their plates a detailed reflection of their tastes, sports, or idiosyncracies. Within limits, one is bound to admit that they are justified'.

186 Ivor Novello

The bookplate of Ivor Novello (1893–1951), the composer, actor and manager whose real name was David Ivor Davies, was designed for him by Philip Armstrong Tilden (1887–1956). Tilden was an architect, but having time on his hands in 1918–19 wanted to occupy himself with lucrative work, and determined on the designing of *ex-libris*. A friend helped him to obtain commissions, and he happily produced romantic compositions for, among others, Edward VIII as Prince of Wales, The Princess Royal, Lady Juliet Duff and members of the Sassoon family. In his architectural career he built country houses, worked for Lloyd-George at Churt and Winston Churchill at Chartwell, and restored historic buildings; he also did murals, was a governor of the Old Vic and Sadlers Wells theatres, and wrote a novel, *Noah*, in 1932. One of the houses he restored was later to be the North Audley Street home of Lady Aberconway (see No. 187).

187 Christabel and Henry McLaren

Rex Whistler (1905–1944) was educated at Haileybury, and after one 'unpromising' term at the Royal Academy Schools was immediately accepted by Tonks at the Slade. He was soon engaged in mural work, including the refreshment room at the Tate in 1927, and by 1930 had finished his wonderful illustrations for *Gulliver's Travels*. In so prolific an output of work as his it is not surprising that bookplates had their place, and though there are few of them they include some consummate little designs. His bookplates are recorded in the author's *The Bookplate Designs of Rex Whistler*, 1973, which illustrates also some of his preliminary drawings—including three for this *ex-libris* of 1932. Most of Whistler's bookplates were for friends, and Christabel and Henry McLaren (later Lord and Lady Aberconway) were among them. One sees here with what success the artist contrives to suggest the interests and preoccupations of his friends. In the library interior are bookshelves and a trophy, indicative of Lady Aberconway's love of writing, reading and music; their busts—labelled with initials—are above the shelves; and beyond there is a garden with a splendid fountain, for Lord Aberconway was President of the Royal Horticultural Society and presented the gardens at Bodnant to the National Trust. It is also a notably and essentially beautiful design—and Christabel loved beauty in its multifarious forms. Rex Whistler also made bookplates for Loelia, Duchess of Westminster, Lady Diana Duff Cooper, Lord Rothschild and Audrey Pleydell-Bouverie —the last a design in colour which was a peace-offering from Rex Whistler for forgetting to attend a dinner party in 1939.

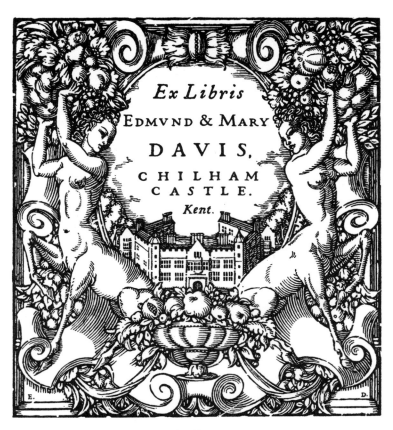

184

185

186

187

188 Elizabeth R

This bookplate was engraved for Her Majesty Queen Elizabeth the Queen Mother as Queen Consort in 1942. The work of Stephen Gooden, CBE (1892–1955), it is one of a series of seven outstanding *ex-libris* for the Royal Family which the artist had begun in the reign of Edward VIII. Five of them are recorded in Campbell Dodgson's *An Iconography of the Engravings of Stephen Gooden*, 1944. The first three (CD. 151–3) were for the Royal Library at Windsor Castle, and in their final states have the cypher of George VI. The CBE was conferred on Gooden in recognition of the fact that the St. George and the Dragon design of the second was adapted for the George Medal, designed by Kruger Gray (see No. 172). In 1942 there followed two bookplates for Her Majesty, the larger of which is shown here; the smaller depicts a crowned lion with a book in its paw (CD. 183–4). The last two, subsequent to the *Iconography*, were plates for the Princesses Elizabeth and Margaret, both probably engraved in 1946. The original designs for the Queen's large *ex-libris* were sold some years ago by Elkin Mathews, Ltd, who purchased the contents of Gooden's studio at his death. They include a variant design, illustrated in their catalogue, which makes an interesting comparison with our illustration and a lovely tapestry—shown in the *Illustrated London News* for 2nd December 1950—which Gooden designed for Her Majesty. Though the tapestry was not finished until September 1950, Gooden had begun designing it in the Spring of 1941, so it may have exerted some influence on the bookplate design. Stephen Gooden, the son of a picture dealer, studied at the Slade. He served in the First World War, and in the 1920s engaged in book illustration, notably for the Nonesuch Press; his bookplate designs number forty-three.

189 Grace Elvina Trillia Marchioness Curzon of Kedleston

Grace Elvina, widow of Alfred Duggan and daughter of J. Monroe Hinds of Alabama, United States Minister in Brazil, married as his second wife the 1st and last Marquess Curzon of Kedleston, the statesman. She published *Reminiscences*, 1955, lived latterly at Bodiam Manor in Sussex, and died in 1958. Her bookplate was engraved by George Taylor Friend (1881–1969). The son of Robert and Mary Friend, his father's hobby of wood-carving may have encouraged his son's interest in art, for at fourteen he was apprenticed to James F. Barnard of Holborn, under whom he learnt engraving on gold and silver. Friend became a distinguished teacher at the Central School of Arts and Crafts, and in 1912 set up his own workshop in Holborn, where he carried on engraving for over half a century. The first of over 500 bookplates from his hand dates from 1911, and his work shows consistently sound lettering and skill in heraldic design. He engraved the Stalingrad sword, and was awarded the OBE in 1954 for services as a teacher of engraving. See P. C. Beddingham's *The Bookplates of George Taylor Friend*, 1972.

190 Leo Wyatt

Leo Wyatt (b. 1909), who engraved this *ex-libris* for himself, was one of Friend's pupils. He was apprenticed to Dacier Baxter, who had an engraving shop in the West End of London, and concurrently studied at the Central School. After working in the City, and for a short time with Waterlows, the printers, he went to the provinces, and from 1947 to 1961 was in South Africa. There he extended the range of his work by teaching himself wood-engraving (see No. 260). He is the only British bookplate engraver working today who is outstandingly skilled in both copper and wood-engraving, and while the former show the influence of Friend his wood-engravings—which are mostly book labels—show that of Reynolds Stone (see Nos. 197 and 254). Most of his 250 *ex-libris* date from after his return to England. There is an article on him, with a check-list, by the author in *A Arte do Ex-Libris*, Lisbon, 1976, and it was reprinted with an expanded check-list in the *Year Book* of the American Society of Bookplate Collectors and Designers, 1977.

191 John Roland Abbey

Among amateur bookplate engravers of this century, Henry John Fanshawe Badeley, 1st Lord Badeley, KCB (1874–1951), was most prolific. The son of Captain Henry Badeley, he was educated at Radley and Trinity College, Oxford, and in 1897 won first place in a Civil Service competition for a clerkship in the Parliament Office. So began a distinguished life's work which led to his being appointed Clerk of the Parliaments in 1934. His hobby, however, was engraving, which he studied under Sir Frank Short at the Royal College of Art. He was for some years secretary of the Royal Society of Painter-Etchers and Engravers, and engaged much in bookplate work. Though of variable quality, and weakest perhaps in the treatment of mantling, his bookplates number 220, and some are very fine. They include *ex-libris* for Queen Mary, Queen Ingrid of Denmark, Princess Helena Victoria, Princess Victoria of Schleswig Holstein, Princess Beatrice and the Duchess of Gloucester. One of his two bookplates for the House of Lords Library is printed from the original copper as frontispiece to his *Bookplates*, 1927, an illustrated publication by the Print Collectors' Club of a lecture he delivered in November 1925. The plate shown here is the smaller of two he engraved for Major John Roland Abbey, the noted book collector, and dates from 1933.

188

189

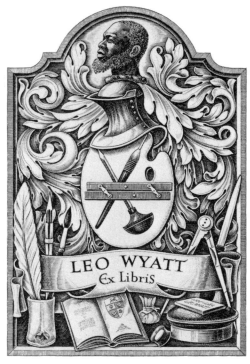

190

191

192 S(acheverell) S(itwell)

John Piper (b. 1903) was educated at Epsom College and studied at the Royal College of Art. His pictures and water-colours, which include a remarkable series of views of Windsor Castle, have earned him an international reputation; and his lithographs have made his work available to a wider public. He has designed few *ex-libris*, but one for David Horner (of an elaborately decorated window supported by sculpture and the name imposed on the glass) and another, shown here, for Sir Sacheverell Sitwell are very memorable. This subject is taken from the initials of Sir Sitwell Sitwell (d. 1811) graven on a lead cistern of c. 1805 in the garden at Renishaw, the family home. Piper has also designed bookplates for Marie Sargant, James Sassoon and William Whitfield.

193 Miriam Rothschild

This wood-engraving for Miriam Rothschild dates from 1932 and was the work of Eric Gill (1882–1940), perhaps the most influential and important bookplate artist of the century. If it is impossible here to summarise Gill's significance and talents it is also unnecessary, for they are widely recognised: he created type-faces, including 'Gill Sans' and 'Perpetua'; carved inscriptions and, as a sculptor, his work includes the Westminster Cathedral 'Stations of the Cross'; and among about 1,000 engravings from his hand were illustrations for *The Four Gospels*, 1931 and other major books. He engraved over fifty *ex-libris*, mostly on wood but some on copper; and several engravings were adapted for the purpose with letterpress. They are all recorded in John Physick's *Catalogue of the engraved work of Eric Gill*, 1963. In view of his importance and the range of his work two bookplates are shown here: Miriam Rothschild's recalls his *Canticum Canticorum*, 1931, in style, and the Harrison plate of three years later is commented on below.

194 Austen St. Barbe Harrison

Austen St. Barbe Harrison (1892–1976) was the architect of Nuffield College at Oxford and designed several buildings in Jerusalem during the Mandate; since Gill designed some plaques for the Jerusalem museums c. 1934, the connection may have led to a commission for this bookplate, which was engraved in the following year. The cupid design was later used as an illustration in Gill's *Last Essays*, 1942, and in *Essays*, 1947, and recalls, also, Gill's 'Apocalypse' of 1936.

195 (Universal Ex-Libris)

The Book Society commissioned 'universal' *ex-libris* for use of members from such artists as Edmund Dulac, Rex Whistler and Robert Gibbings, and it was an idea which has been too little exploited since. Robert Gibbings (1889–1958), the wood-engraver, author and book designer, must have been familiar with bookplate design from his childhood, for his maternal grandfather was Robert Day of Cork, sometime Vice-President of the Ex Libris Society. He engraved, however, very few, and most of them in his earlier years. Apart from the plate shown here, those engraved on wood were for E. L. Allhusen, Cora Kilconnel, Amanda Menhinick, Alex McLachlan, George William Miller, William Penne-father, William Smart, and Gibbings' own *ex-libris*, a crossed graver and quill with the initials 'R.G.'. There were also copper engravings for University College, Cork, Brigadier J. F. Leslie, Colonel Sir William Onslow and Norah Eileen Pike. In addition, two wood-engravings depicting reeds, which originally appeared as illustrations in *Coming Down the Wye*, 1942 and *Lovely is the Lee*, 1945, were adapted with letterpress inscriptions as bookplates by his sister-in-law, Patience Empson. Gibbings' first book was published in 1921, and in 1924 he acquired the Golden Cockerel Press (which, incidentally, printed several labels with cockerel motifs for use at the press). He also did work for the Limited Editions Club, and from 1936 to 1940 lectured in book production at Reading University. In 1939 he began to explore the Thames, and by the middle of the next year had completed *Sweet Thames Run Softly*, the first of seven such books to be produced during the next seventeen years.

196 Ruth L. Bensusan

This print in reproduction can give no idea of the beauty of the delicate green and red colouring of this engraving, one of several *ex-libris* for members of the family of Lucien Pissarro (1863–1944). Pissarro was the eldest son of Camille Pissarro, the impressionist painter; he came to England in 1890, became naturalized in 1916, and is well-known for his engravings, paintings and the productions of his Eragny Press. Many of the last were editions of French classics, superbly printed and bound, and often with illustrations in colour. Pissarro married Esther Bensusan, who also engraved some of his bookplate designs. Details of the respective parts they played in this can be found in the catalogue of his work at the Ashmolean Museum, Oxford. In addition to the composition shown here and their own plate, which reads 'Ex Libris Esther and Lucien Pissarro, The Brook, Hammersmith', there are engravings for J. M. A[ndreini], J. S. L. B[ensusan], S. L. Bensusan, Mary F. Cassola, Harry Alfred Fowler, Dr. T. H. Gaillard and Orovida C. Pissarro. Some show a most imaginative and subtle use of colour.

192

193

194

195

196

197 Hugh Trevor-Roper

The handsomely-illustrated book on the engravings of Reynolds Stone (b. 1909), published by John Murray in 1977, includes over 160 examples of his *ex-libris* and shows the superb quality of his work, which has inspired formal contemporary design. Stone was at school at Eton, where his father was a housemaster; and at Cambridge he became the first graduate apprentice at the University Press under a scheme inaugurated by Walter Lewis. F. G. Nobbs, overseer of the composing room, and Eric Gill, whom he met by chance and visited at Piggotts for a fortnight, were prime influences on him, and the engraving of letters has largely occupied him ever since. His title-pages, illustrations, devices and bookplates are widely known; but he has also engraved on stone, his commissions including the inscription of Sir Winston Churchill's memorial in Westminster Abbey. The pictorial plate for Professor Hugh Trevor-Roper shown here is a fine example of Stone's pictorial engraving and lettering, and a book label for David John Gilson is also illustrated (No. 254); other bookplates include two for the Prince of Wales and a pictorial with a view of Coppins for the Duchess of Kent.

198 David Keir

Joan Hassall (b. 1906), the daughter of the artist John Hassall and sister of Christopher Hassall (d. 1963), studied at the Royal Academy Schools. While there, as a kindness to a friend attending a wood-engraving class in danger of closure, she agreed to join the course and found engraving on wood 'very much more like remembering than learning'; two years later she saw the work of Thomas Bewick, which was an inspiration and gave her a new sense of direction. Her first published work was the title-page for her brother's *Devil's Dyke*, 1936, since when she has illustrated many books. They include *Cranford*, 1940, *Our Village*, 1946, Andrew Young's *Collected Poems*, 1950, the enchanting little Saltire Society chapbooks, and the Limited Editions Club *Poems of Robert Burns*, 1965. The first of about forty engraved or drawn bookplates was made for A. P. Polack about 1932, and earned her 12s. 6d. (62½p). Others include a four-colour engraving for Kathleen Finlay Horsman and this beautifully appropriate 1969 design for David Keir. He was a writer all his life, but served in the Navy during the Second World War; and the open pages of the book show the town hall of his home town and the University of Edinburgh. Her *ex-libris* for H. Raymond Barnett is also shown (No. 253).

199 The Tonbridge Theatre & Arts Club

This trophy design was engraved on wood by George Mackley (b. 1900). Born at Tonbridge, where he still lives, he studied under Noel Rooke and taught as art master at schools in Kent and Surrey from 1921 to 1945, when he became a headmaster. He wrote and illustrated *Wood Engraving*, 1948, and his statement in that book that 'a small block can often be as aesthetically significant and as powerfully expressive as yards of canvas bearing pounds of paint' is amply demonstrated by his remarkable work. In addition to the plate illustrated here he has engraved bookplates for Marinus Buis, Elizabeth Mary Halliday, Julia Peckham, Timothy Peckham, D. Keith Robinson, SERA (Surrey Educational Research Association) and J. R. Toller.

200 Roger Lockyer

Frank Martin (b. 1921) read History at Oxford and then served in the Army before studying at the St. Martin's School of Art, London. Since that time he has been a free-lance artist and a senior lecturer at Camberwell School of Arts and Crafts. For the first fifteen years of his professional life he was much engaged in book illustration and wood-engraving, but since about 1965 has been a print-maker on a larger scale, many of his subjects relating to the world of films. Among his *ex-libris* are engravings for himself, Philip Beddingham, Jill and Michael Poole and his design for Roger Lockyer.

201 An Ambassador Book   Books Across the Sea

Diana Bloomfield (b. 1915) explained in a talk to The Bookplate Society: 'The first introduction I had to mermaids was in very early engraving days; I had just done a bookplate for the Monotype Corporation, and Beatrice Warde, who was a friend, asked me to do a bookplate for *Books across the Sea*. She said, "Can we have a mermaid swimming, with a book, from America to England and then one swiming back again?". Well, the lettering was child's play compared to those mermaids, for, as you can imagine, almost anything would look vulgar. It was an extremely difficult bookplate to do, and I finally did it in a very naïve way and made them look like jolly ladies having a holiday at Brighton'. The full story of Diana Bloomfield's account of her engraved work and bookplates can be found in 'A Fearful Joy', a transcript of her talk, published in *The Private Library* for Spring 1974. She studied at the Harrow School of Art and The Institute, Hampstead, and has taught lettering, painting and engraving at The City Literary Institute; her book illustrations include Walter de la Mare's *Come Hither*, 1960, *The Crystal Cabinet*, 1962, and *The Green Roads*, 1965. There is an article by Philip Beddingham on her *ex-libris*, which number about sixty, in the 1969/70 *Year Book* of the American Society of Bookplate Collectors and Designers.

197

198

199

200

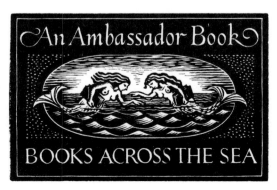

201

202 J(ames) L(ey) W(ilson)

James Wilson's bookplate was commissioned for a collection of books relating to the countryside and was engraved by Richard Shirley Smith (b. 1935). Shirley Smith was educated at Harrow, where he had the good fortune to live almost next door to David Jones, who gave him encouragement and insight into the challenges of an artist's creative life and sponsored his application to the Slade. He left the Slade in 1960 for two years' individual study in Rome, where he taught himself wood-engraving, and has been a free-lance since. His book illustrations include work for the Golden Head Press, The Folio Society, Oxford University Press, Faber and Faber, André Deutsch and the Limited Editions Club—for which he superbly engraved illustrations for *The Poems of P. B. Shelley*, 1971. There is an article on his bookplate designs by the author in *The Private Library* for Summer 1977.

203 H. Montgomery Hyde, Lamb House

After studying commercial art at Harrow School of Art, Michael Renton (b. 1934) served an apprenticeship with S. Slinger Ltd., a firm of commercial engravers in London, concurrently attending classes in life-drawing, lettering and etching at the City and Guilds of London School. He became a free-lance engraver in 1960 and three years later moved to Rye, where he finds the local countryside an inspiration to his work. His bookplates are finely lettered and some show the frontage of houses—including this *ex-libris* for H. Montgomery Hyde, the barrister and author; it depicts the doorway of Lamb House in Rye, which has been the home both of the novelist Henry James and his kinsman Montgomery Hyde, also of E. F. Benson and Rumer Godden. How neatly the artist here marries a pictorial subject with a label which could serve on its own in smaller books. There is an article by Keith Clark on Renton's bookplates in *The Bookplate Society Newsletter* for June 1975, and on his engraved work in general in *Sussex Life* for April 1978.

204 Dartington Hall

It is a matter for regret that Lynton Lamb (1907–1977) designed few bookplates, and none in his latter years, for he had a good understanding of how to make an essentially uncomplicated *ex-libris* design memorable. This plate for Dartington Hall dates from c. 1949; others were designed for J. S. Addison, Nicholas Flower, Neil Forsyth and William Scudamore Mitchell. Lamb was born in India, was at school at Kingswood, and studied at the Central School of Arts and Crafts, 1928–30. He was on the staff at the Slade from 1950, and became production adviser at the Oxford University Press. A popular and fine book illustrator, painter, engraver and lithographer, he designed the 2s. 6d. to £1 stamps for the new reign in 1955.

205 Martin Rees

This attractive little bookplate for Martin Rees is by Simon Brett (b. 1943), who studied engraving under Clifford Webb at the St. Martin's School of Art, London in the early sixties. He then spent some years in Mexico and Provence, during which engraving took second place to painting. Since 1971, however, when he took up a post at Marlborough College he has devoted more time to engraving, and has made forty-five bookplates. They include plates for the Department of Prints and Old Master Drawings of Sotheby & Co., and P. & D. Colnaghi & Co Ltd. There is an article by Keith Clark on Brett's bookplates in *The Bookplate Society Newsletter* for September 1975.

206 Agnes Dunlop

Agnes Dunlop (the novelist Elisabeth Kyle) chose for her bookplate an Italian scene in a Chippendale frame, with her initials as a novelist on the open book in the foreground. It was engraved on wood by William McLaren (b. 1923), who from 1940 to 1946 studied at the Edinburgh College of Art as a pupil of Joan Hassall (see Nos. 198 & 253). A free-lance since that time, his work has included book jackets and illustrations (particularly for Beverley Nichols' books), portraits, landscapes, murals and decorative furniture, on the finishes of which he is an expert. His bookplate output has been small, but has covered thirty years, and includes plates for Liliana Barou, Marc de Prainty, Sir William Hutchison, who became President of the Royal Scottish Academy in 1950, and Lady Mary Russell. There is a brief article on McLaren's bookplates by the author in *The Bookplate Society Newsletter* for December 1976.

207 Michael Brown

John Lawrence (b. 1933) studied at Hastings School of Art and the Central School of Arts and Crafts, since when he has done free-lance work. He taught for two years at Maidstone, then at the Brighton School of Art, and since 1960 has taught one day a week at Camberwell. A distinguished book illustrator, his most recent work has included *Rabbit and Pork* and *The Blue Fairy Book*, 1975, *Watership Down*, 1976 and *The Shepherd's Calendar*, 1978. The bookplate for Michael Brown shows a pigeonnier just behind the owner's farmhouse in the south-west of France, an area where one sees many of these dovecotes, some of them highly decorated. Lawrence's other wood-engraved bookplates have been for the author, Professor William Butler, James L. Wilson (whose bookplate by Richard Shirley Smith is No. 202), and a universal *ex-libris* which is being retailed by an American firm.

202

Ex Libris
H. MONTGOMERY HYDE
Lamb House

203

Dartington Hall

204

MARTIN REES

205

Ex Libris

GIARDINO DEI BOBOLI

AGNES DUNLOP

206

MICHAEL BROWN

207

II BOOK LABELS

208 Robert Reid

This label, in a volume of St. John Damascene, *Opera*, Basle, 1535 in Aberdeen University Library, is one of the two earliest British *ex-libris*. The other is a different setting of the same wording, printed on two lines and larger, in a copy of *Decretales*, Paris, 1527 at the National Library of Scotland; it is illustrated in an article by the author in *Miscellany*, No. 1, 1978. There is no evidence which is the earlier label, for *Decretales* was originally a gift to the library at Kinloss by Abbot Thomas Chrystall, but they may date from c. 1538 when Reid had a fine fire-proof library built for the Abbey. Reid became Abbot in 1528 and died in 1558. He resigned the abbacy in favour of his nephew before 6th April, 1553, but continued to be styled Abbot.

209 Robert & Edmund Tredway

King's College, Cambridge was the first of a number of colleges and institutions to use printed labels for gifts of books, and they were first produced during the provost-ship of Roger Goad, 1569–1610, who moved the books to the south chantries of the chapel and doubtless solicited gifts from Kingsmen. The earliest records a gift by Francis Walsingham in 1586. The Tredways, who gave a copy of Suarez' *Commentariorum*, 1604, were sons of John Tredway of Easton-on-the-Hill in Northampton-shire; both matriculated sizar from King's College at Michaelmas 1609. Edmund was admitted to Gray's Inn in 1614, and his will was proved in 1617. Robert (d. 1653) was knighted in 1642; he married Alice, the daughter of Anthony Thorold of Hough in Lincolnshire.

210 Elias Ashmole

Only one print is known of this in its undated setting, in a little printed folio entitled *Insigel und Wappen Eines Fursichtigen Ersamen und weysen Raths und der Lohlichen Gemainen stats,* 1555 (MS. Ashmole 797, folio 61) in the Bodleian Library. A unique dated example with the same border, reading 'Elias Asmole oweth, this BOOKE. 1635', is illustrated in the author's *Early Printed Book Labels,* 1976. The undated one is slightly later, for the border shows more wear, and both may be ascribed to the printer Thomas Purfoot, who used the ornament in two books. He also used it for the 1633 label reading 'Edward Audley oweth, this BOOKE', prints of which are in the de Tabley and Franks Collections (The use of *owe* for *own* was not unusual at this time). Elias Ashmole (1617–1692), the antiquary and astrologer, was born at Lichfield, and became a lawyer. He served with the King's forces in the Civil War, held office in the excise and elsewhere after the Restoration, and presented his collection of curiosities to Oxford University in 1677. Whether the Ashmole armorial in the Viner Collection was an *ex-libris* is not clear, but he used a portrait plate as a frontispiece in fifteen of his manuscript volumes.

211 Mistris Elizabeth Large

The only recorded print of this is in the Simpson Collection. It was not pasted in, but printed on a large sheet and added probably when the book was bound. On the leaf's reverse are manuscript dates and notes of the Primate family, recording baptisms, marriages and deaths from 1609 to 1665. A number of early bookplates and labels seem to have been printed and bound up in this way, including the Sandcroft (No. 212) and a 1616 example for Hugh Paine of Lion Halles. This occurs in a copy of *The Bible, Geneva version*, printed by Robert Barker in 1616, which was sold at the 1965 Antiquarian Book Fair by Mr H. W. Pratley. As the catalogue for this explains: 'One impression was . . . printed on the back of the final leaf of the Apocrypha; another impression was taken off on a separate sheet, and bound in before the New Testament', while the first of the impressions was printed 'on an available space in the text on the original printed sheets'. Mr Pratley suggests that Barker himself may have undertaken the printing of these.

212 William Sandcroft

This label in a compartment frame is in the library of Emmanuel College, Cambridge, where there is another with identical border and the inscription 'Symbolum amicitiæ NICOLAI HARE, Generosi'. They may have been printed at the same time, but the Hare is pasted in and the Sandcroft is printed on a blank leaf. The books in which they occur came from the library of Archbishop Sancroft, and it seems likely that they were reciprocal gifts from Sancroft and Nicholas Hare (though the archbishop, unlike his uncle, who was Master of Emmanuel, usually spelt his surname without the 'd'). There is a note in both volumes that they were saved from the Fire of London. The arms in the compartment are those of the Stationers Company, which occur also on the 1633 labels of Francis Anderson, William Earn-shaw, Nicholas Gildredge and Richard Stone, the 1684 Elizabeth Grey label (see note to No. 218), and that of Mary Barcock, 1700.

213 Thomas Bendish

Another typical example of an early gift label, this occurs in Cambridge University Library (Sayle 8588) and the library of St. John's College, Cambridge. The son and heir of Sir Thomas Bendish of Steeple Bumpstead in Essex, Thomas Bendish (c. 1607–c. 1674) matriculated from St. John's College in 1624; he was admitted to the Inner Temple in 1626, and succeeded his father as baronet in 1636. A fervent royalist in the Civil War, he sent £3,000 to the king at Newcastle, which led to his estates being sequestrated and a fine of £1,500 in 1644. In 1647 he was sent as ambassador to Constantinople, where he remained about fourteen years.

Ex libris domini Roberti Reid , Abbatis à Kynlos.

208

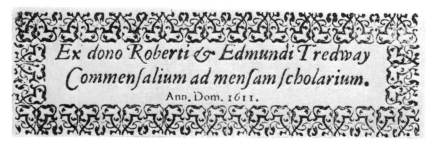

209

210

211

212

213

214 George Anderson

This label within a decorative border occurs in a copy of *The Bible in Englishe,* 1550, printed by Whitchurch, now in the Library of Harvard University. A note in J. F. K. Johnstone and A. W. Robertson's *Bibliographia Aberdonensis* indicates that the label is from the press of Edward Raban (d. 1658), and the word 'Bible' is in manuscript. Since J. H. Slater, in *Book plates and their value,* 1898, lists this *ex-libris* with 'Buik' instead of 'Bible' it appears that there is a variant copy. This view is supported by two manuscript inscriptions in the Bible, in both of which cases 'Book' is spelt 'Buik'. The first reads 'This Buik pertinis to David Anderson, burges of abd. anno 1573', and he has added underneath a statement about the disposal of the volume (1580); the second reads, 'This buik pertinis to me George Andersone ye Sone to ye David Andersone'. George Anderson (or Andersone) (d. 1638), was the eldest son of William Andersone. He was admitted burgess of Aberdeen on 6th January, 1616, and in 1628 was charged with others before the Privy Council with having written and uttered certain pasquils, or lampoons, including one against the Provost of Aberdeen. On subsequently denying the charge on oath he was assoilzied, or acquitted. His wife, who had earlier been wife to Robert Mar, burgess of Aberdeen, was Jean, daughter of Alexander Chalmers of Cults, who was sometime Provost. The use of the phrase 'appertaineth to' for 'belongs to' occurs on several early Scottish labels, including one reading 'This Book appertaineth unto the calling of the Wrights of Glasgow' (the Wrights formed one of the fourteen Incorporations of the Trades of Glasgow and was originally united with the Masons and Coopers), and in a manuscript inscription in the 'Bible . . . given to the Hospitall of ABERDENE, by Gilbert Hervie, elder, Burges of the sayd BURGH, May 18, 1631', the printed label in which was also the work of Raban. Edward Raban, who was an Englishman of German descent, was printer first in Edinburgh, then St. Andrews, and finally in Aberdeen, to which he moved in 1622, establishing himself at 'The Townes Armes' upon the Market Place.

215 (John) Rodeknight

John Rodeknight (d. 1615) of Warwickshire matriculated sizar from Queens' College, Cambridge at Michaelmas 1583. He graduated BA in 1587/8, was a fellow from 1592 to 1605, and was master of King's College School from 1600 to 1615. He was buried at St. Botolph's, Cambridge. The compartment border used here also occurs on a gift label reading 'Donum Joannis Suckling Militis. 1618' now in Cambridge University Library (Syn. 8.61.120), pasted into a folder with no accompanying book; the print is, however, cut very close. The label may record a gift from Sir John Suckling, father of the poet, who was secretary of state to James I in 1622 and died in 1627.

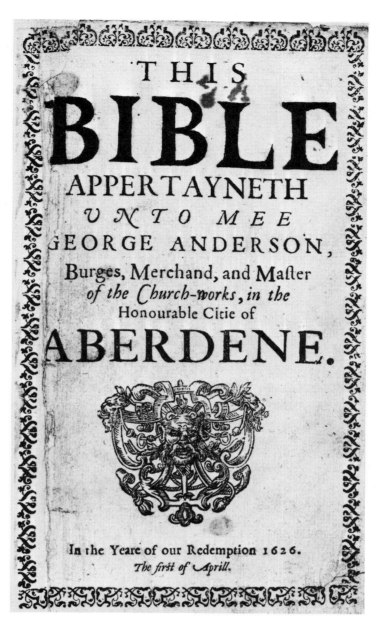

214

215

216 Martha Simcox

There are two printed book labels with this border: the Martha Richards, 1669 and the Martha Simcox, 1670, but it has not been possible to establish a relationship between them. The latter declares itself a book label by its inscription, and the Richards (which is in the Simpson Collection and is illustrated in *Early Printed Book Labels, 1976*) shows evidence of use in a book, and has manuscript inscriptions reading 'There is a Human Face at each corner' and '—9 July 1669. Note. The New Theatre at Oxford, the gift of Dr. Sheldon Archbishop of Canterbury was opened. Dr. South University Orator made a speech upon the occasion'. The Simcox label is in the Henderson Smith Collection at the National Library of Scotland, Edinburgh. The style and rarity of these labels suggest they may have served also as keepsakes, presented to visitors to printing presses on receipt of a small fee, for some details of which see p. 15. The particular compartment frame used here is an especially crude piece of engraving.

217 Doctor Johnston

Nathaniel Johnston (1627–1705) was a physician and antiquary of Pontefract and London. He was an MD of King's College, Cambridge, and became a Fellow of the Royal College of Physicians in 1687. He was a friend of Ralph Thoresby, the Leeds antiquary, who in his Diary (i.39) records that Johnston 'was pleased to adopt me his son as to antiquities'; he left collections on Yorkshire antiquities, and his chief work was *The Excellency of Monarchical Government,* 1686. A copy of this book offered in Maggs Bros. Catalogue 937 had on the licence leaf the following long presentation inscription: 'To the Honourable Sr. Henry Marwood Baronet. Honourable Sr. In testimony of the due respect & Honor I owe you I present this Treatise to yr favourable acceptance who am Sr. yr most humble servant N. Johnston. At Mr George Watsons in Leycester Streete near Leycester fields. Jan. 11, 1685/86'. The label, which is in the bookplate collection at Chelsea Public Library, probably dates from about this time, for the *Dictionary of National Biography* records that it was not until 1686 that he fell out of practice in Yorkshire and moved to London, where he is described as living at the 'Iron balcony' in Leicester Street. Wood dined with him there in September, 1688. He became a high tory pamphleteer, but suffered pecuniary distress and skulked a great many years avoiding declaration of his residence. He died in London.

216

Doctor Johnston,
At Mr. George Watson's,
the Corner House in Ley-
cester-street, near Leyce-
ster-fields.

217

218 Elizabeth Grey

In several respects this is a most interesting book label, and only one complete print is known to survive. The inscription is in red in an elaborate border printed in black. One notices first how delightfully appropriate the inscription is to its pictorial frame; but the frame, which probably comprises four separate pieces of engraving, depicts military costume of the 1615–20 period—and is about eighty years earlier than the printing of the label. It can be precisely dated because of the existence of a second setting, from which it appears the decorative border has been cut away. Of the same shape as the compartment illustrated, and also printed in red, the second setting originally read: 'ELIZABETHÆ GREY. Ex Dono BENJAMINIS OAKE. The Christian Life is a Warfare. Anno 1697'. This inscription has, however, been amended by erasing the 'S' of 'BENJAMINIS', thereby denoting a reciprocal gift. That both were printed at the same time is evidenced by the fact that wet ink has imprinted the inscription shown here on the back of the mutilated print. Gum adhering to the pictorial frame of our illustration shows that this was also at some time covered over, suggesting that the decoration was perhaps favoured by neither recipient.

This label, like several others, indicates how oddments of engraving surviving among a printer's stock were pressed into service for decoration of book labels. Two even more extraordinary examples of late usage of borders exist, one of them a keepsake reading 'Mrs. Sarah Adkinson, Born April 26. 1679', which dates from between 1702 and 1714, though the large title-page engraving which frames it was used in twenty-five books between 1600 and 1635. This and the two Grey labels referred to are in the author's collection, but there is another Elizabeth Grey label, dated 1684, which may well have belonged to the same owner. This is in the Perez Collection at the National Book League, and shows, printed in black, the red block of a two-colour title-page which is illustrated as Fig. 163 in McKerrow & Ferguson's *Title-page borders used in England and Scotland 1485–1640*: *The Psalter*, printed by H. Denham, 1579. This was therefore also used for a book label over a century after its first appearance. The colour-block (printed upright, not on its side as in the Grey label) served as title-page to *A Briefe Introduction to Syntax*, printed by Thomas Harper in 1631, and his initials are retained on the 1684 book label; it shows the arms of the Stationers' company.

ELIZABETHÆ GREY

Ex Dono

Benjaminis Oake.

The Christian's Life is a Warfare.

FATA VIAM INVENIENT

INVIA VIRT NULLA EST

218

219 The Parish Church of St. Andrew in Fersfield

It is rare for the press which printed an early book label to be indicated, and this example is of unusual interest, quite apart from its size. The historian of Norfolk, Francis Blomefield (1705–1752) is more elusive as a man than most of the county historians, for his life centred around a small country parish, and his family had been rooted in Fersfield for generations; they were yeomen and minor gentry, but not armigerous, and married into local families of equal rank. Blomefield was only fifteen when he started working towards his *History of Norfolk* in 1720, and that work shows us the man: unmoved by the world's natural beauties, unstylish and unromantic, yet dedicated to antiquarian detail—and certainly in the registers which he was to keep later as rector of the parish, meticulous and undoubtedly sensitive in his eye to accuracy and the worth of good folk. Though his people had tilled the land, four immediate generations had married heiresses or coheiresses of modest means, and all are recorded in the quarterings of his Jacobean bookplate engraved by W. H. Toms, which must have been made about the time Toms set to work on the copper plates for Blomefield's *History*. Blomefield here adopted the arms of the Bromefildes of Kent, and showed these arms on his memorial to his parents. Between 1720 and 1733 he spent £175 16s. (£175.80) in exploring the county to gather material for his *History*, and in 1724 entered Gonville and Caius College, Cambridge, where he took his degree three years later. His career seems to have been early planned, for when he was only three years old the next presentation to the living of Fersfield was bought by his father from Lord Richardson—and rather conveniently, the rector, John Barker, died just about the time Blomefield was ordained. He was installed as rector in 1729, and remained there until his death. By 1733 he was planning publication of his work, which he was modest enough to refer to as a 'Topographical Essay', and the question of a printer arose. There was none in nearby Diss, so he approached a printer named Chase in Norwich, but his establishment was unequal to the job. Blomefield was worried, as he confided to the Bishop of St. Asaph, about 'stolen copies, which is too often the case in such subscriptions', so he decided to install a printing press in the rectory at Fersfield. At about this time Francis Hoffman, an engraver (see No. 52), was introduced to him as 'Something low in circumstances, but a man well-bred', one who might 'romance a little in conversation', but he would 'cut and design finely'. Hoffman boasted of his skill, was provided by Blomefield with an apartment, and set to work. He stayed three weeks, 'agreed for a large parcel of work, and cut several of the things, all of which he ran away with'. Poor Blomefield then had to search again, and was put in touch with a pewter-engraver, William Pennock of Lewin Street in Aldersgate Street, London. It was not however, until 1739, three years later, that the first part of the work was published. In the meantime this label was printed at the Fersfield press, and on March 12th 1742/3 another book label from the same block, much worn, was printed for William Howard of Norwich (see the author's 'Francis Blomefield and his History of Norfolk' in *The Bookplate Society Newsletter* for September 1978). The only print of this seen, however, has the ornamental border cut away, but the inscription states that it was 'Printed at Fersfield'. The same ornamental border, the authorship of which is unknown, also occurs on a keepsake in the John Johnson Collection at the Bodleian Library, Oxford, with a six-line verse in praise of, presumably, Gutenberg, though his name is not mentioned, and an inscription beginning 'Robert Marsham. On the AUTHOR of PRINTING'. It is dated 1759. For fuller details of Blomefield see 'Cursory Notices of the Rev. Francis Blomefield, the Norfolk Topographer' by S. W. Rix (who designed the bookplate shown here at No. 124), in *Transactions of the Norfolk and Norwich Archaeological Society*, 1849; and 'The Rector of Fersfield, a Bicentenary Tribute', by R. W. Ketton-Cremer, in the same journal for 1952.

220 Miss Elizabeth Gregor of Trewarthennick

Though this has the appearance of a keepsake—and may have been printed as such—it was nevertheless used as a book label, and the example illustrated is in the Viner Collection. It also occurred in the Marshall Collection, and Ellis of Bond Street offered a print or prints for sale in his catalogues of 1908 and 1909. The Gregors were resident in Truro in the middle of the seventeenth century, and Henry Gregor was mayor in 1677. John Gregor of Truro purchased Trewarthenick about 1640, and expanded his estate considerably elsewhere also. Francis Gregor (1686–1762) was a learned man, interested in antiquities and politics; he married twice, firstly to Maria Radcliffe Kempe, a widow, and secondly to Dorothy Harris of Pickwell—and it seems probable that Elizabeth may have been his daughter. The last of the family in direct line, Charlotte Anne Gregor, died unmarried in 1825 and bequeathed her estates to Loveday Sarah Glanville (later Gregor), the daughter of Francis Glanville, Esq., of Catchfrench, a relation by marriage. An article by Christine Hawkridge on Sarah Loveday Gregor's memoirs, which contained much information on the family history, can be found in *Journal of the Royal Institution of Cornwall*, new series, Vol. VI, Part I, 1969. Trewarthenick is near Grampound in Cornwall.

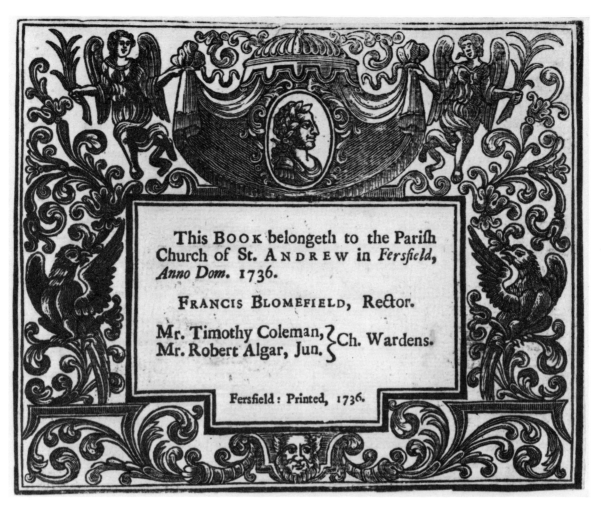

This BOOK belongeth to the Parish Church of St. ANDREW in *Fersfield*, *Anno Dom.* 1736.

FRANCIS BLOMEFIELD, Rector.

Mr. Timothy Coleman,
Mr. Robert Algar, Jun. } Ch. Wardens.

Fersfield: Printed, 1736.

219

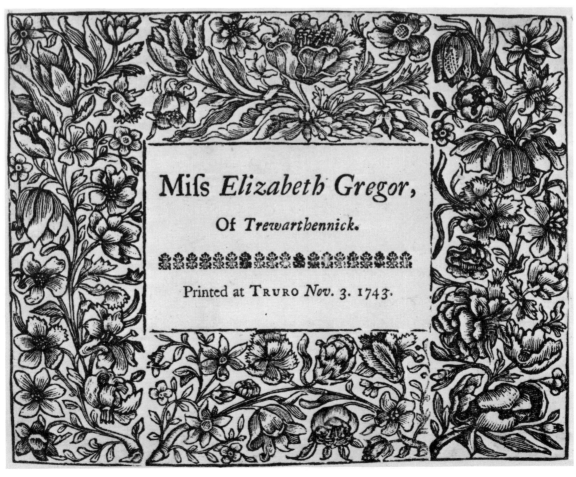

Miss *Elizabeth Gregor*,

Of *Trewarthennick.*

Printed at TRURO *Nov.* 3. 1743.

220

221 Sheppard Frere

Sheppard Frere (1712–1780) was the son of Edward Frere of Thwaite Hall, Suffolk. He was at school at Bury Grammar School under Mr Kingsman, was admitted a fellow-commoner at Trinity College, Cambridge in October 1732, and was admitted to Lincoln's Inn in 1734. He married Susanna, the daughter of John Hatley, Esq., and purchased an estate at Roydon in Norfolk, where he died; he was buried at Finningham. The border ornament of this label first appeared on the 1714 label of Thomas Thurlin, which records a gift to St. John's College, Cambridge, and it became the most familiar Cambridge label ornament of the period. This example, like a number of others, occurs in two settings, slightly differing in the placing of their ornaments but both including the arbitrary question marks as space-fillers. Viner noted a print of the label dated 1752, but the date was probably added in manuscript. Frere later used a Jacobean bookplate with single arms.

222 Kingston, of Dorchester

This and the Frome label (No. 224) show the sort of engraved borders which were used occasionally for book labels about the middle of the eighteenth century. Though Jacobean in style it would be impossible to be precise about the date of its printing, for these borders were sometimes re-used many years after their engraving (see No. 218). It was, however, definitely used as a book label, for the print in the author's collection has the shelf-mark D.14 in ink above, and other examples show evidence of removal from books.

223 Mr. John Tourner

John Tourner's printer went to some trouble to create an elaborate and distinctive ex-libris for him, albeit with six very worn pieces of ornament. Engraved blocks of the kind shown here were much used for the embellishment of books, and a most interesting study by K. I. D. Maslen of the relief cuts used by the William Bowyers, father and son, printers in London from 1699 to 1777, The Bowyer Ornament Stock, was published by the Oxford Bibliographical Society in 1973. Maslen illustrates 319 cuts used over those years, and notes that the Bowyers appear to have bought their blocks—which were engraved by hand—new. The upper and lower blocks of the Tourner label may be compared with Bowyer Nos. 94 and 105; both are, of course, of different engraving and consequently vary a little in their line, but Bowyer was using both designs as early as 1735, and continued to use No. 94 until 1759. Though—as is the case with so many book labels—there is not sufficient evidence to identify John Tourner, he might possibly be a descendant of one of the Turners who had some prominence in seventeenth-century Midhurst. Nicholas and Edward Turner are listed in the Hearth Money levy of 1670 (two of only five on the list designated 'Mr'), Nicholas having nine chimney hearths and Edward four.

224 T. Frome

Like the Kingston label (No. 222), this employs an eighteenth-century compartment frame, but it has an additional row of ornaments to separate the inscription from the date. One notices also in this period the increasing incidence of references to place of residence, in itself a useful evidence of the wider adoption of ex-libris. A particularly large number of book labels relate to East Anglia, but some noteworthy examples belong to the West Country. R. Goadby, the Sherborne printer, used a label, and printed one in 1759 for Matthew Hodge, bookseller and binder in Tiverton; and from Bristol there is a very handsome little series of labels, the work of one engraver, for Edward, Gregory and Richard Ash and Thomas Whitehead, all of that place, and Joseph Beck of Frenchay. Other interesting Bristol labels, slightly later in date, were for I. Banister, John Plant Fry, and Sophia and Rebecca Ring; and 'Samuel Gomond, Merchant, No. 38 Princes-Street, Bristol' used a number of engraved labels (see also No. 242).

225 John Bancks

The George Bickhams, father and son, were very active engravers, and their work included portraits, engravings after old masters, frontispieces and illustrations; they also published some books under their own name, including school textbooks by Daniel Bellamy (for whom they made a Jacobean pictorial bookplate). The younger George produced humorous cuts and was an early political caricaturist. Between them they engraved about twenty ex-libris, but the design shown here was the only label. Apart from its charming composition, it is an early instance of the use of Chippendale ornament, which was to dominate bookplate design until about 1775. It was the work of the younger Bickham, for it can be seen that the signature reads 'Jn' as Fincham records it (Hamilton mis-read it as 'Sc').

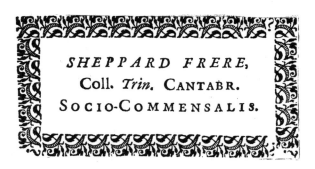

221

222

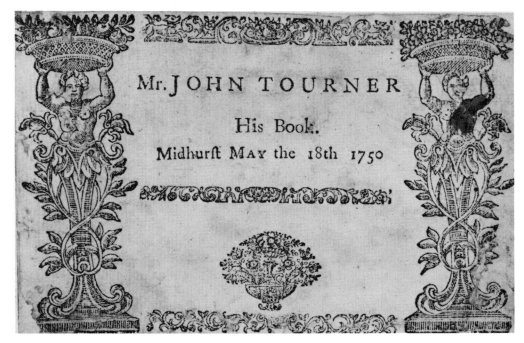

223

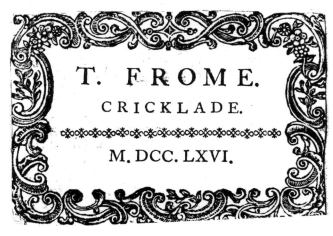

224

225

226 David Garrick

The actor David Garrick (1717–1779) used this *ex-libris*, which on account of its lettered content fits happily amongst the labels, though the balance of its text and decoration is so equal that it could as appropriately be classified as a bookplate. Its elegant design, with the bust of Shakespeare, mask and musical instruments, etc., occurs printed from two coppers, slightly varying in details (see *Bookman's Journal & Print Collector* for January 1922 and Carlyle S. Baer's article in the 1961/2 *Year Book* of the American Society of Bookplate Collectors and Designers, where this question is discussed). Both of the coppers were composed and engraved by John Wood, whom Fincham identifies as that John Wood who was supposed to be a pupil of Chatelain, was employed by Boydell, and died about 1780. One of the original coppers was sold at Sotheby's in a sale of printed books, 18th–21st June, 1928, and seems to have come into the possession of Anthony Prinsep (1882–1942), manager of the Globe Theatre in London, 1918–28, whose bookplate was printed from the same copper. Garrick had offered marriage to the actress Peg Woffington, but married in 1749 a dancer named Eva Maria Violetti (d. 1822), the reputed daughter of a Viennese citizen named Veigel. Though Garrick's books were dispersed in 1823 in a ten days' sale at Saunders', his widow bequeathed certain volumes, and a book label records this. It reads, 'This Book, which formed part of the Library of DAVID GARRICK. Esq., was, amongst others, bequeathed by Mrs EVA MARIA GARRICK, his Relict, to GEORGE FREDERICK BELTZ, Lancaster Herald, one of the executors of her Will', and a print of it occurred in a copy of *Leonidas*: *A Poem*, 1739 (see *The Ex Libris Journal* for June 1893).

227 Joseph Tylee, Organist, Bath

This beautifully engraved label is amongst the most attractive compositions of its period, and belonged to Joseph Tylee (1736–1794), who was organist at Bath Abbey from 1767 until his death. A ledger stone near the organ there records that his wife's name was Mary, and that three of their children—James, Edward and Joseph —died in childhood in the late 1760s. Tylee became organist in succession to Thomas Chilcot, who held the post from 1725 to 1766, and had a Chippendale bookplate engraved in 1757 by William Milton of Bristol (see Nos. 75, 86).

228 Richard Kaye, L.L.S., of Lincoln's Inn

Sir Richard Kaye, 6th Baronet (1736–1809), was the second son of Sir John Lister Kaye, 4th Bart., of Denby Grange in Yorkshire, by his second marriage. Kaye matriculated from Brasenose College, Oxford in 1754 (BCL 1761; DCL 1770), and was admitted to Lincoln's Inn on 15th April, 1755. He became dean of Lincoln in 1783, archdeacon of Nottingham, and was rector of Marylebone in Middlesex and of Kirkby Clayworth in Nottinghamshire; a fellow of the Royal Society and of the Society of Antiquaries, he was also a chaplain to the king. He married Mrs Mainwaring, relict of Thomas Mainwaring, Esq., of Goltho in Lincolnshire and daughter of William Fenton, Esq., of Glassho near Leeds, and died without issue. He was buried in Lincoln Cathedral. The arms shown on this book label are those of Kaye (Argent two bendlets sable), with the mark of cadency of a second son. There is another label of similar design to this, but without mention of Lincoln's Inn and dated 1758; and Kaye also used a Chippendale armorial-pictorial, with a cherub seated on the bracket at lower right reading a book. It occurs in two states and has the same quarterly arms as his father's Jacobean plate: Kaye quartering Copley (?), Lister and Savile; and both states have the mark of cadency. The first is signed, 'Wm. Golbey sculp Horse-Shoe passage Blow-blader Street'; the second is unsigned, has the field of the third quarter of the arms corrected to ermine, and has the motto altered. Golbey is not listed by Fincham, but his signature occurs also on the Brice Fisher Chippendale, at the time of the engraving of which Golbey was living in Foster Lane.

229 Wm. Mountaine, Esqr., F.R.S.

Few Chippendale engraved labels are as large as this, and few are so specific in their inscription and date. *Ex-libris* of schools and colleges make an interesting study in themselves, and examples in the Franks Collection are listed and shown separately, along with royal bookplates and those of universities, ecclesiastical, parochial and public libraries, etc. Closely related are the 'premiums' which academic institutions had specially printed to mark gifts of books for outstanding work. A number of Irish institutions made a speciality of these, and Trinity College, Dublin had many different labels printed. It is pictorial designs, however, which show the greatest adventurousness on the part of their engravers. Several, including a premium plate for Enniskillen School, depict Athene, the goddess of wisdom; the most beautiful of all is one for the Hibernian Academy, a rich Chippendale which shows her crowning a scholar with a wreath; and Apollo performs a similar function for a suitably humble little seeker after truth at Athy School.

La premiere chose qu'on doit faire quand on a emprunté un Livre, c'est de le lire afin de pouvoir le rendre plutôt.

Menagiana. Vol IV.

226

227

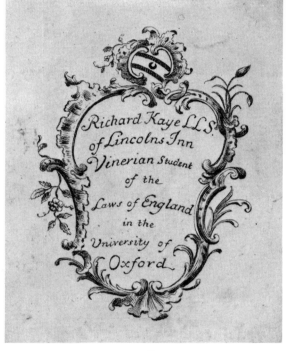

228

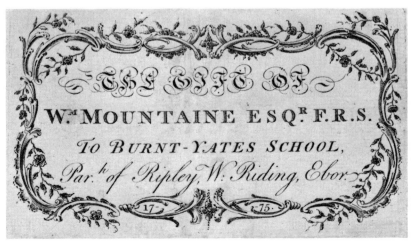

229

230 John Holmes of Holt in Norfolk

John Holmes (c. 1703–1760) was master of Gresham's School at Holt in Norfolk for thirty years, and was author of several works, including *The Art of Rhetoric made easy*, a history of England, and Latin and Greek grammars. His love of the last subject is apparent from his extraordinary engraved label. It is a paradigm of most of the tenses of the Greek verb τυπτω (I beat, strike), showing alternative forms found in the works of some authors, and is really just a 'pretty conceit'. Entitled 'Explanatory tree of a Greek verb', it chooses one which is not particularly interesting or strange, for many others have also 1st and 2nd Aorist forms. The lettering is, however, interesting, with the two forms of τ, and σ as δ, etc. A tablet to the memory of Holmes and his wife, Jane, in Holt Church, was erected by his only daughter, Jane Burrell. It records—in the earnest idiom of the time—how he exerted 'his Abilities to facilitate the Education of Youth in which endeavour he received generous Encouragement from his generous patrons the Fishmongers' company', and how his wife 'was a woman happily qualified to fulfill the Duties of her Station. The children ever experienced in her a Maternal Tenderness, the parents a conscientious attention to their Persons and Morals'.

231 Catharine Houghton

This and the label following reveal, but with comparatively little elaboration, a feature of a number of labels of the 1760–90 period: the arrangement of ornaments in unusual patterns. As a group, they repay investigation: some are merely quaint, others very imaginative, and they were the work of printers in various parts of the country. Among them are dated labels for John Deane, Junior, of Reading, 1766; Richard Gunn, 1771; Edward Hawksworth of Lambourn, 1771; John Ogilvie of Douglas, 1787; Mary Burrow, 1788; and William Lloyd of Maes-annod in the Vale of Clwyd, 1764, which is unusual in that it names the printer, J. Ross of Carmarthen. Undated examples include one for Lancelot Dinsdale of Newcastle, and a very symmetrical but delightfully ornamented label for Margaret Young.

232 M. Wright

The second example showing oddly arranged ornaments is, like the first, totally unidentifiable—as is the case with the majority of simply inscribed labels. Only two impressions of it have been seen, one of them in the Liverpool Public Library Collection. There is a lengthy article on 'Wright book-plates' by Arthur J. Jewers, in *The Ex Libris Journal,* September–December 1906, which discusses principally a group of armorials but illustrates another printed label, a little earlier than this, for 'Mr. JOHN WRIGHT'.

233 James Affleck

There are four book labels of the Affleck family of Dalham Hall in Suffolk, and three of them belonged to the children of Gilbert Affleck, who in 1705 married Anne, the daughter of John Dolben. She bore him seventeen children. Gilbert (1711–1763), the third son, was admitted pensioner at Trinity College, Cambridge in 1731. While there he had a label printed for himself, with a border of the Frere type (see No. 221), and another with the same border printed for his sister Ann. Gilbert was ordained in 1736 and became rector of Dalham in the same year; he married Elizabeth, the daughter of Richard Clopton, in 1746. Whether the simple name label without border for Gilbert Affleck belonged to him or his father is not evident. His younger brother James (1716–1784) used the engraved label shown here; it is very unusual but approximates closely to a label for Eliza Dolben, who may perhaps have been a cousin on his mother's side. James matriculated from Christ Church, Oxford in 1735, became vicar of Finedon in Northamptonshire in 1757, and married Mary Proctor of Clay Coton in that county in the same year. His son James, who succeeded as 3rd Baronet on the death of his first cousin in 1808, used an armorial bookplate with quarterly arms.

234 J. Murden, Comedian, Theatre-Royal

James Murden was one of two comedians who used book labels; the other was Charles Stuart Powell, whose label is illustrated in an article by the author in *Antiquarian Book Monthly Review* for August 1975. The ornaments which Murden used indicate that he was a freemason, and the print illustrated is still pasted on a page, with the signature 'Jas. Murden 1764' on the back. A note indicates that it was removed from a copy of *History of King Lear a Tragedy, revived with alterations by N. Tate,* 1760 (the version in which Cordelia survives and marries Edgar).

235 T. S. Evans, Mathematical Master, Christ's Hospital

Thomas Simpson Evans (1777–1816), eldest son of the Rev Lewis Evans of Bassaleg in South Wales, married in 1797 Deborah Mascall. He was a notable mathematician. About that year he seems to have taken charge of William Larkins' private observatory at Blackheath, and when Larkins died in 1800 was taken on as an assistant at the Royal Observatory at Greenwich. Sometime between 1803 and 1805 he became mathematical master under his father at the Royal Military Academy, Woolwich, moving in 1810 to New Charlton; and in 1813 he became master of the mathematics at Christ's Hospital. His library is said to have been one of the most valuable collections of mathematical and philosophical works in the kingdom, and his bookplate shows the Pythagoras proposition of the First Book of Euclid. Other bookplates showing the 47th Theorem include the beautiful pictorial, designed by Espin, engraved by B. Howlett, for 'T. Espin Teacher of the Mathematics, Louth, Lincolnshire', and the spade shield pictorial of 'William Burney A.M. Mathematician'.

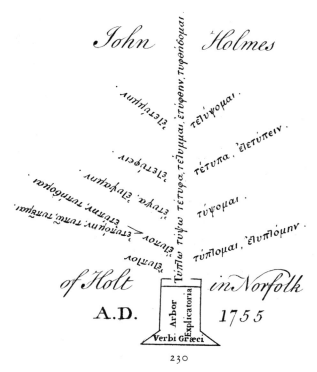

230

231

234

232

233

235

236 James Hadley Cox

James Hadley Cox's very elegant label shows the nice balance which marks the most attractive work of this period. He was the son of the Rev Hadley Cox, and matriculated from Christ Church, Oxford in 1771 at the age of sixteen (BA 1775).

237 Lady Burnaby

Tied wreaths of palm featured much on Georgian *ex-libris,* but similar wreaths had earlier been seen on a handful of mid-seventeenth century plates. Among the latter, the Marsham (No. 9) has a wreath of bay, the Bysshe (No. 16) has palms, and the Eynes and Southwell bookplates have acanthus-like sprays.

238 Robt. Ewing, Baker

It is interesting to contrast this neatly engraved label for a Glasgow baker with the humbler printed version of similar design which Lord Barrymore (see No. 240) used at Eton. A number of engraved labels compare closely with the Ewing in composition, including one for Alexr. McCallum of Greenock.

239 Philip D'Auvergne, L.L.D., F.R.S.

Philip d'Auvergne (1755–1816) had an extraordinary career. Born in St. Helier, Jersey, youngest son of Captain Charles d'Auvergne, he entered the Navy and in 1770 was gazetted to the Royal Yacht; two years later on the *Flora* he was presented to Catherine the Great, who found him personable and offered him employment. Though he declined, the story indicates the charm which was later to serve him favourably. He was wounded at the bombardment of Falmouth in 1775; cut off from the fleet by the French he burnt his first command to avoid capture; he was court-martialled but honourably acquitted; and as First Lieutenant in the *Arethusa* he was taken prisoner in 1779 when she was wrecked off Ushant. By coincidence the Prince of the tiny principality of Bouillon, Godefroi de la Tour d'Auvergne, with only a 'legless, witless and childless' son as heir, wished to adopt a son, and was about to choose La Tour d'Auvergne, later Napoleon's First Grenadier of France, when he heard of the prisoner of his name. He had him paroled, saw and approved of him, and sent his chaplain to try to trace kinship with the Jersey family. Philip was returned to duty, given command of the *Lark*, made Commander, and in assisting his Commodore to found a British colony was sent to a desert island called Trinidada seven hundred miles off Brazil to survey and perhaps colonize it. While surveying there his ship was totally wrecked, but he awaited the Commodore's arrival with thirty men and some prisoners. The Commodore arrived and was impressed (his despatch to the Admiralty described the four-mile rock as 'a jewel fit to adorn the British crown'); he landed stores, told d'Auvergne to stay, and sailed home. The colonizers were apparently forgotten, but got away in December 1782 by attracting the attention of Indian ships, which took them to Madras. In London d'Auvergne found the Prince waiting; genealogists had been obliging and he wanted

Philip as his heir. Peace had also given d'Auvergne the chance to study, and at Dorpat in Livonia he obtained an LLD in 1785; the next year he was elected FRS. Another spell at sea was curtailed by ill-health, but in 1791 the Bouillon Assemblée Générale petitioned the Prince on the succession, and he presented Philip to them. On 4th August it swore loyalty to him as Prince Successor. In the French Revolution, however, the Prince joined the Sanscullottes and invited the National Guard to dinner, and d'Auvergne thought it time to return home. The Prince died in 1792 and was succeeded by his son. d'Auvergne returned to duty and admirably commanded gunboats in defence of the Channel Islands and organised a secret service, 'La Correspondance'. In March 1802 England made peace with Napoleon, and—as the Prince's son had died—d'Auvergne went to Paris to claim his inheritance, but was arrested as a spy. It caused a sensation, but the British ambassador obtained his release. d'Auvergne resumed duty when in 1803 the war broke out again; his promotion accelerated, and by 1814 he was Vice-Admiral of the Red. When in March that year Napoleon was banished to Elba, d'Auvergne rushed to Paris, the King recognised his claim, and he was welcomed at Bouillon; but with Napoleon's return questions of inheritance prejudicial to blood relations were raised, the Duke of Rohan was given right to the title, and there it rested. d'Auvergne died suddenly soon after, and suicide was suggested, for he had lost, and litigation had ruined him. d'Auvergne used four *ex-libris*: a spade shield with supporters, pictorial armorials by Barnes and C. Tows, both dated 1793 and giving his title, and this label which cannot be earlier than 1786.

240 Lord Barrymore, Eton Coll.

The son of Richard Barry, 6th Earl of Barrymore and Lady Emily Stanhope, third daughter of William, Earl of Harrington, Richard Barry (1769–1793) succeeded as Earl before the age of four. He had this label printed while a boy at Eton; its design is a stock pattern which, with differences in engraved detail, is not uncommon. Similar examples were used by 'G. NORRIS, NORFOLK, 1782' and 'ISAAC SHARPLES, HITCHIN, HartfordSHIRE [sic]'. He became MP for Heytesbury, but his life was to be short, and Sir Egerton Brydges described both the man and his demise: 'With talents to shine in a course of honourable ambition, with wit, good nature, and engaging manners, he shone a meteor of temporary wonder and regret, by freaks which would have disgraced Buckingham or Rochester, until the accidental explosion of his musket, while he was conveying some French prisoners from Folkestone to Dover, as captain in the Berkshire militia, put an end to his trouble and his follies on 6 March, 1793'. He left no issue, and was succeeded by his brother.

241 J. Jones, Sheffield

A slightly later label than the others shown opposite, reflecting the move away from strict symmetry.

236

237

238

239

240

241

242 L. & M. A. Schimmelpenninck

This and the other labels shown opposite show how utilitarian many of these *ex-libris* became in the nineteenth century; and the point is even more clearly made by comparison with the pictorial plate which Mary Anne Schimmelpenninck (1778–1856) used before her marriage. Born Mary Anne Galton, her pictorial—which has the rather delicate grey etched line of most of her family's bookplates—shows a female classical figure in a petasus, or winged helmet, with a globe, lyre and palette, etc., in a landscape. Her brother S. Tertius Galton's bookplate is a pictorial with another female classical figure holding an open book and leaning on the pediment of a broken column. An engraved label inscribed 'S. Galton' may have belonged to her father Samuel Galton; and two bookplates inscribed 'Galton' were probably also his: an armorial-pictorial of Athene, who leans on an oval bearing the family arms; and a spade shield armorial in an oval wreath (a variant of this shows differences in the wreath). Mary Anne married in 1806 Lambert Schimmelpenninck of Bristol, who was connected with the shipping trade there. It was not, however, until about 1811, when her husband found himself in financial difficulties, that Mrs Schimmelpenninck turned to the writing which earned her a certain fame. Her books included a sketch of the modern history of the Moravians, and *The Theory and Classification of Beauty and Deformity*, 1815. A second book label for husband and wife contains the address '8 Berkeley Square, Bristol'; and after her husband's death in 1840, when she retired into seclusion, she used a label with the address 'Harley Place, Clifton'. She was a cousin of the Gurneys of Earlham—who used a number of bookplates, notably in the nineteenth century—and Elizabeth Fry (née Gurney) described her as 'one of the most interesting and bewitching people I ever saw'. The inscription from the Psalms against borrowing which occurs on this label became very familiar in this century, but it first appeared on the motto ribbon of the 1756 Chippendale armorial of Sherlock Willis.

243 Justin, Archdeacon of Pentonville

Who exactly 'Justin' was is not clear, for Pentonville appears never to have been an archdeaconry, but the inscription of this label is both unique on British *ex-libris* and sufficiently light-heartedly admonitory to merit inclusion. A rough translation reads: 'This book belongs to Justin Archdeacon of Pentonville; if anyone takes it away may he be baked in a baking pan—may he be rolled over and over in Purgatory— may he be accursed! Amen!!' A more familiar Latin tag, often written in manuscript on scholars' books, was:

> Hic liber est meus,
> Testis et est Deus;
> Si quis me quaerit,
> Hic nomen erit,

or a variant of the same; and this was sometimes accompanied by a neat little gallows and dangling figure. There were, not surprisingly, other variants on the gallows theme, and a personal favourite is the manuscript inscrip-tion which was found in a copy of *Coke upon Littleton*, 1628, and read: 'Mary Cudmore her booke a men and he that doth booke stayl he shal be put in exter Gayle although he ware a felfet cote he shall go up by the ladder and done by a rope, Katren Cudmore'.

244 Henry Charles Douglass

Henry Charles Douglass was admitted pensioner at Corpus Christi College, Cambridge in 1868 and was ordained priest five years later. After several curacies, the first of which was at Upper Chelsea, he became incumbent of St. Matthew's, Ealing, where he remained almost continuously between 1876 and 1916; he died in the church during a service in August of that year. His otherwise very pedestrian book label contains a little anthology of favoured thoughts on the value of books, and reflects the taste of its period in the quotations from the now largely forgotten Crabbe and Overbury.

245 Charles Cotton

These verses are much rarer on book labels than the ones shown at No. 250, perhaps because of the necessity to rhyme the second line of the second verse with the name of the owner. The same verses were, however, used by George Wightwick, a Plymouth architect and author, who re-arranged the second to read:

> And whomsoe'er this book shall find
> (Be't trunk-maker or critick),
> I'll thank him, if he'll bear in mind
> That it is mine, George Wightwick.

Though 'criticks' were perhaps a rhyming necessity, this seems a little hard on 'trunk-makers', and one wonders which of their number may have particularly offended. These simple verses are exceeded in verbiage by the twenty lines of amiable doggerel which Hardy ascribed to Charles Clark of Great Topham Hall, near Witham in Essex—though they were not confined to his use. Entitled rather ungraciously 'A Pleader to the Needer when a Reader', this abounds in puns, and the occasional gleams of humour which Hardy claims for it have less heat and light to offer today's reader. W. J. Hardy, in his *Book-plates*, devotes a whole chapter to inscriptions in condemnation of book-stealing or book-borrowing, and in praise of study, and de Tabley deals with them at length, but with a keener eye to earlier and continental examples. See also E. Wilson Dobbs' listing of scholars' manuscript verses on ownership in *The Ex Libris Journal* for June 1900.

No.

<hr>

L. & M. A. Schimmelpenninck,
𝔅𝔯𝔦𝔰𝔱𝔬𝔩.

<hr>

The wicked borroweth and payeth not again.

Psalm xxxvi. 21.

242

Hic Liber est JUSTINI *Pentonvillæ Archidiaconus;*
Quem siquis abstulerit—in Sartagine coquatur—
In Purgatorio rotatur—et Anathema sit!   *Amen!!*

243

This Book is the property of
HENRY CHARLES DOUGLASS
(King's College, London.   Corpus Christi College, Cambridge),
EALING, MIDDLESEX.

<hr>

" Blest be the gracious Power, who taught mankind
To stamp a lasting image of the mind."—*Crabbe.*
" Read not to contradict and confute, nor to believe and take for granted, nor to find talk and discourse, but to weigh and consider. Some books are to be tasted, others to be swallowed, and some few to be chewed and digested."—*Bacon.*
" A good book is the precious life-blood of a master spirit embalmed and treasured up on purpose to a life beyond life."—*Milton.*
" I cannot think the glorious world of mind,
Embalmed in books, which I can only see
In patches, though I read my moments blind,
Is to be lost to me."—*Overbury.*

244

𝔐𝔬𝔯𝔲𝔪 ℭ𝔢𝔯𝔱𝔲𝔰 𝔄𝔪𝔬𝔯.
—:—:—:—

" To whosoe'er this book I *lend*,
I *give* one word—no more :
They, who to *borrow* condescend,
Should graciously *restore.*

And whosoe'er this book should find
(With neither *name* nor *lot* on),
I'll thank him if he'll bear in mind
That it is mine—

CHARLES COTTON."

245

246 Charlotte Mary Yonge

The novelist Charlotte Mary Yonge (1823–1901) used this simple printed label, the lettering and ornament of which are typical of the latter half of the nineteenth century. The daughter of William Crawley Yonge (who, incidentally, used a die-sinker armorial bookplate with quartered arms) and Frances Mary, the daughter of Thomas Bargus, vicar of Barkway in Hertfordshire, she was brought up at Otterbourne near Winchester, where her father had a small estate. By her own record she was clumsy, inaccurate and inattentive as a child, and an inordinate shyness remained throughout her life. She nevertheless taught in the local Sunday School for seventy-one years; and John Keble's appointment as incumbent at nearby Hursley was a key event in her life and led to her enthusiasm for the Oxford Movement. Keble encouraged her in a sort of literary evangelism, and vetted her manuscripts for her. A prolific writer, *The Heir of Redclyffe*, 1853, was her first highly successful novel, and her work had a remarkably wide appeal; she was also for thirty-eight years editor of the *Monthly Packet*. A small typographic label, reading 'From the Library of Charlotte M. Yonge', was placed in some of her books at her death (see No. 256). Books from the library of her friend John Keble (1792–1866), the clergyman, poet and Tractarian, given to Keble College, Oxford, on its foundation in 1870, are marked by a printed label in Latin which occurs in two settings.

247 Andw. Lang

Andrew Lang, Sheriff Clerk at Selkirk, used an engraved label which was the work of one of the Kirkwood family of engravers in Edinburgh. Though Fincham does not list this—or any other label—among their work, the Lang and a label for William Humphry of Greenock bear the Kirkwood signature. (Neither did Fincham feel able to distinguish their armorial work from that of a Dublin engraver of the same name at that time). When Thomas Bewick visited Edinburgh in 1823 he visited James Kirkwood, who was by then retired and 'up in years', and he notes in his *Memoir*, 1862, that Kirkwood 'led the way to excellence particularly in writing engraving, in which he was succeeded by his son and grandson'. The lettering of this example suggests a fairly late date.

248 John Huxtable

The John Huxtable label is a Victorian adaptation of the festoon labels which had been popular since the 1780s (see Nos. 238 and 240), and appears to be a simpler, later and less impressive version of the label for 'MR. REDHEAD, CUMBERLAND', which has an intricately detailed border. It is shown here, in preference to the other, as a very late interpretation of a long-familiar style.

249 Angelo C. Hayter

This copperplate label was reproduced lithographically to mark a gift to his son Angelo from Sir George Hayter (1792–1871), the portrait and historical painter. Sir George studied at the Royal Academy Schools, and after brief service in the Navy began exhibiting as an artist. He studied in Rome, spent some time in Paris, and was appointed portrait and historical painter to Queen Victoria on her accession; he became her 'principal painter in ordinary' in 1841, and was knighted the following year—but as an artist he was competent rather than brilliant. Labels such as this, recording gifts within a family, are rare, but many *ex-libris* have had manuscript annotations of a similar kind.

250 F. Tylor

No verses on nineteenth-century labels enjoyed such popularity as the ones seen here. Hardy states that they were composed early in the century and produced by C. Talbot of 174 Tooley Street as 'universal' *ex-libris*, the name to be added in manuscript. Whether or not this was so, other printers took advantage of the idea, for the author's collection has an example printed by G. Booth, Hyde, and another with the additional inscription: 'Printed at the Imperial Miniature Press, In the Royal Gallery of Practical Science, Lowther Arcade and Adelaide Street, Strand. Published by J. Gathercole, at the Gallery'. For those who spurned the muse of such verses—and several hundred didn't—there was always prose, even sometimes at length: 'Hear! Hear! I say Mr. Reader, I want to speak with you. When you borrow my book, pray return it in good time. I did not lend it you to keep it, nor yet make it dirty. Pounds worth of experience make me insert this. That is all at present. Good morning. But stop, Friend, for a moment, only one moment longer!—Don't keep my book twelve months in your possession, and then cry out, Dear, dear! of whom did I borrow this book?—I am sure I forgot. But—remember—there is such a person as William Coombs, In Bradford, Wilts.'

251 William Haworth, F.S.A.

The Rev William Haworth (d. 1904) was succentor of York Minster and Vicar of St. Sampson's, York; he was elected a fellow of the Society of Antiquaries in 1897. His label was therefore printed in the seven years around the turn of the century, and that one would have supposed it earlier merely indicates how little design changed in some areas. The ornamental addition of a vignette had been long established; there were, for example, several very crudely printed labels from the Newcastle area in the time of Thomas Bewick, embellished with little cuts after his manner.

246

247

248

249

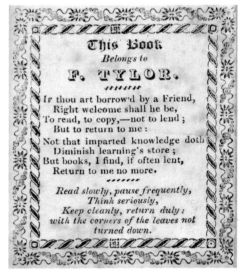

250

251

252 Edward Burne-Jones

Sir Edward Burne-Jones' bookplate for Frances Horner is No. 130, but this label for his own use was one of a series printed at the Kelmscott Press on 25th February, 1898, in Kelmscott Golden Type. Others printed at the time were for Emery Walker (at No. 3 Hammersmith Terrace; his No. 7 Hammersmith Terrace label is later and perhaps printed by line-block), Charles Fairfax Murray, May Morris, Laurence W. Hodson, H. C. Marillier, John and Margaret Mackail (she was Burne-Jones' daughter), and a posthumous label for William Morris' own books. The last is not to be confused with a similarly worded label in Lining Jensen Oldstyle No. 2. A Golden Type label for George Dunn was printed later; and many similar labels were produced from drawn lettering or using variant types.

253 H. Raymond Barnett

This *ex-libris* in the manner of a printer's mark, engraved by Joan Hassall in 1943, occurs printed in black and in red. Her other book labels include two designs for Janet Camp Troxell: the first, printed in black and in red, shows the name in a floral and leafy oval; the second—for a Rossetti collection—has the initials 'JCT' in black on a yellow design incorporating Dante Gabriel Rossetti's personal letter-heading device. One of Miss Hassall's bookplate designs is shown (No. 198); but for fuller details of her work see Ruari McLean's *The Wood Engravings of Joan Hassall*, 1960, and an article in the Winter 1974 number of *The Private Library* which contains the text of a talk she gave to The Bookplate Society in 1972.

254 David John Gilson

Reynolds Stone (See No. 197) achieves a perfect balance of ornament and lettering on any scale, and this recent label has been printed by Will Carter of Cambridge in three different colours: brown, green and a strong black.

255 Lytton Strachey

Lytton Strachey (1880–1932), the critic and biographer, used this label by his friend Dora Carrington (Mrs. Ralph Partridge). She studied at the Slade, became an artist and decorator, and with her husband kept house for Strachey at Tidmarsh and Ham Spray—committing suicide two months after his death. Strachey also used a pictorial bookplate, inscribed with his full name; it is signed by Halsey Ricardo, dated 1899, and shows, through a presumably stone window frame, a tree and fruits in the foreground and two old ships on the ocean beyond.

256 JMB (Sir) James M. Barrie

This very simple label was printed after his death to mark the books of Sir James M. Barrie (1860–1937), the playwright and novelist, author of *Peter Pan*. The use of similar labels for the books of literary men has not been uncommon, and examples include designs for Charles Dickens (See No. 144), W. T. Watts-Dunton, E. M. Forster, Thomas Hardy, Augustus Hare, John Masefield, William Morris (See Note to No. 252) and Charlotte Mary Yonge (See No. 246). Though these were posthumously printed, they are bibliographically useful.

257 Rene Leo Mendez

Peter Reddick (b. 1924) studied at the Slade School of Fine Art from 1948 to 1951, and though most of his bookplates have been pictorials he has engraved several labels, including one for the Slade. The example illustrated here was printed with letterpress to mark a memorial gift of books to a hospital. There is not space to show the whole label, but it reads: 'Given in memory of Rene Leo Mendez who died on 28 April 1953 aged 29. In his eleven years at St. Mary's he enriched the lives of all he met. His friendliness and sincerity, his wit and charm and his steadfastness in adversity are a lasting inspiration to all his friends. In his living and in his dying he set an example not to be excelled'. A wood-engraver, Reddick's book illustrations have included four books for the Folio Society, and *The Poems of Robert Browning* for the Limited Editions Club; he has taught for many years, and is in the graphics department at Bristol Polytechnic.

258 Nial Devitt

Designed in 1972 by John Smith, at that time senior lecturer in art at the Mary Ward College, Nottingham, this unusual label was printed on the hand-press at Stanbrook Abbey in 1973 in a chocolate-brown colour.

259 John Carter

The bibliographer John Waynflete Carter (1905–1975) used several book labels, two of them engraved by his cousin Reynolds Stone. This example, however, is one of two which were drawn for him by his brother Will Carter, the Cambridge printer. It is a typical example of Carter's elegant label designs, which are printed photographically reduced from drawings of much larger size. Will Carter (b. 1912) founded the Rampant Lions Press which he runs with his son, Sebastian Carter—who also, incidentally, has designed some book labels.

260 June & George Ratcliffe

Details of Leo Wyatt's career are given with the illustration of his own copper-engraved bookplate (See No. 190), but a large proportion of his distinguished *ex-libris* work comprises wood-engraved labels, and this design dates from 1974.

261 Basil Harley

This label was the work of David Kindersley (b. 1915), who trained for two years under Gilbert Ledward and was apprenticed to Eric Gill from 1935 to 1936. He established his own workshop in 1946, with associates, and engages in an impressive variety of work, including letter-cutting on stone. This design, dating from 1974, was for Basil Harley, Managing Director of the Curwen Press.

FROM THE LIBRARY OF
EDWARD BURNE-JONES
THE GRANGE NORTH
ENDROAD FULHAM ✿ ✿

252

H. RAYMOND

RB

BARNETT

253

David John
Gilson

254

LYTTON
STRACHEY

255

From the Library of

JMB

Sir James M. Barrie

256

RENE LEO
MENDEZ

257

EXLIBR
ISNIAL
DEVITT

258

John Carter

259

June &
George
RATCLIFFE

260

BASIL
HARLEY

261

[155]

SELECT BIBLIOGRAPHY

This is divided for convenience into two sections, the first listing standard works of general use to the student and the second recording particularly specialised or slighter studies; a brief comment is included on the contents of the latter list. Monographs are excluded, but are referred to in the notes facing the illustrations where appropriate. J. H. Slater's *Bookplates and their value*, 1898, and E. Almack's *Bookplates*, 1904, are excluded on grounds of inaccuracy.

I

Arellanes, Audrey Spencer. *Bookplates, A Selective Annotated Bibliography of the Periodical Literature*, Detroit, Gale Research Company, 1971

Castle, Egerton. *English Bookplates*, London, Bell, 1892, new and enlarged edition, London, Bell, 1893

de Tabley, see Warren

Ex Libris Society. *Journal of the Ex Libris Society*, Ed. W. H. K. Wright, Volumes 1–18, London, A. & C. Black, 1891–1908

Fincham, Henry W. *Artists and Engravers of British and American Book Plates*, London, Kegan Paul, Trench, Trubner & Co Ltd, 1897

Fuller, George W. *A Bibliography of Bookplate Literature*, Washington, Spokane Public Library, 1926, republished by Gale Research Company, Book Tower, Detroit, 1973

Hamilton, Walter. *Dated Book-plates*, London, A. & C. Black, 1895

Hardy, W. J. *Book-plates*, London, Kegan Paul, Trench, Trubner & Co Ltd, 1893, second edition, same publisher, 1897

Howe, E. R. J. Gambier. *Catalogue of British and American Book Plates bequeathed to the Trustees of the British Museum by Sir Augustus Wollaston Franks*, three volumes, London, British Museum, 1903–1904

Howe, E. R. J. Gambier. *Catalogue of the . . . Collection of Book-plates of the late Julian Marshall*, London, Sotheby, Wilkinson & Hodge, 1906

Labouchere, Norna. *Ladies' Book-plates*, London, Bell, 1895

Marshall, see Howe

Vaughan, Herbert M. *The Welsh Book-plates in the Collection of Sir Evan Davies Jones, Bart.*, London, A. L. Humphreys, 1920

Warren, the Hon. J. Leicester. *A Guide to the Study of Book-plates*, London, John Pearson, 1880, second edition (as Lord de Tabley, but published posthumously), Manchester, Sherratt and Hughes, 1900

II

Badeley, J. F. *Bookplates*, a lecture delivered to the Print Collectors' Club on Wednesday November 18th, 1925, London, Print Collectors' Club, 1927. A pleasantly written and illustrated introduction to the subject; it contains three original prints

Burke, Henry Farnham. *Examples of Irish Bookplates from the Collections of Sir Bernard Burke*, privately printed, Peckham, W. Griggs, 1894. A fine picture book of eighteenth century Irish bookplates, most of them rarities, but no text

Burke, Henry Farnham. *Examples of Irish Bookplates from the Collections of Sir Bernard Burke; supplementary volume*, privately printed, Peckham W. Griggs, 1894. As the last.

Griggs, W. *83 Examples of Armorial Book Plates*, privately printed, Peckham, W. Griggs, 1884. Illustrations of early and rare bookplates, with a brief but useful description of the plates and their owners

Griggs, W. *147 Examples of Armorial Book Plates* (Second Series), privately printed, Peckham, W. Griggs, 1892. Further illustrations of seventeenth and eighteenth century bookplates, including many of ecclesiastics, but without text

Guthrie, James, Ed. *The Bookplate Magazine*, London, Morland Press, 1919–1921. The lightweight text hardly warrants the price one is sometimes asked for these booklets, but they are interesting to Guthrie, Rodo and Brangwyn collectors

Guthrie, James, Ed. *The Bookplate*, The English Bookplate Society, Pear Tree Press, 1921–1925. As the last

Howard, Joseph Jackson. *The Wardour Press Series of Armorial Bookplates. Baronets*, London, Mitchell and Hughes, 1895. Mostly eighteenth century bookplates well illustrated, and with excellent genealogical details of their owners

Lee, Brian North. *Early Printed Book Labels, A catalogue of dated personal labels and gift labels printed in Britain to the year 1760*, Pinner, Private Libraries Association & The Bookplate Society, 1976. A record of over 500 book labels, with about 100 illustrations, and appendixes on early American labels, printers' gifts and book stamps.

Oliver, Vere Langford. *West Indian Bookplates, being a first list of plates relating to those islands*, London, Mitchell, Hughes & Clarke, 1914 (reprinted from *Caribbeana*). A useful catalogue with genealogical details; the bookplates are, of course, almost entirely English work. Details of particular plates are given in subsequent issues of *Caribbeana*, and a second list was published in the July 1917 issue

Rylands, John Paul. *Notes on Book-plates (ex-libris) with special reference to Lancashire and Cheshire examples*, privately printed, Liverpool, T. Brackell, 1889. Useful for those studying the book plates of the locality.

Severin, Mark F. *Making a Bookplate*, London & New York, Studio Publications, 1949. A well-illustrated book of mainly modern examples, particularly helpful for those who wish to design, or commission, bookplates

Severin, Mark, and Reid, Anthony. *Engraved Bookplates,*

European Ex Libris 1950-1970, Pinner, Private Libraries Association, 1972. This sets recent British bookplates in the context of European work since 1950, and is superbly illustrated

Studio, The. *Modern Book-plates and their designers*. London, Studio, 1898–1899. This special Winter Number of the *Studio* is full of information and illustrations for those who study and enjoy the 1890s period

Vaughan, Herbert M. *National Library of Wales Catalogue of the Aneurin Williams Collection of Book Plates*, Aberyst-wyth, 1938. The record of a miscellaneous collection, containing a number of bookplates of poets, authors, artists, doctors, lawyers and clerics, but few early plates. Its identification of owners is useful

Viner, George Heath. *The Origin and Evolution of the Book-plate*, London, The Bibliographical Society, 1946, reprinted by the University Press, Oxford from Trans-actions of the Bibliographical Society, *The Library*, June 1946. A brief article of six pages, but thoroughly sound in its text

ACKNOWLEDGEMENTS

I thank Her Majesty Queen Elizabeth the Queen Mother for gracious permission to reproduce her bookplate by Stephen Gooden. I also acknowledge the kind permission of the Trustees of the British Museum and the National Library of Scotland, the Provost and Fellows of King's College, Cambridge, the Master and Fellows of Trinity Hall, Cambridge, the Warden and Fellows of New College, Oxford, the Treasurer and Masters of the Bench of the Honourable Society of Gray's Inn, and the Librarians of Cambridge University Library, the Bodleian Library, Oxford, Aberdeen University Library, The Dartington Hall Trust, Emmanuel College, Cambridge, Harvard University Library, Kensington and Chelsea Public Libraries, The National Trust, Queens' College, Cambridge, The United Society for the Propagation of the Gospel and Winchester Cathedral for permission to reproduce bookplates. Similar thanks are also due to Mr Douglas Percy Bliss, Mrs Diana Bloomfield, Mr Simon Brett, Mr Will Carter, Mr Nial Devitt, Miss Agnes Dunlop, Mr David Gilson, Mr Basil Harley, Miss H. E. Harrison, Miss Joan Hassall, Mr Ellic Howe, Mr H. Montgomery Hyde, Mr David Kindersley, the Hon. Mrs Miriam Lane, Mr John Lawrence, Mr George Mackley, Mr Frank Martin, Mr William McLaren, Mr John Piper, Mr Peter Reddick, Mr Michael Renton, Sir Sacheverell Sitwell, Bart., Mr Richard Shirley Smith, Mr Reynolds Stone, Mrs Diana Trappes-Lomax, Professor Hugh Trevor-Roper, Mr Laurence Whistler and Mr Leo Wyatt. For information and advice I am grateful to Mr Iain Bain, Mr Albert Garrett, Mr Kenneth Guichard, Mrs Nina Griggs and Mr David McKitterick. Among collector friends I am grateful to Mr Philip Beddingham, Mr Keith Clark, Mr James Wilson, and Mr John Simpson who was as ever generous in sharing his knowledge of early bookplates and allowed me to reproduce a label in his collection. Mr Anthony Pincott and Mr Peter Summers gave invaluable assistance and advised on the improvement of the text, and Mr Pincott helped me also in the preparation of the index. Finally, I should like to thank the Librarian of the Society of Antiquaries, Mr John Hopkins, Mr Reginald Williams of the Department of Prints and Drawings at the British Museum, and the staff of the reference department at Chiswick Public Library for unfailing courteousness and helpfulness in my researches.

INDEX